For God's Sake

For God's Sake

The Christian Right and US Foreign Policy

LEE MARSDEN

ZED BOOKS
London & New York

For Gill

For God's Sake: The Christian Right and US Foreign Policy was first published in 2008
by Zed Books Ltd, 7 Cynthia Street, London N1 9JF, UK
and Room 400, 175 Fifth Avenue, New York, NY 10010, USA

www.zedbooks.co.uk

Typeset in Monotype Van Dijck by illuminati, www.illuminatibooks.co.uk
Cover designed by Andrew Corbett
Printed and bound in the EU by Biddles Ltd, King's Lynn

Distributed in the USA exclusively by Palgrave Macmillan,
175 Fifth Avenue, New York, NY 10010, USA

A catalogue record for this book is available from the British Library
Library of Congress Cataloging in Publication Data available

ISBN 978 1 84277 884 5 hb
ISBN 978 1 84277 885 2 pb

Contents

PART III

Acknowledgements

Very special thanks to all those friends, family and colleagues without whom this book would not have been possible. In particular I would like to thank the Social Science and Law School at Oxford Brookes University for generously funding travel to the United States; colleagues in the British International Studies Association US Foreign Policy working group, Brookes and the University of East Anglia for commenting on drafts of chapters, especially Stuart Croft, Martin Durham, John Street and Heather Savigny. Importantly, I wish to thank Ellen McKinlay, an exceptional editor, two anonymous reviewers and the team at Zed for their hard work and invaluable advice, which has made the book better than it would otherwise have been, although the usual disclaimers apply about any mistakes being my sole responsibility. Thanks to all the interviewees who gave generously of their time and especially Brian Grim of the Pew Forum on Religion and Public Life, for lunch and a sense of perspective. Last, but by no means least, thank you to my stepson Isaac Hogg for research on Blackwater, to my father Dennis Marsden, an unpaid but not unacknowledged researcher, and to Gill, whose patience knows no bounds.

Abbreviations

ACLU	American Civil Liberties Union
AFA	American Family Association
AIPAC	American Israel Public Affairs Committee
BMENA	Broader Middle East and North Africa
CBN	Christian Broadcasting Network
CCC	Campus Crusade for Christ
CEDAW	Convention on the Elimination of All Forms of Discrimination Against Women
C–FAM	Catholic Family and Human Rights Institute
CFBCI	Center for Faith-Based and Community Initiatives
CFI	Christian Freedom International
CFR	Council on Foreign Relations
CIPAC	Christians' Israel Public Action Campaign
CNP	Council for National Policy
CSI	Christian Solidarity International
CSW	Commission on the Status of Women
CUFI	Christians United for Israel
CWA	Concerned Women for America
ECI	Evangelical Climate Initiative
EPA	Environmental Protection Agency
EPPC	Ethics and Public Policy Center

ERA	Equal Rights Amendment
ERLC	Ethics and Religious Liberty Commission
EU	European Union
FBO	faith-based organization
FCF	Free Congress Foundation
FETV	Far East Television
FOF	Focus on the Family
FRC	Family Research Council
GOP	Grand Old Party (Republican Party)
HSLDA	Home School Legal Defense Association
IASPS	Institute for Advanced Strategic and Political Studies
ICC	International Christian Concern
ICES	Interfaith Council for Environmental Stewardship
IFAS	Institute for First Amendment Studies
IFCJ	International Fellowship of Christians and Jews
IPCC	Intergovernmental Panel on Climate Change (UN)
IRD	Institute on Religion and Democracy
ISA	Interfaith Stewardship Alliance
LeSEA	Lester Sumrall Evangelistic Association
MEPI	Middle East Partnership Initiative
METV	Middle East Television
NAE	National Association of Evangelicals
NASB	New American Standard Bible
NED	National Endowment for Democracy
NGO	non-governmental organization
NTM	New Tribes Mission
OBI	Operation Blessing International
PFM	Prison Fellowship Ministries
PHC	Patrick Henry College
PNAC	Project for the New American Century
PPF	Persecution Project Foundation
SIL	Summer Institute of Linguistics
TBN	Trinity Broadcasting Network
TVC	Traditional Values Coalition
UN	United Nations
USA	United States of America
USAID	United States Agency for International Development
VOM	Voice of the Martyrs
WCF	World Congress of Families
WFPC	World Family Policy Center

Preface

The Christian Right have become one of the hottest topics in academic debate and the media in both American domestic politics and foreign policy. Undergraduate and Master's students are increasingly producing dissertations on the subject and Ph.D. students are preparing to offer their insights to the debate over the next few years. Security Studies and US foreign policy specialists are busily reinventing themselves as experts on the Christian Right, to move into the rapidly emerging field of Religion and International Relations in the same way as others have become experts in terrorism. In many ways I am making a similar journey but one that brings with it a slightly different angle.

Hitherto much of the work on the Christian Right's involvement in US foreign policy has been written by antagonists eager to alert the world, or their readers at least, to the dangers that the movement poses to US foreign policy interests. To this end polemics have been produced emphasizing the unrepresentative lunatic fringe of the Christian Right, which if it seizes power will turn America into a theocracy and send the world hurtling towards Armageddon. The

Christian Right have been variously characterized as fascists and theocrats with the president in their thrall, intent on world domination. In deciding to write on the Christian Right and US foreign policy I wanted to discover what the movement, if it was a movement, really believed and how those beliefs translated into attempts to influence their country's foreign policy. In other words, I wanted to consider the Christian Right on their own terms rather than seeking the evidence to support preconceived ideas.

My own journey in writing this book actually spans the past quarter-century, from spiritual conversion in 1981 through sixteen years as a conservative evangelical involved in leadership with Pentecostal and renewalist churches, including ordination in a Word of Faith church, part of an American fellowship of churches, serving as pastor. During this time I taught, preached and believed in the Bible literally, including creationism. Attendance at university as a mature student in 1996 began a process of questioning these beliefs as I was exposed to the teachings of Hume, Weber, Durkheim, Marx and Foucault by sociologists and philosophers at the University of East Anglia. As my personal journey has progressed from the certainties of fundamentalism to the doubts of liberal secularism, it appears that for many others around the world the opposite is true, as religious fundamentalism becomes a significant actor in international politics.

This personal experience of conservative evangelicalism, familiarity with the teachings of the main actors in the Christian Right, and an experiential understanding of their world-view, provides a perspective that is different from that of most other academics writing in this area. I am aware that, having distanced myself from the movement, there is a tension between new and former sets of beliefs. The passage of ten years before writing on this theme hopefully enables greater objectivity, which is complemented by a social scientist's desire to get to the evidence rather than convince conservative evangelicals of any supposed error of their ways. I wanted to provide a more comprehensive coverage of the Christian Right's involvement in foreign policy than has previously been produced, by considering those areas of foreign policy that affect the whole world, including the War on Terror, the Palestinian–Israeli dispute, global warming, democracy promotion, humanitarian intervention and human rights, and to discover whether the Christian Right really have become an integral part of the US foreign policy process. It is to be hoped that *For God's Sake* will contribute to understanding the movement's role in US foreign policy and serve as a resource for academics, students and foreign policy practitioners alike.

Norwich
January 2008

Introduction

In less than three decades right-wing Christians have become major players in domestic American politics to such an extent that no politician, Republican or Democrat, can afford to overlook their influence. While much has been written charting the domestic rise and influence of the Christian Right, this book examines for the first time the movement's impact on US foreign policy, an area of vital importance not just for American national interests but for the future of world peace. This has become one of the most important and divisive issues in global politics today. The emergence of the Christian Right as a key player in US foreign policy has until recently been largely off the political and academic radar, because their activities have been conducted behind closed doors in the White House, Congress, the United Nations and the Republican Party. The academic focus on neoconservatives and Bush foreign policy has distracted attention from a movement that in the long term may have far more influence on the future direction of US foreign policy. This book is an attempt to redress the balance.

From being a fringe interest group on the edges of the Republican Party, conservative evangelicals now form part of the base of the party and occupy senior positions from local party level to the presidency itself. Towards the end of the Clinton presidency, this group expanded its activities to play an increasingly important part in US foreign policy. *For God's Sake: The Christian Right and US Foreign Policy* is an attempt to chart the rise of conservative evangelicals' involvement in and growing influence on US foreign policy. During the Bush administration, conservative evangelicals have been granted unprecedented access to, and consultation with, the White House, home of a self-proclaimed born-again Christian president. Rather than standing on the outside looking in, conservative evangelicals are inside the corridors of power, seeking to influence policy decisions and exercising their electoral power.

The increasing influence of the Christian and Religious Right has concerned many on the left, traditional Republicans, and America's allies and enemies abroad. In recent years, a number of fine books have been written detailing and exposing how right-wing religious Christians have sought to influence US foreign policy in specific areas. Writers such as Esther Kaplan (2005), Jennifer Butler (2006), Kevin Phillips (2006), David Domke (2004), Doris Buss and Didi Herman (2003), Tim Weber (2004) and Allen Hertzke (2006) have made a valuable contribution in highlighting this change of emphasis. These books have tended to concentrate on certain subgroups such as dominionists within the Religious Right, or specific areas of Christian involvement such as Israel, religious persecution or family values. *For God's Sake* stands on the shoulders of such giants as Kaplan, Sara Diamond and Clyde Wilcox, and attempts to provide for the first time an overview of the broad ambit of conservative Christians' involvement in US foreign policy during the Bush administration. In doing so, I am mindful of the injunction of Richard Land, president of the Southern Baptist Convention's Ethics and Religious Liberty Commission: rather than seeking to ridicule or present a distorted image, this book represents an effort to 'take conservative religious people seriously instead of writing them off as fanatics' (Land, 2007: 191). In taking them seriously, far from writing them off as fanatics the evidence presented here reveals an aggressive and determined political force intent on influencing US foreign policy just as they have dominated the domestic agenda over the past eight years.

Who Are the Christian Right?

Already in these first few paragraphs the reader will have noticed a variety of terms being used to describe the Christian Right, including 'Religious Right', 'born-again Christians', 'conservative evangelicals', 'religious conservatives' and 'dominionists'. Herein lies a problem when seeking both to understand and to define the Christian Right as a movement. Authors, statisticians, pollsters and journalists all experience similar problems in describing the phenomenon. Clyde Wilcox defines the Christian Right as 'a social movement that attempts to mobilize *evangelical* Protestants and other orthodox Christians into conservative political action' (Wilcox and Larson, 2006: 6). Wilcox points out that the movement consists of many overlapping agendas and has no one organization or spokesperson to represent them. Instead, there are a combination of social-movement organizations, leaders, activists and members, the core constituency of which tend to be white evangelicals (Wilcox and Larson, 2006: 7–9). This working definition is quite useful but requires some further qualification.

The term 'Christian Right' in this book applies to conservative evangelicals and right-wing Catholics within the Republican Party whose religious persuasion determines their attitudes to political questions. This grouping consists of organizations, politicians, activists and supporters who are generally Protestant evangelicals, but also includes right-wing Catholics supportive of conservative moral and fiscal values on issues such as abortion, sexuality and free markets. They may influence the Democratic Party on specific issues but do not organize within the party because of their opposition to core Democratic social and fiscal values. The Christian Right are politically active conservatives, united in their opposition to abortion, euthanasia, stem-cell research, homosexuality, same-sex marriage, promiscuity, secularism and big government. Out of a total population of around 300 million people in the United States, around 60 million have identified themselves with the ideas of the Christian Right in 2004 (Green et al., 2005; Haynes, 2007). This figure includes politically conservative Catholics, many of whom are among the 36 per cent of Catholic adults (around 14 million) who identify themselves as charismatics (Pew Forum, 2006a: 90–91).

A profile of a member of the Christian Right might look something like this: a white evangelical member of a nuclear family, living in a Southern state; mom stays home looking after the kids, who are educated at home, and dad lives with the family and goes out to work. The family attend church at least once a month, and quite likely more than once a week; mom and dad vote Republican and support the war in Iraq, watch Christian television and Fox News, and support one or more Christian parachurch organizations encouraging them to be politically active. Such a stereotype, however, fails to recognize that the Christian Right are becoming increasingly diverse, although they remain united around social conservatism. There are many black conservative evangelicals, in particular among Word of Faith and Pentecostal churches, who are certainly members of the Christian Right. According to Barna Research group, divorce rates among born-again evangelicals may actually be higher than in the general population (Wicker, 2000). Clearly, most conservative evangelicals do not choose or cannot afford home schooling for their offspring, or for mothers to stay at home. Conservative evangelicals are not exclusively concentrated in Southern states but are in all states.[1] They comprise a flexible grouping that becomes energized and activated around core issues of both domestic and foreign policy. This political engagement distinguishes the movement from other Christians who either do not share this conservative agenda or are religious without political partisanship.

The Christian Right are a subgroup of the Religious Right, which comprises conservative Christians including Protestant evangelicals, Pentecostals, charismatics, fundamentalists, Catholics, sects and cults, including the Church of Jesus Christ of Latter-day Saints (Mormons), Worldwide Unification Church (Moonies), and Christian Scientists. Socially conservative Jews, Muslims, Hindus and Buddhists would also be included in this wide-ranging definition. Only those Protestants and Catholics who are socially conservative and politically active are included in the Christian Right; this excludes the vast majority of members of mainstream Protestant and Catholic churches, where a more inclusive and tolerant social gospel is taught.

The movement is evangelical in both religious and political contexts, commissioned to evangelize and convert believers of other faiths or none to a narrow version of Christianity in which a conversion experience, being born again, is the minimum requirement for entry. Conservative Catholic Republicans adopt a similar evangelical zeal in seeking converts to social conservatism but do not insist on religious conversion. This can create tension between different parts of the movement, with some evangelicals (left and right) doubting Catholics' salvation but nonetheless willing to work with them and incorporate them within the movement in order to achieve mutual objectives. Evangelicals are defined by this proselytizing imperative and can be either liberal or conservative, African American, Hispanic or white, but in order to be incorporated within the Christian Right the common denominator is social and fiscal conservatism. Opinion poll surveys tend to regard white evangelicals as the core of the Christian Right and Republican support, but this is potentially misleading and fails to account for the considerable differences and political volatility among evangelicals.

Pentecostals are Protestant and evangelical but are differentiated from other Protestant groupings by their emphasis on baptism in the Holy Spirit with the initial evidence of speaking in other tongues, also known as glossolalia (1 Corinthians 14:5, 13; Acts 1:4, 2:1–4, 10:44–46, 19:6). Other Christians, including Catholics, who emphasize and practise the gifts of the Holy Spirit within church meetings are charismatics, and, just as Pentecostals, can be liberal or conservative, with the latter qualified for membership of the Christian Right. Fundamentalists, like many but not all evangelicals, will adopt a narrow literalist interpretation of the Bible that seeks to apply their interpretation of 'biblical truths' to everyday life. Many fundamentalists have a pessimistic view of the state of the world and withdraw from political involvement, concerning themselves with their own walk with God amidst a fallen humanity. Fundamentalists today represent a small and relatively insignificant section of the Christian population of America. They can really only be considered members of the Christian Right when actively engaged in the political sphere to promote a conservative agenda.

Theological streams

Within these various strands of Christian Right religious affiliation, there are also two streams of theological emphasis that affect political involvement and are of more significance than biblical literalism, the importance of baptism in the Holy Spirit or proselytizing. These are Christian Nationalism and Christian Zionism. Christian Nationalism incorporates concepts of theocracy known as Dominion Theology and Reconstructionism (Goldberg, 2007). These were popularized by the late Rousas Rushdoony, father of the Christian Reconstructionist movement, in his *Institutes of Biblical Law*. Dominion Theology takes as its starting point verses from the first chapter of Genesis, in which God gives humanity dominion over his creation:

> And God said, Let us make man in our image, after our likeness: and let them have dominion over the fish of the sea, and over the fowl of the air, and over the cattle, and over all the earth, and over every creeping thing that creepeth upon the earth. So God created man in his own image, in the image of God created he him; male and female created he them. And God blessed them, and God said unto them, Be fruitful, and multiply, and replenish the earth, and subdue it: and have dominion over the fish of the sea, and over the fowl of the air, and over every living thing that moveth upon the earth. (Genesis 1:26–28)

Rather than simply interpreting the above verses as an imperative for humanity to be a good steward of the earth, dominionists use them as the starting point to insist on Christian domination of the political and economic system. For dominionists, only Christians are capable of governing according to God's will, and therefore non-Christians should effectively be excluded from political processes. Dominionists consider that Old Testament laws should still be applicable, with punishments, including the death penalty, for breaking any of the Ten Commandments. They argue in favour of dominionist churches appropriating all the social functions of the state (Beliles and McDowell, 1989). Reconstructionist writers, including Rushdoony (1973), Gary DeMar and Peter Leithart (1988), George Grant (1985), H. Wayne House and Thomas Ice (1988), constantly emphasize the necessity for Christians to 'subdue' and 'exercise dominion' over the earth and evil. According to such thinking the United States, and indeed the world, can be rescued from disaster only by applying Old Testament law and having Christians controlling government. Although dominionist and Reconstructionist thinking has been applied in a domestic context, the idea also has efficacy in foreign policy for believers who consider Christian governance necessary for a fallen world (Berlet, 2005).

Reconstructionists adopt extreme positions on adultery, abortion and homosexuality, even advocating the death penalty for such 'offences'. Under such a theocratic system a new economic order based on Christian economics, where God provides through the giving of church members rather than through income tax, would be introduced (North, 1989). As with all groupings and subgroupings within the Christian Right, dominionists operate on a continuum, with hard dominionists advocating a complete takeover of US institutions and the establishment of a theocratic state, whereby the Constitution and Bill of Rights are interpreted as supplementary to Biblical Law. Hard dominionists, including Reconstructionists and Earl Paulk's Kingdom Now theology, are unwilling to compromise with secular bodies and those Christians who do not accept their theological beliefs. Soft dominionists, such as the late D. James Kennedy of Coral

Ridge Ministries, seen until his death in 2007 on American television screens every Sunday morning, stop short of calling for a theocratic state and work within the existing political system to achieve their objectives (Berlet, 2005; Diamond, 1995b). Hard dominionists such as George Grant, former executive director of Coral Ridge Ministries, however, take their desire for a theocratic state to its logical conclusion and seek Christian dominion over not just America but the world:

> Christians have an obligation, a mandate, a commission, a holy responsibility to reclaim the land for Jesus Christ – to have dominion in the civil structures, just as in every other aspect of life and godliness.
>
> But it is dominion that we are after. Not just a voice.
>
> It is dominion we are after. Not just influence.
>
> It is dominion we are after. Not just equal time.
>
> It is dominion we are after.
>
> World conquest. That's what Christ has commissioned us to accomplish. We must win the world with the power of the Gospel. And we must never settle for anything less. (Grant, 1987: 50–51)

As scary as these sentiments might be, Richard Land is probably right in his assessment of liberals' preoccupation with dominionism (Land, 2007: 190), although, as we will see, they are influential in certain aspects of Christian Right thinking on foreign policy. A group with far more significance in terms of influencing the administration are Christian Zionists. Christian Zionists have become an increasingly important subgroup within the Christian Right, especially under the leadership of the late Jerry Falwell and the Moral Majority and more recently under John Hagee and Christians United for Israel (CUFI). Christian Zionism, which predates Jewish Zionism, gained influence through the teachings of nineteenth- and twentieth-century revivalist preachers Darby, Moody and Sunday, and the teachings of the Scofield Study Bible.

Christian Zionism teaches that human history can be divided into seven time periods or dispensations from the Garden of Eden (a literal belief in creationism) through to the Second Coming of Jesus.

According to such beliefs, we are now in the end times of the sixth dispensation awaiting the Second Coming of Jesus. Crucial to the return of Christ is a series of biblical prophecies that are to be fulfilled centring on the State of Israel and fulfilment of the Great Commission to take the gospel into the entire world. The creation of the State of Israel in 1948, the conquest of the West Bank and reunification of Jerusalem are considered signs that Christ's return is imminent. Christian Zionists believe that America, and indeed the world, will be judged according to their dealings with Israel. In such thinking, Genesis 12:3 refers to the blessings and curses of God being dependent upon how people treat the Jewish people: if America blesses (stands up for and supports) Israel, then God will bless America; if it does not, then America will suffer.

For Christian Zionists there is still a separate covenant between God and the Jewish people, and a further covenant with the church. Thus US relations with Israel are seen as being the most important aspect of American foreign policy, and the War on Terror and democracy promotion in the Middle East are viewed primarily through this lens. For a large, albeit declining, section of the Christian church, this view is rejected in favour of replacement theology, which stresses that the church has replaced Israel as God's chosen people. This tends to be the view of most mainstream denominations, including Presbyterians such as Coral Ridge Ministries, while most of the 17-million-strong Southern Baptists, Pentecostal, fundamentalist and charismatic churches have since the 1967 Six Day War been firmly in the Christian Zionist camp. Christian Zionists are democrats rather than theocrats and span both main political parties, although they are predominately Republican.

Many members of the Christian Right do not fit comfortably within either of these two subgroups, including the US president himself (Mansfield, 2005: 153). For them their politico-theological perspective is democratic but they tend to identify the promises of God with America, rather than Israel or the church. In such thinking, America is a Christian nation in which patriotism is next to godliness.

For them, God has blessed America, is blessing America, and will continue to bless America because American values of freedom and liberty have sprung from a Judeo-Christian ethos and possess universal applicability. The argument goes that if God has blessed the United States with great wealth and natural resources, it therefore behoves it to export its values to the rest of the world, with significant implications for US foreign policy.

Researching the Christian Right

With so many different churches, organizations and individuals making up the amorphous Christian Right, the parameters of research into the movement can be problematic. The movement is constantly transforming, with patriarchal figures such as Rushdoony, Falwell and D. James Kennedy dying, new leaders such as Hagee and Parsley emerging, and others including Haggard, Reed and DeLay enmeshed in scandal. The 2006 mid-term elections removed two leading contenders for the Republican presidential nomination, Senators George Allen and Rick Santorum, from the Senate and the presidential race. The present patriarchs and matriarchs of the movement, who include James Dobson, Tim and Bev LaHaye, Pat Robertson and Richard Land, presently command the attention of the political elite, but a new generation is waiting to emerge.

In researching the role of the Christian Right in US foreign policy formation, I have conducted interviews with leading figures within the movement and the Bush and Clinton administrations, attended Christian Right meetings and conferences, observed countless services and television broadcasts, studied Christian Right literature, and listened to sermons, speeches and television broadcasts from leading figures within the movement. I have made extensive use of congressional administration reports, records, and the websites of Christian Right organizations to keep updated on the claims and influence of the movement. I have received regular newsletters and updates from a variety of organizations active in the international arena. In addition

I make use of the now extensive literature on the Christian Right, by friend and foe, to build a detailed picture of what they stand for, how they are organized, and the extent of their impact and significance on US foreign policy. This influence becomes more significant when one considers that mainstream Protestant denominations are declining at a dramatic rate, from 29 million in 1960 to 22 million in 2003 (24 per cent), while Pentecostal, charismatic and Southern Baptist churches have grown exponentially (Russell Mead, 2006).

A Christian Nation?

America is a country in which the overwhelming majority of its citizens believe in God and claim to be Christian. In any one month, at least half the population will have attended church at least once. While religion in Europe has declined over the course of the twentieth and early twenty-first centuries, in America it has gone from strength to strength. America is clearly a nation of Christians, but is it also a Christian nation? This debate has raged since the earliest Puritan settlers fled Europe to start a new life in America and continues to be a source of contention. Samuel Huntington contends that America has been an Anglo-Protestant country for the past three hundred years. White Anglo-Saxon Protestant values, he argues, have been of central importance in defining who and what America is. When immigrants have entered the country, they have embraced Protestant values. However, the influence of Catholic immigration has changed the USA from 'a Protestant country into a Christian country with Protestant values' (Huntington, 2005: 60–61, 92). According to Huntington, these values shape the way Americans think about themselves and their role in the world. For him, 'America is a predominantly Christian nation with a secular government' (Huntington, 2005: 83).

Many on the Christian Right would take issue with Huntington's description, believing that the original intention of the Founding Fathers was to establish one nation under God, which was added to the Pledge of Allegiance by act of Congress in 1954. The Supreme

Court in 1811, 1892 and 1931 described Americans as a Christian people or Christian nation, but it is difficult to avoid the conclusion that the Founding Fathers purposed to maintain a separation between church and state to avoid the sort of repression their ancestors had suffered in Europe (Huntington, 2005: 98). The US Constitution is a secular document, which does not mention Christianity or Jesus Christ. The only two references to religion are contained in Article VI, which states that 'no religious Test shall ever be required as a Qualification to any Office or public Trust under the United States', and in the First Amendment, which forbids the establishment of religion and any attempts to prevent its free exercise. Thomas Jefferson and James Madison led the way in seeking to allow religious freedom while opposing the establishment of religion. Jefferson introduced an 'Act for Establishing Religious Freedom' in 1779 (passed in 1786) and wrote a letter to Danbury Baptists in 1801 calling for a 'wall of separation between church and state', which has become the definitive interpretation of the First Amendment. Madison's 'Memorial and Remonstrance Against Religious Assessments' in 1785 expressed his opposition to a proposal by Patrick Henry to tax all Virginians for the support of Christian ministers. Further confirmation of the outlook of the Founding Fathers is clearly set out in the Treaty with Tripoli, 1797, passed unanimously by the US Senate, with Article 11 stating that the 'Government of the United States is not, in any sense, founded on the Christian religion'.

The Christian Right agitate to break down the wall of separation at every opportunity, adopting the role of victim that places them in the position of suffering persecution for their beliefs. The enemy is considered to be a liberal secularism, devoid of moral values, that would seek to erode Christian freedoms and traditional American Judeo-Christian values. At home, this archetypal enemy includes the American Civil Liberties Union, People for the American Way, Americans United for Separation of Church and State, and the Democratic Party. In foreign policy, the enemy comprises secular institutions such as the United Nations and the International Criminal Court, which would seek to influence US policy on social, moral, fiscal, humanitarian or military matters. Alexis de Tocqueville noted in 1835 this intimate relationship between Christianity and American identity:

> It must not be forgotten that religion gave birth to Anglo-American society. In the United States, religion is therefore mingled with all the habits of the nation and all the feelings of patriotism, whence it derives its force. (de Tocqueville, 1998: 181)

De Tocqueville considered that the separation of church and state was the strength of the American system, where 'religious institutions have remained wholly distinct from political institutions'. Such was, and is, the hold of Christianity on the American public mind that it has become 'a religion which is believed without discussion' (de Tocqueville, 1998: 181). The clear separation between church and state identified by de Tocqueville has been severely eroded by the Bush administration, with its faith-based initiatives and the involvement of the Christian Right in decision-making processes.

Throughout American history, a combination of Protestantism and patriotism has helped shape American domestic and foreign policy. A series of 'Great Awakenings' or religious revivals during the eighteenth and nineteenth centuries – under George Whitefield and Jonathon Edwards in the 1730s to 1740s, Charles Finney in the 1820s, and Dwight Moody and Billy Sunday in the 1890s to 1900s – helped develop an individualistic Protestantism. The combination of a highly individualized religion and economic prosperity during the twentieth century helped develop a distinctive American gospel. The secularization of this American gospel forms the basis of the American Creed, American Civil Religion and American Exceptionalism.

The American Creed is an ideological commitment to the democratic, legal and individualistic principles enshrined in the American Constitution, Bill of Rights and Declaration of Independence. It is a fervent belief in the wisdom of the Founding Fathers and principles of life, liberty and the pursuit of happiness. Seymour Martin Lipset describes the key distinguishing features to be an abiding belief in liberty, egalitarianism (of opportunity rather than outcome), individualism, populism and laissez-faire (Lipset, 1973: 63–4). This glue binds American society together and draws it into alliances and relationships with the rest of the world, developing bonds with those of similar persuasion and seeking to convert those nations that resist. For preachers, televangelists and politicians in the Christian Right the American Creed is the clearest expression of the favour God has bestowed on America, and it comes with an imperative to share the good news of freedom and prosperity with the added bonus of salvation for those who believe.

The other pillar of the American gospel is American Civil Religion or civic nationalism. This seeks to unite Americans of all religious faiths and denominations around a civil religion that is Christian in origin but now embraces all Americans around the shared values of the American Creed. Huntington considers that American Civil Religion – which excludes atheists, whom he considers 'outsiders' in the American community (Huntington, 2005: 82) – comprises four main elements. It presupposes a Supreme Being and belief that Americans are either God's 'chosen' people, or as close to it as it is possible to be, with a mission to do 'good' in the world. Religious allusions and symbols are prevalent in US public rituals and ceremonies, and the national ceremonies themselves assume a religious aura and perform religious functions (Huntington, 2005: 104–5). This intermingling of the civil and religious creates a hybrid faith that is undergirded by an exceptionalism which contends that the United States was chosen by God to fulfil a unique role in the world. Every time the Pledge of Allegiance is recited or *The Star-Spangled Banner* sung such beliefs are reinforced.

The perpetuation of such beliefs serves to construct an American identity that presents American foreign policy with particular challenges. There remains a constant tension between realist approaches to US foreign policy, which only consider national security interests, and liberal approaches, which would seek to promote the moral values defined in the American Creed. Traditionally, American presidents have pursued narrow American self-interest but have clothed realist policies in liberal or moral rhetoric. Realism is the default position of US foreign policy, but occasionally liberal and more recently neoconservative policies have sought to export American values. Neoconservatives advanced an agenda that had been prepared in opposition during the Clinton years. They advocated a Reaganite foreign policy based on increased military strength and the promotion of American values abroad by democratization and open markets, getting rid of hostile regimes, and assuming global leadership in pursuit of US principles and interests (PNAC, 1997, 1998). The events of 11 September 2001 provided Bush with an opportunity to pursue liberal/neoconservative policy options, enthusiastically embraced by Christian Right organizations and politicians concerned with foreign affairs.

George W. Bush's Base

The Christian Right have become an important story in American politics because of the efforts by Karl Rove, Bush's master strategist, to adopt a 51 per cent winning strategy. Following the awarding of the presidency to George Bush by the Supreme Court's decision to stop counting votes in Florida in 2000, Rove determined to gather right-wing evangelicals to the Bush cause by concentrating on moral issues of concern to them. In this way his man could govern effectively and achieve his objectives with the support of just 51 per cent of those who voted; that is, rather than compromising and seeking to dilute social, fiscal and security objectives, embracing the Christian Right would enable Bush to achieve his objectives. The Christian Right, as an organized movement, could be relied upon to vote and work to secure the election of their preferred candidate, particularly when that candidate was 'one of their own' and committed to delivering results on issues of concern to them. The strategy was extraordinarily successful. Indeed, it subsequently resulted in 74 per cent support for Bush from white evangelicals in the 2004 election, ensuring that he remained in office, despite opposition in the country to the Iraq War.

Rove's strategy did not represent a gamble but rather reflected a determination on the part of the Christian Right to influence the political agenda and gain more influence in the Republican Party. The Christian Right emerged as a forceful player in the Republican Party following the humiliating defeat of Barry Goldwater by Lyndon Johnson in the presidential elections of 1964 (Goldwater only collected fifty-two electoral college votes). Paul Weyrich, one of Goldwater's advisers, was determined to avoid such humiliations in future by expanding the base of the Republican Party. In 1973 he formed an influential think-tank, the Heritage Foundation, and courted members of Pentecostal, charismatic and fundamentalist churches to become involved. Along with fellow conservative Catholics Richard Viguerie and Terry Dolan, Weyrich brought together Howard Phillips, Ed McAteer and Morton Blackwell to establish the Moral Majority under Jerry Falwell, bringing conservative evangelicals national attention and helping secure Ronald Reagan's election victory the following year. In 1981, Weyrich and Tim LaHaye were also instrumental in the formation of the Council for National Policy (CNP), which brought together leading members of the Christian Right, corporate executives, financiers, gun lobbyists, and political operatives within the Republican Party. A decade later, the Moral Majority gave way to the Christian Coalition; through it, and myriad specialist parachurch organizations, the Christian Right became established as a permanent feature of the American political process.

Christian Right organizations mobilized their supporters, encouraged them to join and take over local Republican parties throughout America and to participate in elections at every level. They have been extremely successful in working the democratic process to ensure maximum support for their political and religious perspective. Not only Bush but also numerous congressional representatives and senators owe their seats to the active involvement of the Christian Right in their constituencies. The Christian Right support candidates with the expectation that the candidate will deliver them specific benefits in terms of their political objectives. In domestic politics, the expectation has been that Bush and the Republican Congress would tighten controls on abortion, stem-cell research, same-sex marriages and gay rights, while permitting prayer and the teaching of creationism in schools, and providing support for abstinence programmes. In addition, social welfare provision would be removed from the state and subcontracted to faith-based organizations. There is the expectation of regular consultation with Christian Right leaders on all issues affecting them and their members, including appointments to the administration and to the Supreme Court. Many of those expectations have been fulfilled over the course of the Bush presidency.

Successes have led to increased confidence on the part of leaders of the movement and a desire to extend that influence to the foreign policy arena. Organizations such as Focus on the Family (FOF), the Family Research Council (FRC), Concerned Women for America (CWA), the Institute on Religion and Democracy (IRD), and the Eagle Forum have turned their attention towards seeking to advance their socially conservative moral values in the United Nations and World Congress of Families. Organizations have been eager to apply for faith-based-initiative funding to deliver humanitarian assistance abroad while evangelizing. Other groups have sought to highlight issues of religious freedom, campaigned in support of Israel, or used the War on Terror to advance their own agendas; still others have sought to minimize the significance of global warming and environmental degradation. The Christian Right during the Bush presidency have become increasingly involved in foreign affairs. This book charts that progress by examining key areas of interest for the movement.

For God's Sake details how the Christian Right have managed to become an important actor in US foreign policy, attempting to advance interests in accordance with their own world-view. The book divides into three parts, with a conclusion. Part One provides a solid foundation that considers what the Christian Right believes and teaches, before detailing how it has gained and continues to gain in influence. It pays attention to the theology and world-view of the Christian Right and considers how the movement operates. In Part Two the focus is on key political and ideological concerns including democracy promotion, human rights, humanitarian assistance and the environment, and how the Christian Right have sought to influence policy in these areas. Part Three concentrates on the Christian Right's influence on US foreign policy approaches towards Israel and the War on Terror.

The Christian Right in America have worked hard to be in a position to influence significantly the country's foreign policy decision-makers. Chapter 1 looks at the different agendas of the Republican Party and the Christian Right and the way in which they have been able to influence successive presidents and their administrations, congressional representatives and senators through effective lobbying, think-tanks, fund-raising and voter registration. An examination is made of those Christian Right organizations specifically engaged in foreign affairs, before considering how conservative evangelicals seek to extend their influence into the future through the growth of Christian Right training colleges and organizations which seek to develop the next generation of political and foreign policy decision-makers. Chapter 2 examines the proselytizing imperative of Christian Right organizations. The evangelistic impulse aims at the worldwide conversion of believers of other religions and none to the one true faith. This chapter explores the range of missionary activity carried out by the Christian Right during the George W. Bush administration, including radio, televangelism, charity works, missions, and religious crusades abroad and how gaining converts to an Americanized gospel promotes capitalism and support for US foreign policy objectives.

Chapter 3 considers democracy promotion under the Bush administration. Democracy promotion has always played a key role in US foreign policy strategy. Organizations such as the National Endowment for Democracy (NED) were set up as anti-communist organizations intended to undermine leadership in countries that did not share America's liberal democratic tradition. In recent years, anti-communism has been replaced by a pro-democracy stance that seeks to encourage or impose free-market democracy on all nations. George Bush's powerful religious–democratic rhetoric, identifying him as a member of the Christian Right, reaches out to this constituency, both domestic and international. The chapter analyses the appeal of democratization around the world for the Christian Right.

The Christian Right in the United States have developed great expertise in advancing their cause, and Republican foreign policy interests more generally, by using heightened concern for the normative issues of human rights and humanitarian assistance. They have managed to focus attention on real and imagined Christian persecution abroad in order to receive funding for their work and to gain access to countries hostile to proselytizing. Chapter 4 considers how Christian Right organizations have successfully attracted government finance through faith-based initiatives to fund relief and development projects while propagating an American gospel overseas. The chapter further examines how Christian Right attitudes on family values and morality adversely affect humanitarian assistance in the fight against HIV/AIDS and disadvantage women in both the global North and South. Further consideration is given to attempts to promote the Christian Right's domestic policy concerns abroad, drawing attention to the Bush administration's granting of privileged NGO observer status at the United Nations and international forums to Christian Right groups. The chapter emphasizes the role of Christian Right groups in promoting an agenda that undermines a woman's right to choose an abortion and discriminates against homosexuals.

Chapter 5 focuses on the increasingly important area of environmental politics. The Christian Right have traditionally taken a dominion theology or Reconstruction approach to environmental matters, based on Genesis 1:26–29, in which humanity rules over creation. Such an approach espouses the abundance of natural resources and leads to opposition by some Christian Right groups to environmentalism, including a denial of global warming. The chapter examines Christian Right attitudes to climate change and highlights divisions within the movement over the issue of anthropogenic global warming. Such divisions grow out of differing interpretations of scripture and approaches to global poverty. The chapter presents the arguments from environmental, or creation-care, evangelicals and counter-arguments from the Christian Right mainstream within the Stewardship of Creation grouping, before analysing the impact of both camps on Bush strategy.

Chapter 6 details Christian Zionist action on behalf of Israel. The Christian Right have been among Israel's leading supporters both within and outside successive administrations. Traditionally Israel has derived its support in America from the Jewish lobby and, in particular, the efforts of the lobbying group American Israel Public Affairs Committee (AIPAC). In recent years, however, the most vociferous and influential support has come from the Christian Right. This chapter examines that influence by considering the eschatological basis of Christian Zionist support for the nation of Israel and their interaction with the Israel lobby. In considering this influence, attention is paid to the modus operandi of Christian Zionists and how they have sought to influence the foreign policy decision-making process. Case studies, including the 2006 Israel–Hezbollah war and the Middle East Road Map, are used to illustrate the strength of the Christian Zionist movement in America and how this has shaped US Middle East policy.

Chapter 7 extends the previous chapter's focus on the Middle East by focusing on the global War on Terror. Many sections of the Christian Right regard Islam as the major enemy facing America today. In this chapter, we revisit Samuel Huntington's clash-of-civilizations thesis and demonstrate how the Christian Right have used the events of 9/11 to seek to persuade the government to press for religious freedom and opportunities for them to proselytize in Muslim countries. Christian involvement in Muslim countries is a sensitive issue that is further complicated by perceptions of the US military as a Christian army. An examination of this claim is undertaken, considering both the make-up of the armed forces and the role of Christian Right-financed mercenaries. The chapter continues by exploring the part leading members of the Christian Right, such as Franklin Graham, Jerry Falwell and Hal Lindsay, have played in fanning Islamophobia at home and abroad through their sermons, broadcasts, briefings and writings. The chapter concludes by considering whether the long War on Terror is shorthand for a war against Islam.

The book concludes that since the events of 9/11 the Christian Right have had greater opportunities to influence US foreign policy than ever before. They have seized those opportunities provided by the Republican Party, Congress and the George W. Bush administration to influence, to reinforce and, in terms of humanitarian assistance, to deliver US policy on democracy, human rights, foreign aid, the environment, Israel and the War on Terror. The Christian Right have enjoyed success in many areas during the Bush years and are currently training up a new generation of leaders who are intent on maintaining US foreign policy according to a narrow set of religious beliefs in perpetuity. Christian Right influence is damaging to US interests in the short, medium and long term and is likely to engender continued hostility for many years to come.

PART I

I

Open Doors in the Corridors of Power

Over the past three decades, the Christian Right have developed into a sophisticated and relatively coherent political force with their roots firmly in Republican Party soil. Whatever the outcome of the 2008 presidential election, it is inconceivable that the Christian Right will not have played a significant role in the nomination of the Republican candidate. Such expectations are a fitting tribute to a movement that has come of age and is able to mobilize millions of voters behind a narrow range of socially conservative moral issues. The Moral Majority and, later, the Christian Coalition have proved invaluable in delivering Republican victories in three presidential and six congressional elections. The Christian Right's ability to mobilize supporters behind the Republican cause is not guaranteed, however, and there are limits to their ability to turn out the vote, particularly when concerns other than socially conservative ones dominate elections. Over the course of the George W. Bush presidency the Christian Right have increasingly sought to extend domestic success to the international arena on an equally narrow range of special interests. In this chapter, we will consider the background to the movement and examine how it seeks to influence the executive and legislature. This will enable an understanding of the religious and political motivations of the movement, and of the politics of mutual dependency between the Republican Party and the Christian Right, which will inform discussions in later chapters on specific foreign policy interventions.

Influencing the White House and Capitol Hill

The relatively recent phenomenon of organized Christian Right political involvement began in the 1970s, but there are antecedents. Most presidents have claimed to be practising Christians and have transferred the rhetoric, at least, of civil religion and the American Creed to foreign policy. President Truman's early decision to recognize the State of Israel was due in no small part to his Christian belief (Clifford, 1992: 7–8). Richard Land would claim that Wilsonianism represented an evangelical foreign policy with its roots firmly in Woodrow Wilson's Presbyterian evangelicalism.[1] However, the 1970s mark a departure in this general principle of evangelical engagement with the political process. During this period, there was a shift among conservative evangelicals, particularly in the South, from the Democrats to the Republican Party. Democrat support for civil rights, the Equal Rights Amendment, abortion and increasing secularization threatened traditional evangelical values and caused those who held them to question their long-standing allegiance to the party. Kevin Phillips attributes this political shift to the reform legacy of four Southern Democratic presidencies: Truman, Johnson, Carter and Clinton (Phillips, 2006: 179). In a rapidly changing society, where traditional gender roles, sexual morality, marriage and traditional Christian beliefs were increasingly contested, conservative evangelicals sought security in their traditional values.

The election of born-again Southern Baptist Jimmy Carter to the presidency in 1976 should have signalled a restoration in Democrat fortunes among white evangelicals in the South. Conservative churchgoers were unimpressed, however, with Carter's record in office and disappointed by increased secularization, a poor economy and weak foreign policy. Those leading evangelicals determined to construct a politically active Christian Right, committed to becoming an integral part of the Republican Party and its most significant voice, capitalized on such frustrations. From the time Carter took office in 1977 until Reagan's inauguration, no fewer than twelve evangelical organizations were formed that would help shape the course of American politics, and eventually US foreign policy, to the present day.

Christian Right Organizations

In 1977 the American Family Association (AFA), Focus on the Family (FOF), and the National Federation for Decency were established. These concentrated their attention on promoting traditional family values and a socially conservative political agenda, although Focus on the Family would emerge to become one of the main conservative evangelical actors in foreign affairs. The following year saw the formation by Robert Grant of the organization Christian Voice, which would become highly influential. Christian Voice organized evangelical Christians across denominations to become involved in the political process, introducing the innovative Congressional Report Card, which has since been taken up by other Christian Right organizations, showing supporters the voting performance of congressional representatives and senators on a range of issues highlighted by Christian Voice as relevant to its members' interests. Members and supporters mobilized behind a campaign entitled 'Christians for Reagan' and began the process of politicization of conservative evangelicals, almost exclusively within a Republican Party context. The organization was a precursor to the emergence of some of the most important Christian Right groups in this period. In 1979, Ed McAteer established the Council of 56 Religious Roundtable, which brought together leading conservative evangelical and Catholic businesspeople, preachers, financiers, military and politicians in regular meetings to help shape a conservative political agenda, which they sought to introduce into the Republican Party.

In the same year, the success of previous organizations inspired the formation of the Moral Majority and Bev LaHaye's Concerned Women for America (CWA), an organization dedicated to resisting the Equal Rights Amendment (ERA) and upholding traditional moral values. The CWA and LaHaye's Institute have been significantly involved in foreign affairs from the time of the founder's personal support for Reagan's policy of arming the Nicaraguan Contras (Brozan, 1987). Perhaps even more significant for the fortunes of the Democratic Party in the South was infighting among the Southern Baptists, Carter's own denomination. Richard Land, an Oxford-educated Anglophile with great presence and later a confidant of President George W. Bush, succeeded in taking control and steering the formerly moderate denomination into an overtly conservative political and religious direction, enabling Reagan to take all but Carter's home state in the South in 1980 and all eleven Southern states in 1984.

In 1980 the National Affairs Briefing, the Council on Revival and Lou Sheldon's Traditional Values Coalition (TVC) were formed, adding to the active political engagement by a new wave of Christian Right organizations. Most organizations concentrated exclusively on domestic policy, and moral values in particular, but where they did focus attention on foreign policy, as in the case of the Religious Roundtable, Phyllis Schlafly's Eagle Forum and Christian Voice, it was to support calls for a strong defence and resolute anti-communism. The organizations often shared members and worked in the same narrow areas of interest. Although overwhelmingly white evangelical, they increasingly reached out to Catholics and other conservative groups with shared interests in opposing the secularization of American society. The Institute on Religion and Democracy (IRD) and the Family Research Council (FRC), two organizations that would come to play an important part in Christian Right advocacy in international affairs, were set up during Reagan's first administration, in 1981 and 1983, respectively.

Council for National Policy

A secretive organization known as the Council for National Policy (CNP) was set up in Reagan's first year in office, 1981. The CNP, like the Religious Roundtable, sought to bring together movers and shakers within the emerging Christian Right. Unlike McAteer's group, however, the CNP sought to include business magnates, financiers, corporate executives, media moguls, judges, conservative Republicans and politicians, as well as Christian Right leaders. The CNP today claims a membership of over 600, and is committed to the 'free enterprise system, a strong national defense, and support for traditional western values'.[2] The CNP does not lobby government; rather, it is a group that seeks to build close personal relationships in a shared endeavour to achieve common goals. The group's secretive nature reflects an approach to the political process that seeks to achieve objectives without accountability or scrutiny by the democratic polity. The membership list is confidential but was leaked for several years during the 1990s by the now defunct Institute for First Amendment Studies (IFAS).

The CNP's membership list and executive board read like a who's who of the Christian and conservative right. Members have included congressional representatives Dan Burton, John Doolittle, Ernest Istook, Jack Kemp and former Leaders of the House Richard Armey and Tom DeLay. Senators include D.M. 'Launch' Faircloth, former chair of the Senate Foreign Relations Committee Jesse Helms, Jon Kyl, Republican whip Trent Lott and Don Nickles. Other political leaders include former attorneys general Edwin Meese and John Ashcroft, Reagan domestic policy adviser Kenneth Cribb, and former health and human services secretary Tommy Thompson. Morton Blackwell served as a special assistant to Ronald Reagan in the White House and tycoon Joseph Coors organized a kitchen cabinet with regular access to the president, in the Executive Office Building, until removed. Gary Bauer was White House adviser on policy development. Phyllis Schlafly served on Reagan's Defense Policy Advisory Group and advocated strongly in favour of Star Wars. Eagle Forum actually became an NGO with special consultative status at the United Nations with the Economic and Social Council (IFAS, 1998; Leaming and Boston, 2004).

Leaders of Christian Right organizations represented in the CNP include: Paul Weyrich; Pat Robertson, founder of the Christian Broadcasting Network and the voice of Christian America for much of the world; Charles 'Chuck' Colson, former member of the Nixon administration, sentenced to prison for his part in the Watergate scandal, and founder of the Prison Fellowship Ministries in 1976; James Dobson, a leading Christian commentator on child raising and the family, and the founder of FOF; Michael Farris, founder of the Home School Legal Defense Association and Patrick Henry College, a training centre for future Christian Right political leaders. Also Tim and Bev LaHaye, Ed McAteer and Christian Reconstructionist writer Gary North are members, as are Tony Perkins, one of the leading second-generation Christian Right leaders and president of the FRC, and Ralph Reed, former head of the Christian Coalition and adviser to the Bush campaign in 2000. In 2006, Reed failed in a bid to become lieutenant governor of Georgia, after being implicated in the Abramoff lobbying scandal, involving Native American gambling money (Stone, 2006). The list also includes Rick Scarborough, founder of Vision America and a leading force in turning out Christian Values Voters in 2006 and 2008. Others have included the late Rousas Rushdoony, D. James Kennedy, Jerry Falwell and Bill Bright, founder of Campus Crusade for Christ (CCC). The thrice-yearly meetings of the CNP provide an excellent opportunity for Christian Right ministers to meet with like-minded financially wealthy backers and key opinion formers to determine strategy for influencing Republican administrations.

Key members of the CNP and benefactors of this and other organizations include Ed and Elsa Prince, who have supported the FRC, Howard Ahmanson Jr, who has supported Rushdoony's Chalcedon movement, Weyrich's Free Congress Foundation (FCF), the Rutherford Institute and the think-tank Council on Foreign Relations (CFR).[3]

The Coors brewing magnates have generously supported FCF and conservative think-tank the Heritage Foundation. The DeVos family, founders of the Amway direct-selling organization, have financed FRC and Robert Schuller Ministries. The brewing and energy company family of Herbert and Nelson Bunker Hunt have supported Christian Broadcasting Network (CBN), Campus Crusade for Christ, the Summer Institute of Linguistics (SIL) and Wycliffe Associates (IFAS, 1998; Leaming and Boston, 2004).

This secretive network equipped the Christian Right with major resources, which they were later able to supplement through the giving of organization members and supporters. Under the Reagan administration, the Christian Right enjoyed unprecedented access to the White House through the CNP and Joseph Coors's kitchen cabinet. Edwin Meese had served as Reagan's chief of staff during his governorship in California and played a pivotal role throughout Reagan's double term as president. Meese later went on to work at the Heritage Foundation, a think-tank to which he had earlier promised that 'this administration will cooperate fully with your efforts' (Leaming and Boston, 2004).

The Christian Right and Reagan foreign policy

In terms of foreign policy, the Christian Right directed their efforts towards anti-communist initiatives advocated overtly and covertly by the administration. Ever since Karl Marx called for the abolition of religion, that 'opium of the people', in his *Introduction to a Contribution to the Critique of Hegel's Philosophy of Right*, communism has been viewed as the arch-enemy of Christian evangelicals. The persecution of Christians by communist authorities throughout the world served to strengthen this hostility. The Christian Right therefore enthusiastically supported Reagan's arms race and his powerful invective against the Soviet Union. A meeting of the National Association of Evangelicals (NAE) was an obvious setting for Reagan's 'evil empire' speech, and the Christian Right remained his most fervent supporters. Oliver North and General John Singlaub, former head of the

World Anti-Communist League, both members of the CNP, were involved in the covert military operations in Central America and in the supporting of the Nicaraguan Contras that did so much to discredit the Reagan administration. Jerry Falwell's Moral Majority, Pat Robertson's Freedom Council and the Heritage Foundation were among a number of right-wing groups involved with the Reagan administration's Outreach Working Party on Central America, devising strategy and propaganda in support of a campaign of targeted killings and other anti-communist activity (IFAS, 1998; Diamond, 1995a). Christian Right support for US oil and business interests in South America (Perkins, 2006), the Contras and fellow evangelical Rios Montt in Guatemala have all had long-term repercussions for America's relationship with countries in its self-proclaimed backyard.

Christian Voice and the Unification Church

A more surprising source of Christian Right funding came from Sun Myung Moon's Unification Church, which, through the Coalition for Religious Freedom and the American Freedom Coalition, supported Christian Voice and collaborations with Christian Right leaders including Tim LaHaye, Don Wildmon, Hal Lindsay, Paul Crouch (Trinity Broadcasting Network), James Robison, Jimmy Swaggart and D. James Kennedy (IFAS, 1998). In the quest for power, conservative evangelicals have been prepared to jettison long-standing theological objections to Catholicism, the Unification Church and, later, the Mormons, preferring to achieve temporal political objectives rather than seeking to maintain theological integrity (Shupe and Heinerman, 1985). They were willing to make common cause with any group that espoused conservative social values, a belief in free enterprise, and virulent anti-communism.

From Bush to Bush

Although Ronald Reagan was, and remains, the Christian Right's favourite president, his vice president was not guaranteed the succession. Pat Robertson, a Southern Baptist converted to Assembly of God minister, challenged George H.W. Bush for the presidency. Robertson's campaign resulted in caucus victories in Alaska, Hawaii, Nevada and Washington, with near misses in three other states. Vice-President Bush went on to win the nomination, but in order to do so was obliged to reach out to the Christian Right by publicly proclaiming his connections with conservative evangelical leaders and detailing his own faith in his book *Man of Integrity*. Bush Senior enlisted his son, George W., to be his liaison with the Christian Right, recognition of the increased national influence of the movement. Once elected, however, Christian Right influence on the administration diminished as the new president oversaw the end of the Cold War, sought to distance himself from the Iran–Contra scandal, and embarked on the Gulf War. Robertson, in the meantime, developed the Christian Coalition, replacing the Moral Majority, which by 1989 had run its course.

Facing re-election in 1992, Bush Senior was not so fortunate: the Republican vote split because of the independent candidacy of Ross Perot and the appointment of an all-Southern Democrat ticket of Clinton and Gore in 1992. Undeterred, conservative evangelicals continued to campaign electorally and within the Republican Party to exert as much influence as possible over policy and the nomination process. They were able to do so because of their perceived ability, among fellow Republicans, to mobilize public support and turn it into votes. Conservative evangelicals Richard Armey and Tom DeLay joined forces with Newt Gingrich in writing the Republicans' manifesto 'Contract with the American People' for the mid-term elections in 1994. The mid-terms resulted in the first victory ever for the Republican Party over both Houses of Congress and ushered in Republican domination of the House for twelve years. In spite of this, during the Clinton period Christian Right organizations had very limited access to the executive.[4] Attempts to influence foreign policy went through Congress, newspapers and the Christian media. Two issues dominated the Christian Right's concern in foreign affairs: the religious persecution of Christians in southern Sudan, and CWA's opposition to the Convention on the Elimination of All Forms of Discrimination Against Women (CEDAW) (Oldfield, 2004).

George W. Bush, having observed his father's defeat eight years earlier, determined to harness the support of conservative evangelicals as effectively as Reagan had managed in 1980. Bush Junior had an advantage in that he was a born-again Christian who had built up considerable contacts with the movement as point man in the successful campaign of 1988 (Kristof, 2000). In 1999, George W. Bush spoke at the CNP in a bid to secure Christian Right support and finance for his presidential campaign. A full text of the speech has never been released, leading to suggestions that promises were made behind closed doors to special interests groups but undeclared to the American people (Phillips, 2006; Leaming and Boston, 2004).

The controversial Bush victory in 2000 was secured with 68 per cent of those white evangelicals who voted opting for Bush, a figure that was to increase four years later to 78 per cent. The increased representation and political involvement of the Christian Right have led to over a quarter of members of both Houses of Congress identifying themselves as evangelicals (Russell Mead, 2006). By 2007 every governor, every senator and all but eleven congressional representatives identified themselves by religion (Capitol Advantage, 2007).

Christian Right Activism

The Christian Right have become very accomplished political operators throughout the American polity and have increasingly played a significant role in foreign affairs through involvement in the United Nations and the World Congress of Families. In the following section, the common characteristics of the most successful and active organizations are detailed in order to highlight how they have been able to influence the political process. In order to succeed in American politics, financial resources are a prerequisite and the Christian Right have made every effort to obtain and expand those resources in pursuit of political objectives. As previously discussed, the movement has certain key wealthy benefactors who have provided start-up capital in order to establish organizations, which have then been able to develop through the financial contributions of supporters. Being a conservative movement, the Christian Right encourages entrepreneurship and free enterprise, and it is therefore no surprise to discover that organizations are run as businesses, albeit with tax-exempt status. The most successful Christian Right organizations have balance sheets revealing turnovers of many millions of dollars. Such income serves to maintain a high profile for organizational leaders, plays an active role in the continuous US electoral cycle, and provides Christian Right leaders with the credibility and income to enable them to mix with the country's political elite.

The relationship between the Christian Right and financial wealth has led to scandals that have been an integral part of the movement since the late 1970s. In addition to questions of propriety raised about the connection of leading conservative evangelicals to the Moonie cult, through financial support by the Unification Church, there have been further scandals. Pat Robertson's Operation Blessing ministry diverted airplanes from delivering medical supplies to Congo refugees to transporting diamond-mining equipment for Robertson's African Development Corporation (Palast, 2003: 236–7). The Jim and Tammy Bakker scandal in the late 1980s, which saw Jim Bakker gaoled for fraud and conspiracy involving Praise the Lord Television Corporation and the Heritage USA Christian theme park, also embroiled Jerry Falwell as he failed to restore the fortunes of both television corporation and theme park. More recently, the Jack Abramoff lobbying scandal involving Grover Norquist and Ralph Reed resulted in the resignation of House Majority Leader Tom DeLay, and defeat for Reed in his attempt to become lieutenant governor of Georgia (IFAS, 1998; Carney, 2006).

Under the second Bush administration the Christian Right have also benefited from a new funding source. Federal money now goes to faith-based organizations in a presidential initiative designed to privatize the delivery of social and welfare and provide resources to mainly Christian organizations to enable them to deliver services.

The initiative extends to foreign assistance and enables faith-based organizations to proselytize and recruit members providing that they notionally separate service provision using federal funding from proselytizing financed by their own resources. The faith-based initiative can be regarded as payback for conservative evangelical support for Bush during the elections of 2000 and 2004[5] (Lynn, 2006: 117–47), while also appealing to small-government Republicans.

The Christian Right have become proficient at extracting funds from supporters through regular mailings, financial appeals and television advertising. Such requests are framed in terms of 'love offerings', 'gifts' and 'seed planting', with the inference that the giver is contributing directly to God's work and will be duly rewarded. The Word of Faith and Pentecostal movements have grown particularly adept at preaching a prosperity gospel that proclaims: 'Give, and it shall be given unto you; good measure, pressed down, and shaken together, and running over, shall men give into your bosom. For with the same measure that ye mete withal it shall be measured to you again' (Luke 6:38). The message is clear: the more you give to the organization, preacher or church, the more you will receive. Unfortunately, as many Christians have discovered, the reality is that the more they give, the poorer they get and the richer the leader becomes.

Money and resources are vital, however, for the extensive political activity in which the Christian Right engage in pursuing their objectives. Resources are needed to pay for impressive Internet sites, direct mailing campaigns, literature, television programmes and conferences. Although political donations from non-profit-making organizations are not permitted under US tax law, Christian Right organizations nonetheless provide contributions in kind in terms of time and resources. Advertising campaigns attacking political opponents and supporting policy positions adopted by favoured candidates are used to advance their objectives.

Supporters of Christian Right organizations, however, play a far more important role than simply providing money; their voice becomes all-important in influencing policymakers. Direct mailing, newsletters, magazines, local organizers, radio broadcasts, television programmes and websites keep supporters fully apprised of the latest concerns of Christian Right leaders. Many organizations, such as FRC and CUFI, use rapid action calls to alert members and supporters of impending legislation and other matters that require an instant response. These members and supporters are crucially the constituents of congressional representatives and senators, and represent a significant number of votes that could be lost should a representative decide to ignore or reject their requests. When Congress is in session congressional representatives and senators spend considerable amounts of time away from their constituencies and become particularly sensitive to issues raised by organized groups of voters that could jeopardize their prospects of re-election.

Successful Christian Right groups have become very effective lobbyists, developing close connections with Republicans on Capitol Hill and within the White House. Christian Voice pioneered the congressional report card in the early 1980s, which informed constituents of the voting profile of their representatives and senators on a range of key issues. Other groups, including Eagle Forum, FRC and Christian Coalition, have also adopted report cards, which serve as a powerful tool to enable supporters to engage with their representatives over issues concerning an organization, with the added benefit of intimidating representatives facing re-election into taking notice of those issues. At the CUFI conference in Washington DC in July 2007, some two thousand supporters received packs containing details of every congressional representative and senator and were taught how to lobby. The lobbying prompt illustrates the attention to detail of such organizations and the commitment of Christian Right regular members in being willing to invest the time and expense in visiting the capital to influence the political process.

How to Effectively Communicate with Congressmen and Senators
Preparing for the meeting

- Get informed – Go to your elected official's website and familiarize yourself with who is representing you. What is their religious affiliation? What seem to be their personal interests? What have been the key legislation they have sponsored?

- Have a prepared FACT sheet.
- Once appointment is confirmed, ask about bringing a camera and cameraman to tape a greeting to their constituents that you represent.
- One week prior to meeting, call to reconfirm appointment time as well as who in your group will be attending. Ask for specific instructions for entering their office.

Meeting day

- Dress professionally.
- Arrive early for security processing. Take photo ID.
- Bring FACT sheet.
- Have a designated point person. They will introduce the attendees and present concerns. Others may ask questions or contribute additional information but it is essential to have a designated point person who will also close the meeting, restating concerns.
- Open the meeting by expressing your appreciation for the member's time and for their past support of ___________.
- Stay focused and on task. Do not introduce multiple issues.
- Listen and be responsive. If they request additional information, get it to them as soon as possible.
- Close – 'We hope we can count on your support for …'
- Encourage everyone in your group to send a thank you card upon your return home to the member and the staff that assisted you.

Letter requesting support for Israel

- Use personal stationery – remember that colored paper stands out in piles of white and cream.
- Open with greeting and thanks for prior meeting.
- Use your own words but be sure to include phrases (i.e. 'no more dividing the land,' 'right to co-exist,' 'right to defend herself').
- Be brief and succinct! State points and give back up statement.
- Be encouraging, positive and request support. Don't threaten, bully or slander.
- Close – Express your appreciation for their time and support.
- Ask for a response.

Build a relationship

- Find common issue to agree on and use that as a vehicle on which to build a relationship.

- Work to build ongoing relationship with the member's staff – acknowledge and compliment them.
- Go to local events that elected official will be attending or sponsoring – reintroduce yourself to the member and their staff.
- Send note of encouragement and thanks periodically.[6]

The importance of this document is that it reveals the seriousness of intent that is characteristic of everything the movement embarks on. This is not playing political games; this is devising campaign strategies to win and maintain power and influence. The tactic is to win the support, respect and even friendship of a senator or representative. The initial approach is to flatter the target by knowing about their work and personal life. The offer to bring a camera and camera operator massages the target's ego while offering a free publicity opportunity. As he or she is unlikely to say anything antagonistic to your policy viewpoint, this also provides evidence of at least tacit support for the preferred policy position. The politeness and thank-you card follow-up are all designed to project an image of respect, efficiency and knowledge about the issues. In CUFI's case, the repetition of emotive phraseology is recognition that, as a representative has so many matters to attend to, that the repetition of simple phrases will lodge them in the subconscious mind, whence they will be recalled and become part of the representative's own thought process.

Other organizations adopt similar strategies. David Brog from CUFI also advised attendees to lobby not only congressional representatives and senators but also constituency offices and staffers. Politicians facing re-election and living in the rarefied atmosphere of Washington DC are particularly sensitive to constituency concerns. If the Christian Right are actively engaged at constituency level then the reports back from the home constituency are likely to reflect disproportionate constituency concern for conservative evangelical issues, including foreign policy. Lobbying also extends to rapid response actions, which involve flooding the White House and Congress with tens of thousands of letters, emails, faxes and telephone calls to express approval or disapproval for courses of action highlighted by

Christian Right organizations. This is used to great effect and, again, pressures government to act on the disproportionately represented concerns of Christian Right voters.

Christian missions to America's governing elite also orchestrate lobbying activities. D. James Kennedy's Coral Ridge Ministries ran for a number of years the Center for Christian Statesmanship on Capitol Hill. The mission closed in April 2007 but reopened a few months later under the auspices of Evangelism Explosion International, founded by Kennedy in 1962. The Center seeks to befriend congressional representatives, senators, staffers and interns, with volunteers leading weekly Bible studies, and hosting monthly Politics and Principles luncheons. The organization is evangelistic in seeking to convert its target audience to a conservative evangelical version of Christianity. Those involved with the work of the Center train new converts and produce prayer lists for Washington's top leaders in the executive, congress, judiciary, military, and ambassadors of foreign embassies. The prayer lists contain details of foreign embassies' national days and the birthdays of American leaders. Leaders are made aware that they are being prayed for and made to feel important and valued, which can be very seductive in a political environment in which they are under constant pressure. There are also quarterly retreats to train staffers in evangelistic techniques. Evangelism Explosion is an evangelistic outreach programme designed to aid church growth, which has been exported to 211 countries throughout the world.[7]

The Christian Embassy in Washington DC complements the work of the Center for Christian Statesmanship. It describes its role thus:

> Our purpose is to care for, serve, encourage and equip leaders at the White House, at the Pentagon, in foreign embassies and on Capitol Hill. We help people in these communities to reflect on and integrate their values with their work life to develop personally, professionally and spiritually.[8]

This all sounds very commendable. The subtext, however, is that the Christian Embassy is specifically targeting the most important people in the country either to convert them to their narrow political agenda rather than Christianity or to strengthen those who already share that political agenda. The Christian Embassy also produces a monthly prayer guide and organizes small Bible study groups in which leaders can meet with their peers. On Capitol Hill lunches and dinners, again with a well-known speaker, take place to enhance the esteem of the nation's leaders. Twelve small groups meet on a weekly basis designed to sustain and encourage Christian congressional representatives and senators to share their faith and to govern according to conservative evangelical standards. Presidential appointees and new foreign ambassadors are also targeted with courtesy calls, and seminars are held to familiarize them with Washington DC and discuss spirituality. Ambassadors, their staff and families receive invitations to attend small groups for spiritual reflection and periodic special dinners to encourage networking. The overt emphasis in all such activities is on befriending rather than conversion,[9] which encourages greater receptivity to the conservative evangelical agenda. The Embassy's mission to the Pentagon provides small groups, Bible studies and Wednesday morning prayer breakfasts with keynote speakers open to all military and civilian ranks and grades. These occasions are an ideal opportunity for juniors to be noticed and to interact with seniors and develop informal Christian networks.[10]

The Christian Right is able to exert influence through specific interest and parachurch organizations, with their leaders issuing public statements about areas of concern. This can be in the form of television or radio broadcasts or open letters and advertisements in the press. Such statements usually alert supporters, legislators and the administration of the strength of opposition to a proposed course of action. National and local conferences and meetings serve the dual purpose of highlighting concerns and rewarding favoured politicians with a platform to speak in favour of key issues to core constituencies. Favoured conservative politicians are invited to address students and faculty at leading Christian Right universities, including Pat Robertson's Regent University and the late Jerry Falwell's Liberty

University. They might also be offered seats on the boards of Christian Right bodies and appear on Christian television and radio.

Leading Republican contenders for the presidential nomination and for Congress are invited to speak at Values Voters Summits organized by FRC, FOF and AFA, or to address CUFI's Washington Summit and Night to Honor Israel events around the country. Politicians who are seen to be active in their promotion of Christian Right objectives are feted and presented with awards. John Ashcroft, for example, was named 'Daniel of the Year' in 2002 by *World* magazine; Bill Frist was honoured by the CNP in 2003 (Leaming and Boston, 2004); and the Center for Christian Statesmanship has honoured Dick Armey and Tom DeLay as distinguished Christian statesmen.

Although the Christian Right do not control any significant think-tanks capable of influencing foreign policy decision-making, they are well represented within established ones such as the Heritage Foundation and Council on Foreign Relations. The Hudson Institute (to which Nina Shea transferred her Center for Religion and Religious Freedom from Freedom House) and the Institute on Public Policy and Religion, led by Catholic priest and Bush confidant Richard John Neuhaus, also have a Christian Right presence. Michael Cromartie at the Ethics and Public Policy Center (EPPC) directs an 'Evangelicals in Civic Life' programme that seeks to research the role of evangelicals in public life while bringing together evangelical leaders and promoting evangelical public engagement. The programme hosts meetings on topical issues of relevance to the Christian Right and engages with academics, media and politicians about evangelical political participation. Cromartie, Richard Land and Nina Shea serve on the United States International Religious Freedom Commission, reporting on issues of religious freedom to Congress and the administration. Rick Santorum is now heading a 'Program to Protect America's Freedom' at EPPC, highlighting potential threats to America. Santorum identifies Bolivia, China, Cuba, Iran and 'Islamic fascism', Nicaragua, Russia and Venezuela as threats to the US national interest (Barry, 2007).

The Christian Right in Office

The preceding paragraphs have detailed the approach adopted by Christian Right organization in its attempt to influence key decision-makers under Bush. However the movement has also had insiders in prominent positions throughout the administration, judiciary, military and Congress. The principal member of the Christian Right is the president himself, who owes his election success in no small measure to members of the Christian Right wooed by strategist Karl Rove, and who even employed Ralph Reed, once depicted as the 'right hand of God' on the cover of *Time* magazine, as a campaign consultant in 2000. The president has brought in many other Christian evangelicals at different levels within his administration. In the White House, evangelical Christians filled at least four key positions. Andrew Card served as Chief of Staff; Michael Gerson, chief speech writer; Karen Hughes had the role of communications officer and, from 2005, under secretary for public diplomacy and public affairs; Tim Goeglein's job was deputy director of the White House Office of Public Liaison, and he served as the chief liaison with the Christian Right.

The White House became a place very amenable to Christian evangelicals. David Frum recalled that every cabinet meeting opened in prayer; he was made aware that 'attendance at Bible study was, if not compulsory, not quite *uncompulsory* [*sic*]' (Frum, 2003: 13, 4–5). Megan Gillan, director of communication, coordinated the presidential prayer team, which encouraged members throughout the country to pray for the president, his administration and the US military, especially in Iraq and Afghanistan.[11] The Office of Faith-Based and Community Initiatives, under Jon Dilulio, James Towey and then Jay Hein, also found its home in the White House.

Other important Christian Right appointments have included John Ashcroft as Attorney General (at the time of writing, he is on the staff of Regent University and director of the United States Agency for International Development, USAID); Andrew Natsios, who after leaving office served as Bush's envoy to Sudan; and Don Evans, the first-term Secretary of Commerce. Conservative evangelicals hold office at every level of the administration and are being encouraged to share and exercise their faith as they go about their work. Christian colleges and universities encourage students to secure placements as interns and staffers at all levels of government, in preparation for future public service and to 'witness' to their faith through their work and lifestyle. The Christian Right are no longer outsiders seeking a place at the table but are included within the decision-making process.

Tim Goeglein and Karl Rove, until his retirement, have organized regular meetings with Christian Right leaders and arranged a weekly conference call for prominent Christian Right leaders. The White House consults and/or informs Christian Right leaders before major policy announcements in areas of concern to them, including on Middle East policy, as detailed later in the book. Richard Land and Janice Crouse, Senior Fellow of the Beverly LaHaye Institute, a tenacious and seasoned campaigner on conservative values at the United Nations (UN) and former speechwriter for George H.W. Bush, spoke to me of regular access to the White House and meetings with the president. The president and senior officials have also consulted Christian Right leaders with no apparent foreign policy expertise on the Iraq War. When asked to differentiate between the reception of conservative evangelicals by the Clinton and Bush administrations, she explained:

> Oh, it's night and day for us as Christian conservatives. I was not in the White House for the whole Clinton administration. And recently I was invited as a member of a group of twelve people who sat around the Roosevelt table in the Roosevelt room … across the table is Jim Dobson, beside me is Chuck Colson – you know, a table full of conservative dignitaries – and the president is sitting there asking our advice about Iraq. It was a half-hour meeting, which turned out to be ninety minutes, which I think was significant.[12]

Christian Right organizations have been granted privileged NGO observer status at the United Nations and participation in

US delegations because their views reflect those of the White House (Monkerud, 2005).[13] They also increase their visibility and influence by serving on presidential and congressional initiatives and working parties such as the Commission on Religious Freedom. Fellow members of the Christian Right serving on congressional committees will call on other evangelical conservatives to give 'expert' testimony and briefings before those committees. Leaders of the Christian Right in Congress have been vocal and active in pursuing domestic and foreign policy objectives, especially concerning religious persecution, HIV/AIDS, the War on Terror and Israel. Former House Majority leaders Dick Armey and Tom DeLay, representatives Frank Wolf, Chris Smith, Michael Pence, and Republican whip Roy Blunt receive national recognition as political leaders within the Christian Right. Former Senators Jesse Helms, George Allen and Rick Santorum have consistently articulated and sought to legislate in favour of Christian Right objectives, as have present incumbents Sam Brownback, James Inhofe and Tom Coburn.

Congressional scorecards produced by Christian Right organizations reveal the depth of support for conservative evangelical positions. The FRC/FOF Vote Scorecard on the 109th Congress 2nd Session awarded 121 100 per cent approval ratings, including 5 Democrats. In the Senate 23 senators, all Republicans, earned a perfect score, including Santorum, Allen, Kyl, Inhofe, Coburn, Brownback and Mitch McConnell; 16 of the 22 members of the House Foreign Affairs Committee rated over 85 per cent, including perfect scores for Christian Right stalwarts Dan Burton, Mike Pence and Christopher Smith. Out of 10 Republican US Senate Committee on Foreign Relations members only 3 achieved 100 per cent ratings, including Johnny Isakson from Georgia, David Vitter from Louisiana, and Jim DeMint from South Carolina (FRC/FOF, 2007). These statistics indicate that congressional representatives, having to face re-election every other year rather than every six years, are either far more attentive to or are influenced by the views of the Christian Right, or share those views, than senators.

Christian Right Organizations Engaging in Foreign Affairs

From time to time Christian Right leaders will speak out on foreign policy issues in an individual capacity or on behalf of their organization. They will tend to do this on favourite core issues such as Israel, national security, opposition to communism and Islam in its radical and moderate guises, AIDS, Christian persecution, the United Nations, as well as moral issues concerning sexuality, family planning, prostitution, human trafficking and, belatedly, global warming. Umbrella groups such as the National Association of Evangelicals, Moral Majority or Christian Coalition claim to speak on behalf of millions of members of churches linked to these groups. Ted Haggard, before his resignation, claimed to speak on behalf of the 30 million members of churches affiliated to the NAE, ensuring him regular access to the White House. Richard Land could equally claim to speak on behalf of the 17 million members of Southern Baptist churches. Such leaders are listened to, but effective campaigns to change foreign policy through mobilizing grassroots supporters/constituents are the preserve of a select few organizations, such as FOF, FRC, IRD and CWA, which spend the time and resources seeking to do so alongside their domestic political activity.

Long-standing campaigners on foreign policy issues include IRD, which has connections with three of *Time* magazine's twenty-five most influential evangelicals in 2005: the president Diane Knippers (until her death in 2005), Richard Neuhaus, and financiers Howard and Roberta Ahmanson. Knippers is credited with leading efforts to undermine traditional denominations including United Methodists, Presbyterians and Episcopalians by using IRD to help create divisions by promoting homophobia, support for Israel and conservative foreign and domestic policy (Clarkson, 2007).[14] Richard Neuhaus has been Bush's adviser on issues such as abortion, stem-cell research, cloning and traditional marriage, all issues increasingly fought within the UN. As a prominent Catholic conservative, he has played a pivotal role in persuading American Catholics to back Bush and moral conservatism. Neuhaus also devised the strategy to weaken the influence of liberal mainstream denominations opposed to positions adopted by the Christian Right (Clarkson, 2007).[15]

CNP members and financiers Howard and Roberta Ahmanson have supported IRD over the years and Roberta sits on the board of directors (Clarkson, 2007).[16] IRD has campaigned vigorously on issues of religious persecution, and within the past few years has launched campaigns supporting religious freedom in North Korea and Sudan. Indeed, IRD has been a major force in making Sudan a cause célèbre. IRD has an extensive agenda of domestic and foreign policy objectives in order to advance free-market democracy at home and abroad, emphasizing 'the relationship between Christian faith and democratic governance'.[17] This is significant because IRD's promotion of a free-market agenda provides useful support for the Republican Party and keeps religious freedom to the fore in policy decision-making, precluding the opportunity to adopt realpolitik solutions to international affairs.

Concerned Women for America claims a membership of half a million and in 2002 declared earnings of almost $11 billion. The organization has extended its international interests from a simple opposition to international institutions, and to communism, to seeking to advance traditional family values and opposing feminism and liberal activism in international forums. Foreign policy issues are mainly dealt with by Wendy Wright and Janice Crouse, of the Beverly LaHaye Institute, and extend its opposition to the ERA internationally, through obstructionism and opposition to the UN's Convention on the Elimination of All Forms of Discrimination Against Women. CWA, like FRC and the Eagle Forum, has acquired official NGO status and participated in UN forums. The organization has a daily radio show, broadcast on seventy-five stations, reaching an estimated audience of over 1 million listeners. A variety of CWA publications reaches hundreds of thousands of subscribers and church members each month, which provides the organization with political capital within the Republican Party (Oldfield, 2004; PFAW, 2007a).

All Christian Right organizations claim to be defending a way of life that is fast disappearing under a tsunami of secularism. Regardless of the merits of this claim, CWA is among the most successful in attempting to reverse liberal gains and women's rights. Founder Bev LaHaye and husband Tim are the first family of the Christian Right and wield tremendous influence in Christian and conservative circles. Tim LaHaye was co-founder of the Moral Majority and is co-author of the best-selling *Left Behind* series of end-time novels, which have sold over 70 million copies. The books attempt to convince millions of Americans that God's plan for eternity revolves around Israel. For the LaHayes, Russia, China, the Arabs, Europe and the United Nations are all on the wrong side of history (LaHaye and Jenkins, 1995).

Phyllis Schlafly's Eagle Forum, Tony Perkins's FRC and James Dobson's FOF have also tended to see involvement in foreign policy as being necessary to prevent international institutions dictating policy in America. Together with CWA, they are the most prominent voices in advancing conservative moral values outside America; they do so by promoting and defending those values rigorously at the UN and in dealings with the administration and Congress. These organizations are exceptionally well funded, supported and equipped, enabling them to exert pressure on government confident of the backing of their membership. People for the American Way report that Eagle Forum has 80,000 members and in 2000 had finances of $2.3 million. The organization produces weekly newsletters and monthly reports; also Schlafly has a syndicated newspaper column in one hundred newspapers, and she broadcasts weekly on over four hundred radio stations (PFAW, 2007b).

The FRC, founded by James Dobson with Gary Bauer as its first head, was intended to be FOF's outreach in Washington DC, although the organization has developed significantly since its inception. Under Tony Perkins's leadership, the organization enjoys considerable prestige and authority within the Christian Right. The FRC budget in financial year 2006 was $10.8 million, enabling it to lobby Congress effectively and make its case at the United Nations. Along with FOF, FRC also produces congressional report cards and organizes Value Voters' summits to vet Republican nominees for the presidency and Congress (Boston, 2007). It has sought to develop links with other morally conservative groups though participation in World Congress of Families (WCF) conferences and networks. FRC is actively involved in building international alliances of the Religious Right opposing abortion, stem-cell research, contraception, same-sex marriages, homosexuality, pornography and gender equality. At the World Congress of Families IV conference, held in Warsaw in 2007, FRC was joined by forty other co-sponsoring organizations from the USA, Canada, Mexico, Poland and Italy. US Christian Right groups present included CWA, FOF, American Values and the AFA.[18] FOF, FRC and CWA have more influence in international affairs than the other groupings, due to their activities at the UN.

Over the past twenty years, the major visible power brokers within the Christian Right have been Jerry Falwell, Pat Robertson and James Dobson. Even before his death, Falwell's influence had waned, and Robertson's influence, although still important, has declined noticeably with the demise of the Christian Coalition and his increasingly bizarre utterances on the *700 Club*, a daily news/magazine programme watched by over a million viewers in the USA and millions more in over two hundred countries worldwide. This has left James Dobson as the most significant political figure in the movement; he is the man whose endorsement conservative Republicans most crave. Dobson's FOF organization has around 1,300 employees and attracts revenue of over $137 million for the main organization and a further $25 million for the overtly political FOF Action, a separate company. FOF includes benefactor Elsa Prince as a director and has over 2 million subscribers to a variety of magazines. Dobson produces daily radio broadcasts to 164 countries throughout the world to an audience of over 220 million people, translated into fifteen languages. Dobson also appears on eighty television stations daily (PFAW, 2006). Millions of Christians throughout America have been encouraged to bring up their children according to Dobson's advice in books, readings and broadcasts. Dobson has become increasingly politically active during the Bush administration. As we have seen, he, along with fellow conservative evangelicals, has been consulted by the president on Iraq, and FOF has become more involved in promoting a conservative moral agenda abroad through involvement at the WCF and the United Nations.

Former Majority Leader Dick Armey recalls on one occasion Dobson lobbying him against a trade bill and on another occasion berating the House leadership for 'having failed to "deliver" for Christian conservatives, that we owed our majority to him, and that he had the power to take or jobs back'. Armey goes on to accuse Dobson of orchestrating a campaign against him among his colleagues by accusing him of not being a 'good Christian'. Armey accused Dobson of being a 'thug' and a 'bully', a charge Dobson denies (Armey, 2006; Dobson, 2006a; Blumenthal, 2006). Dobson has a reputation for threatening the Republican Party dating back to a CNP speech he gave in 1998, reported in the *Washington Post*. In the speech, known later as 'Dobson's Choice', the FOF leader asked:

> Does the Republican Party want our votes, no strings attached – to court us every two years, and then to say, 'Don't call me, I'll call you' – and to not care about the moral law of the universe? … Is that what they want? Is that the way the system works? Is this the way it's going to be? If it is, I'm gone, and if I go, I will do everything I can to take as many people with me as possible.[19]

The Republican leadership has been frightened of upsetting Dobson and other Christian Right leaders, because of their popularity and following among conservative evangelicals, which they fear could influence voting preferences. In order to ameliorate the potential problem, during the 109th Congress they organized 'Values Action Teams' to liaise between Congress and the Christian Right; Joseph Pitts headed the House team with Sam Brownback heading the Senate team (Boston, 2006).

Before the mid-term elections in 2006 a Values Voters' summit was arranged by the FRC and attended by leaders and followers of the Christian Right. Leading Republican politicians put their policy positions before Values Voters, in the hope of securing their backing for presidential and congressional elections. Speakers included George Allen, Rick Santorum, Mitt Romney, Mike Huckabee, Newt Gingrich and Sam Brownback. Giuliani and McCain, the leading contenders at the time for the Republican nomination, were pointedly not invited. All the speakers praised Dobson and the other conservative evangelical patriarchs represented (Blumenthal, 2006). Following the Republican defeat in those mid-term elections, Dobson immediately accused the GOP (the Republican Party) of abandoning values voters and bringing about their own downfall (Talhelm, 2006; Dobson, 2006b).

Dobson's importance as a power broker was reflected in the initially stalled campaign of John McCain – Dobson said he 'would not vote for John McCain under any circumstance' (Unruh, 2007). McCain, aware of the importance of this core constituency, has had to retract statements he made about Falwell and Robertson denouncing them in 2000 as 'agents of intolerance'. He subsequently courted Falwell and Robertson, addressing Liberty University and Regent University (Kirkpatrick, 2007). McCain launched a campaign to appeal to conservative evangelical voters called Americans of Faith for McCain, but it failed to ignite his campaign (Cooperman, 2007). He met with John Hagee, who announced to fellow Christian Zionists that McCain agreed with their position on Israel.[20] He later attended the CUFI Washington Summit in July 2007, as part of a continuing rapprochement with the Christian Right, but in spite of this and Sam Brownback's endorsement following his own withdrawal from the Republican nomination race, James Dobson's rejection of McCain's candidacy could prove decisive in weakening his presidential prospects.

The struggle for the 2008 presidential nomination revealed the significance of winning the approval of the Christian Right leadership. It has become apparent that in a campaign with no clearly delineated champion of the Christian Right (Huckabee was the choice of many grassroots conservative evangelicals rather than of the leadership), foreign policy, and in particular the War on Terror, is becoming just as important to conservative evangelicals as the domestic conservative moral agenda. In 2007, Dobson devoted five radio broadcasts to highlighting the threat from radical Islam. The most important question for reporters interviewing Mitt Romney at the National Religious Broadcasters' Convention was 'how does America win against the jihad' (Gilgoff, 2007). IRD and other groups are stressing the importance of addressing religious persecution. Robertson consistently uses his CBN platform to raise the spectre of an Islamic threat to America. Hagee and Christian Zionists are also successfully bringing support for Israel and a tougher stance against Hamas, Hezbollah and Iran to the fore of political discourse. This current generation of the Republican Party, at all levels, is integrally connected and influenced by the Christian Right, but what about the next generation?

The Next Generation

Not content with short-term gains, the Christian Right have actively sought to change irreversibly the political and moral make-up of the country. Jerry Falwell, Pat Robertson, Oral Roberts and Bob Jones have each invested heavily in future generations by building universities to train up young Christians to be future leaders in America. Net Ministries lists over three hundred Christian colleges and universities throughout America, the majority disseminating a conservative evangelical message.[21] The Christian Right commitment to raising up a new generation of conservative evangelicals to assume leadership positions in the American polity starts in childhood. Increasingly, conservative evangelical parents are opting to educate their children at home, rather than risk exposure to liberal ideas. Consistent with the widespread Christian Right belief that America's greatest enemy is secularism, home schooling has become increasingly popular since Michael Farris founded the Home School Legal Defense Association (HSLDA) in 1983 (Smith, 2003). HSLDA, with offshoot Home School

Foundation, is a national membership organization for parents who home-school, to promote and uphold the legal right to home-schooling. HSLDA's objectives are to 'maintain our freedom to homeschool and control the upbringing of our children in the future. We must be proactive in providing virtuous leaders in government and other key spheres of influence in order to preserve our freedoms.'[22]

The home-schooling movement now extends to hundreds of thousands of children across America and is extending its influence to other countries where conservative Christians also seek to control their children's development. HSLDA has formed a political action committee to advance its conservative moral agenda, opposing homosexuality, teaching abstinence instead of sex education, and encouraging teenage participation in the political process on behalf of socially conservative candidates. The organization is critical of the UN, opposing the UN Treaty on the Rights of the Child because 'it would strip parents of much of their authority to educate, train, and nurture their children according to the dictates of their conscience'. Sympathetic representatives and senators articulate such criticism in Congress; and CWA, where Farris was a former general counsel, has led opposition in the UN to the Treaty on the Rights of the Child.

HSLDA encourages members' children from age 11 to 19 to be actively engaged in the political process.[23] In 2004, the organization set up Generation Joshua to educate conservative evangelical home-school students on civic responsibility. Students are encouraged to join Student Action Teams and campaign on behalf of movement-favoured political candidates and voter registration drives to increase voting among sympathetic sectors of the their communities. Students who do particularly well in the Generation Joshua programmes have the opportunity to win a scholarship to Patrick Henry College (PHC).[24] PHC grew out of the home-school movement and is seen by it as a crucial element in the future transformation of American society. HSLDA's board of directors, under the leadership of Michael Farris, founded the college in September 2000. Farris served as president until 2006, from when he has served as chancellor, advising his successor, Professor Graham Walker.

PHC recruits home-school students brought up in conservative evangelical homes and aims to equip them with the requisite leadership skills to provide Christian leadership. The college's mission statement declares its role as preparing 'Christian men and women who will lead our nation and shape our culture with timeless biblical values and fidelity to the spirit of the American founding'.[25] The vision of the college is nothing less than 'the transformation of American society by training Christian students to serve God and mankind with a passion for righteousness, justice, and mercy, through careers of public service and cultural influence'.[26] Students are required to adhere to a strict moral code, which among other things prohibits alcohol, tobacco, swearing, pornography and sexual activity on and off campus. Students need parental permission to date and are encouraged to inform on students who fall short of these standards.[27] PHC trains students to believe in creationism, and that sexual activity is only permissible in a marriage between a man and woman. Governments that permit pornography or homosexuality are considered to be acting immorally and without proper authority in this area. Socialism and communism, in this view, are a considered a violation of God's creation order, which sanctions private property.[28]

PHC is a Christian liberal arts college that received accreditation in 2006, growing to some 350 students. During this period, the college has gained a reputation for achieving academic excellence and equipping students to take their place in US government and the courts. When Farris founded the predominately white evangelical college, he fondly imagined that

> 15 years from now one of our students walks down the aisle at the Academy Awards to receive the Oscar for Best Picture of the Year, and gets a call from his college roommate who is President of the United States. And that's the vision, and we don't want to take second place. We want to raise winners, and people who know how to do what's right and really lead the country. (Rollin, 2001)

Farris's strategy appears to be working, with students winning national debating and court moot competitions. Hanna Rosin, who spent a year and a half embedded as a reporter within the college, reveals a committed, hardworking and serious student body committed to fulfilling their founder's and parents' expectations (Rosin, 2007). Over twenty-two congressional representatives and senators have employed interns from PHC. Seven out of one hundred White House interns in 2004 were from the college, another worked for the Bush–Cheney re-election campaign, one for Karl Rove, and another for the Coalition Provisional Authority in Baghdad. For the first few years Paul Bonicelli, a former staffer on the House International Relations Committee, taught students as dean of academic affairs, providing a clear insight into the workings of US politics (Olsen, 2004; Alden, 2005; Buncombe, 2004). PHC seniors undertake a directed research project designed to be the kind of work an entry-level staffer carries out. Many members of Congress started out as staffers on Capitol Hill and Farris envisages his students doing the same. Out of the 61 students in the graduation class of 2004, 18 acquired governmental jobs, including 2 in the White House, 6 as staffers on Capitol Hill, 8 in the federal agencies and 2 in the FBI (Rosin, 2005). The achievements of PHC are exceptionally impressive for such a young college and are a portent of the ambition of the Christian Right. PHC's narrow and highly partisan biblical interpretation has led to the resignation of nine members of the teaching staff on grounds of academic freedom, but such teething problems have failed to halt the determined progress of Farris and Walker (Henderson Blunt, 2006).

Jerry Falwell's Liberty University, which has a longer history than Patrick Henry College, shares a similar vision of providing a rounded education for over 20,000 students from over seventy countries around the world, including all fifty US states. The university is the largest evangelical university in the world and spends around a quarter of a million dollars a year on its student debating team. Liberty was founded in 1971 and in 2006 achieved the unique distinction of finishing first in the rankings of three national policy debate groups:

ADA, National Debate Tournament, and Cross Examination Debate Association (Pulliam, 2006). Liberty decided at an early stage not merely to produce Bible students and preachers but to train up the next generation of lawyers, business leaders and politicians. Within the university is a full-size replica of the Supreme Court for students to learn debating skills and as an aspiration to place Liberty alumni on the Supreme Court in the future.

Regent University, although smaller than Liberty, is also committed to academic excellence and equipping students to take their place as tomorrow's leaders. Their mission statement pledges to 'equip Christian leaders to change the world'. Regent's 4,000-plus students come from America and all over the world. Pat Robertson's connections enable the university to attract leading conservative figures and international political leaders to address the student body. Former Attorney General John Ashcroft and former Chief of Naval Operations Vern Clark are on staff, and guest lecturers have included Ehud Barak, Newt Gingrich, Rudy Giuliani and John McCain. The university hosts the Clash of Titans debate between leading military and political figures, and the Ronald Reagan Symposium on American Conservatism. The student body has enjoyed success in winning the American Bar Association's 2006 National Moot Court Championship and the 2007 Negotiation Competition, defeating Ivy League opposition.[29]

These leading Christian Right colleges are now competing with Ivy League universities and producing accomplished, well-trained and disciplined students who are equipped to secure employment at the highest levels of the American polity. The problem for America and, indeed, the rest of the world lies in what such institutions do and do not teach. Graduates emerge from PHC, Liberty and Regent Universities strengthened in a narrow range of beliefs about the traditional role of women, and upholding the 'sinfulness' of abortion, pornography, prostitution, homosexuality, communism, socialism, feminism and premarital sexual relations. Students graduate with a missionary zeal to change America over time into a theocratic state.

Conclusion

The Christian Right have enjoyed considerable access into the very heart of government. This is not a recent phenomenon attributable to George W. Bush, but has been a factor in US politics and foreign policy since the Reagan presidency, although access was denied to the Clinton White House. In one sense, Bush has simply reopened the privileged access to conservative evangelicals enjoyed by them twenty years previously. The movement has overcome numerous sexual and financial scandals over the years, and the death of many of its most prominent leaders, but continues to go from strength to strength. The resilience of the movement indicates how successful Weyrich's, Falwell's and Robertson's early efforts to engage supporters in a political crusade have proven. The Christian Right are better organized than they have ever been and all Republican candidates must make their case before Christian Right leaders before their candidacy can be credible. Rather than standing on the outside looking in, the Christian Right are members of and control large sections of the Republican Party, and are actively training up a future generation to continue their crucial role in the American polity.

Although most attention is focused on the Christian Right leadership as the movers and shakers within the political process at home and abroad, it is the ordinary supporter and churchgoer who is the strength of the movement. Conservative evangelical organizations receive considerable support from wealthy benefactors, mostly members of the CNP. However, it is individuals throughout America who are relied on most to subscribe to publications, donate regularly and become involved in political campaigning. The power of constituents and voters responding en masse to the directives of Christian Right leaders to register concern with Congress, the United Nations or the White House, and overwhelming communication systems with emails, faxes, telephone calls, postcards and letters, has an impact on even the most hardened politician. The movement is integrated, with memberships of organizations and churches interlinking and overlapping. The success of the movement has been achieved through leaders being in tune with the concerns of the person worshipping God in their church or living room on Sunday morning. When Christian Right leaders offend their members and supporters, then the Republican Party suffers defeat at the polls as conservative evangelicals register a protest. When the Christian Right leadership at all levels reflect the core values of its supporters, the movement's growth and involvement in the political process bring it ever closer to achieving its objectives. In the next chapter, we will examine how the movement is promoting those objectives internationally.

2

Spreading the Word

> And he said unto them, Go ye into all the world, and preach the gospel to every creature. He that believeth and is baptized shall be saved; but he that believeth not shall be damned. And these signs shall follow them that believe; In my name shall they cast out devils; they shall speak with new tongues; They shall take up serpents; and if they drink any deadly thing, it shall not hurt them; they shall lay hands on the sick, and they shall recover. (Mark 16:15–18)

In considering the Christian Right as a political movement, it is important not to lose sight of the movement's identity as conservative *evangelicals*. Organizations such as the Moral Majority and Christian Coalition have raised the political consciousness of conservative Christians and translated it into power and influence, as we shall see, within the Republican Party. The primary calling for evangelicals, however, is the Great Commission to evangelize given to his followers by Jesus at the end of his earthly ministry (Matthew 28:18–20; Mark 16:15–20). Conservative evangelicals take this command every bit as seriously as their liberal evangelical counterparts do, and spend considerable resources on preaching, teaching, ministering, broadcasting and evangelizing to spread the Christian message throughout the world. The gospel that is propagated bears an uncanny resemblance to American values of self-help, prosperity, private enterprise, individualism and support for Israel. The impact of such teaching and preaching is not intended as an extension of US foreign policy but is an example of soft power by presenting an image of American prosperity and success that is attractive to audiences in developing countries.

Evangelistic Outreach

For the past hundred years, American Christians have been at the forefront of trying to convert the world to Christianity. Evangelicals of all types have led the way in proselytizing throughout the developing world, establishing missions, translating the Bible into native languages and dialects, providing health care and education, building and supporting churches, and making converts, who then proceed to play a role in building the indigenous church. Conservative evangelicals follow in this tradition but many also present a very distinct Americanized version of the gospel that has an impact on fast-growing churches in the global South and former Communist countries. American evangelicals, coming from the richest country in the world, have the benefit of unparalleled resources, enabling them to present their message in a wide variety of formats and with a genuine commitment to preach their understanding of the gospel to all. Members of the Christian Right have been seeking to share their faith internationally for the past few decades, with spectacular results, contributing to the exponential growth of Pentecostal, Word of Faith and charismatic churches, known collectively as renewalism, throughout the world.

Although the role of conservative evangelical denominations such as the Southern Baptists should not be underestimated, the most visible expression of American evangelicalism abroad comes from the renewalist tendency within the movement. Televangelists, including Kenneth Copeland, Paul Crouch, Creflo Dollar, Jesse Duplantis, John Hagee, Benny Hinn, T.D. Jakes, Joyce Meyer, Joel Osteen, Rod Parsley and Pat Robertson, dominate specialist religious channels and the religious component of mainstream US satellite programming. These evangelists are following in the footsteps of veteran Pentecostal and Word of Faith evangelists T.L. Osborn, Oral Roberts and Morris Cerullo, who between them have preached to tens of millions of people across six continents in evangelistic crusades, claiming millions of conversions to Christianity. These evangelists have enjoyed particular success in Africa, Latin America and Asia with ministry that emphasizes the supernatural abilities of the disciples (Mark 16:16–18, 20). They preach literal belief in salvation, damnation, exorcism, speaking in tongues, divine protection, and miraculous healing of the sick. In accordance with Mark 16:20 they believe that the evidence of their favour with God comes from the evidence of 'signs following' their ministry. In addition to hundreds of thousands of converts, they claim the 'signs following' of supernatural healings and deliverances from evil spirits.

While conservative evangelists claim to believe and teach the literal truth of the Bible, despite its many contradictions and errors, the reality is that they, like other Christians, teach a partial Bible based on their favourite passages. It is the partiality of these passages that most interests us in examining the political influence of the movement. For the favourite spokespersons of the renewalist wing of the Christian Right, it is their promotion of a supernatural faith in which God miraculously intervenes to heal the sick, cast out demons and cause people to prosper financially that has tremendous appeal among countries in the global South, where health provision is weak and incomes low. Different evangelists will concentrate on different themes, principally salvation, but increasingly the most popular concentrate on promoting a prosperity gospel that promises viewers, listeners and congregants that as they give money to the evangelist's ministry God will cause them to prosper financially. Alongside core evangelistic messages, ministries are eager to promote a world-view that fits in with their eschatology. This world-view considers modernism, secularism, communism and Islam as pillars of evil in the world. As leading Christian talk-show host Frank Pastore, from Los Angeles KLAA, states:

> I teach conservatives that their principles are fundamentally Christian, and I teach Christians that when they live out their faith, they're fundamentally conservative. If the world is going to be saved from secular communism, European socialism, and the Islamofascist threat, it's going to be America that leads the way. (Trammel, 2007)

Pastore is not an isolated voice. Pat Robertson has been one of the most influential and vocal critics of Islam and its radical manifestation. Robertson uses the *700 Club*, broadcast by CBN, as his personal political and theological platform. The programme airs across America and throughout most of the world via cable and satellite. On 13 March 2006, Robertson derided Muslims who protested against controversial cartoons of the prophet Muhammad as 'satanic' and 'crazed fanatics' motivated by 'demonic power'. He also argued that 'the goal of Islam ... is world domination'. A few weeks later, on 23 May, Robertson described Islam as 'essentially a Christian heresy'. Then, on 29 August, he claimed that there was little difference between radical and moderate Islam:

> So are these extremists something aberrational from the Quran? I'm not sure they are. I would think Osama bin Laden may be one of the true disciples of the teaching of the Quran but you know because he's following through literally word-for-word what it says ... Islam is not a religion of peace. No way.

In case his viewers had failed to understand his concerns, in the 12 June 2007 edition of the programme he clarified the position:

> Ladies and gentlemen, we have to recognize that Islam is not a religion. It is a worldwide political movement meant on domination of the world. And it is meant to subjugate all people under Islamic law.
>
> Now, sure, over here, you've got Islam light and you've got all these various things, but the idea is we don't want just accommodation, we want to take over and we want to impose sharia on you. And before long, ladies are going to be dressed in burqas and whatever garments they would put on them, and next thing you know, men are going to be allowed to have wife-beating and you'll be beheading adulterers

> and so on and so forth. That's Saudi Arabia. We don't want that here in America. If they don't like it here in America, then let them go to Saudi Arabia, to Kuwait, to Yemen, to all those wonderful nations around the Middle East.

Robertson has been almost as scathing about communism and socialism. In one outspoken attack on Hugo Chávez on the 22 August 2005 broadcast of the *700 Club*, commenting on the Venezuelan leader's claims that America was seeking to assassinate him suggested that 'if he thinks we're trying to assassinate him, I think that we really ought to go ahead and do it. It's a whole lot cheaper than starting a war.' Such comments, and the ones above, were broadcast into the Muslim world and into Latin America and provoked outrage from governments and international media. The State Department, in order to avoid a diplomatic incident, was obliged to intervene and insist that Robertson's views were his own and did not reflect government policy. Robertson may be espousing distasteful views but he articulates thoughts that the Christian Right in America are already thinking. As Reverend Barry Lynn, a tolerant minister and zealous opponent of anything tending towards theocracy, from Americans United for the Separation of Church and State, explains, most Americans treat his comments as 'just another foot in the mouth of a man who puts his foot in his mouth regularly'. For people outside America, however, Lynn warns that 'when he [Robertson] pontificates about any matter of world interest it is taken seriously by the world'.[1] Many viewers in the rest of the world will interpret Robertson's statements as reflecting America's rather than simply the sectional views of part of the Christian Right.

Missionary Activity

Radio broadcasting

Radio broadcasting has long been an effective way of communicating the Christian message. In countries where televisions are in short supply or satellite broadcasts or Internet connections are blocked, radio provides a tremendous opportunity to reach large numbers of people. Outside America Christian radio has been largely neglected until recently by the Christian Right, who have preferred television and the Internet as their media. Traditional evangelical organizations including Trans World Radio and Far East Broadcasting Company, both founded within seven years of the end of the Second World War, dominate the market. The conservative evangelical voice can be heard on Lester Sumrall Evangelistic Association (LeSEA) via five shortwave radio stations broadcasting to 90 per cent of the world.[2] Focus on the Family also makes effective use of radio in airing its flagship daily programme *Focus on the Family* on 2,000 facilities in America and hundreds more around the world.[3]

Evangelistic crusades

Apart from one-to-one evangelism, the lifeblood of the evangelical movement is the crusade or outreach event. The evangelistic crusade has been an integral part of American Christianity and the names of the leaders of the Great Awakenings and Spiritual revivals have become part of American folklore. Billy Graham, the best known of the living evangelists, at the time of writing, cannot be considered a member of the Christian Right, claiming to remain apolitical, while befriending and counselling successive presidents. His son and successor in the family evangelistic business, Franklin Graham, however, certainly is a member of the Christian Right. In 2007, Franklin Graham led crusades (festivals) in Ukraine, South Korea, Ecuador and Hong Kong, although the results achieved do not compare with his father's ministry.[4] The personal appearance of Christian Right evangelists proclaiming a gospel of health and wealth at massive evangelistic events, which are replayed on Christian television throughout the world, has proved an infectious combination judging by the numbers attending crusades and subscribing to Christian broadcasting.

The most prominent of the Christian Right evangelists holding large revival crusades outside America are Benny Hinn, Joyce Meyer and T.D. Jakes. In early 2006, T.D. Jakes attracted an audience of nearly 1 million people in Nairobi, Kenya (*The Economist*, 2006). Joyce Meyer preached to 1.2 million people in a four-day conference held in Hyderabad, India, in January 2006 and over the past few years has preached in Rwanda, Uganda, South Africa, Jamaica, Australia, New Zealand and the Philippines.[5]

The undoubted master of the crusade circuit, if judged by the number of times they are featured on Christian television, is Benny Hinn, who draws vast crowds attracted by his measure of a supernatural God healing the sick and casting out demons. Benny Hinn's website is captioned 'winning the lost at any cost' and details the miraculous claims made by the ministry. In conducting dozens of crusades in Africa, Asia, North and South America, Europe, the Caribbean and Australasia, Hinn reports miracles occurring with the blind seeing, the deaf hearing, the lame walking, and the demon-possessed set free. Cancers disappear and relationships are restored. As Hinn prays many people are apparently knocked off their feet or fall over, affected by the anointing of God or group hysteria. Hinn's claims are difficult to substantiate independently, but whether or not he and Morris Cerullo are charlatans, they appeal to audiences excited by charismatic performances that offer transformative power to change lives and heal people's bodies and minds. The ministries claim hundreds of thousands of converts and healings, which in turn helps bring in substantial funds from donors and supporters to sustain the ministry. This suggests that, irrespective of physical evidence, the public clearly perceive, or respond, in a manner which suggests their belief or acceptance of these claims.

Televangelism

Those evangelists conducting crusades have also developed strong televangelist ministries, airing their crusades, conferences, church meetings, and their own specially made programmes on hundreds of Christian and secular networks. Arrays of Christian Right ministers have developed their ministries as parachurch organizations or as pastors of large congregations, and very often both. Christian broadcasting has enabled minsters such as Hinn, Meyer, Jakes, Joel Osteen, Creflo Dollar, Kenneth Copeland, Rod Parsley, Jesse Duplantis, John Hagee and Ron Carpenter to become household names in much of America and within renewalist congregations around the world. The importance of such minsters and television station heads like Paul Crouch and Pat Robertson lies both in their message and in their presentation of a health, wealth and lifestyle gospel closely in tune with conservative American values of free markets, individualism and self-help.

The programmes invariably feature the celebrity preacher teaching the conference or church congregation, and very consciously the television audience, about how to lead a Christian life characterized by success. The preacher, exuding confidence, exhorts the audience to use the word of God (in the Bible) and the authority given to them, in order to triumph over life's difficulties. Audiences are told that, if they only have the faith to act on what the preacher tells them, the Bible says they can enjoy financial prosperity, successful relationships, physical health, godly children and faithful marriages. If they only believe and act upon the words of the preachers then God will bless them, give them inner peace, and a lifestyle that causes them to enjoy success in all walks of life. As the audience responds to the preacher, at the end of the programme some will claim to be born again, healed and set free from the physical, emotional, social and financial problems that beset them. Touched by the ministry, the wider audience is invited to send donations, gifts, 'love-offerings' or 'seed faith' in order to support the work of the ministry and as an indication of faith in God's willingness to grant whatever the preacher has promised. If that opportunity is missed, there is a further chance to buy recordings of the meeting, and of other meetings, as well as films, DVDs, books and even anointed handkerchiefs to heal the sick. Supporting websites enable viewers to register for newsletters, email updates and further opportunities to hear their favourite celebrity preacher, and to donate to the ministry or purchase items in perpetuity.

The celebrity preacher will inevitably be a millionaire,[6] dressed immaculately, well groomed, cosmetically enhanced and preaching a seductive message that seemingly answers all the audience's problems. The preacher presents him- or herself as a success story whose life has been turned around by a relationship with God and the offerings of the viewers. For many in the global South this image of the prosperous American preacher, blessed by God, is an inspirational figure who presents an appealing version not just of Christianity but of American capitalism too; a gospel which tells a story that prosperity is next to godliness, that the key to prosperity is giving to ministries and supporting Israel (Genesis 12:3). The preachers, it would seem, are living the American Dream and convincing their viewers that it is God's will for them to do likewise. Meanwhile the preachers' importance in the American polity is demonstrated as they are feted on Fox Television, CNN's *Larry King Live*, in *Time* magazine and even included in conference calls with the White House.

Many secular and Christian channels provide coverage of Christian Right celebrity preachers' programmes throughout six continents. The ministry of Jesse Duplantis, for example, is aired on secular channels ABC, NBC, CBS, as well as Christian broadcasters such as Trinity Broadcasting Network (TBN). TBN is the world's largest Christian television network, with forty-seven satellites and over 12,000 television and cable affiliates, reaching over 92 million households in the United States alone.[7] Founded in 1978 by television chat-show hosts Paul and Jan Crouch, the network is now the seventh largest network in America, ahead of ABC.[8] It broadcasts via satellite, cable and the Internet, and translates many of its programmes into other languages. There are TBN sites in America; Africa, including Namibia, South Africa and Tanzania; Asia and the South Pacific, including Australia and New Zealand; South America; India; and Europe, including Estonia, Italy and Russia. In February 2007, TBN reached an agreement with Asia Broadcast Satellite to air TBN's programmes throughout the Asia and Pacific region, which includes the heavily targeted 10/40 window of countries lying within 10 and 40 degrees latitude north, home to most Muslim nations, India, China, Indochina, Japan and Korea (TBN, 2007).

Although TBN broadcasts an eclectic range of programmes, including those from Southern Baptists and Catholics, there is considerable bias towards the renewalist ministries – that is, Pentecostal, Word of Faith and charismatic ministries. This bias reflects the Word of Faith inclinations of Paul Crouch, who provided broadcasting outlets for early pioneers of the Word of Faith movement such as Kenneth Hagin and Oral Roberts. The Word of Faith movement is sometimes known as 'name it and claim it' because of its emphasis on believing and confessing that God has delivered what you have asked for even before it has been received. Believers have their money, healing, and relationships restored because they believe that God has said in the Bible that if they are faithful to him then he wants them to be well, prosperous and in the right relationships (Hebrews 12:1; Matthew 6:33).

This teaching is part of an American gospel that has its antecedents in the teachings of E.W. Kenyon and taps into an American culture of self-help, motivational teaching and the culture of success, which permeates the business sales and sporting arenas. There is a considerable amount of borrowing, often unknowingly or unacknowledged, from Norman Vincent Peale's positive thinking, Robert Schuller's possibility thinking, and even neuro-linguistic programming, popularized by Anthony Robbins. This reflects the identification of Christian Right thinking with images of success from business and sports, and with the individualism of the Protestant work ethic, personal responsibility and self-improvement.

TBN programming runs twenty-four hours a day throughout the world, providing maximum coverage for ministries to supplement their domestic and Internet audiences. An examination of the programming of TBN's Asia and Pacific network for one week in September 2007 showed that renewalist preachers dominated the airwaves. Three satellites broadcasting to a potential audience of hundreds of millions aired Paul and Jan Crouch's two-hour flagship programme

Praise the Lord and Pat Robertson's *700 Club* several times every day. Joyce Meyer's *Enjoying Everyday Life*, Rod Parsley's *Breakthrough* and John Hagee's programmes were also broadcast several times a day. Other ministries featured prominently included Benny Hinn's *This Is Your Day* (shown 46 times), T.D. Jakes's *Potter's Touch* (27 times), James Robison's *Life Today* (25 times), Creflo Dollar's *Changing Your World* (18 times), Kenneth Copeland's *Believer's Voice of Victory* (18 times) and Joel Osteen (13 times).

Programme titles are catchy and emphasize the individuality of the viewer and the expectation, through belief in the ministry/God, that lives will be transformed. Viewers are invited to an 'hour of power', to have 'ever increasing faith' or to 'acquire the fire'. Although there is an evangelistic thrust to much of the programming, the ministries deliver biblically based motivational talks focusing on just one verse or part of a verse, often taken out of context to persuade viewers that with God's/their help they can overcome life's problems. The preachers set themselves up as role models, encouraging the audience to become just like them, triumphing over adversity and becoming successful, where success is implied but never stated to be the fulfilment of the American Dream. Afro-American ministers T.D. Jakes, Fred Price and Creflo Dollar in particular have concentrated on being role models to their communities and in promoting a prosperity gospel challenging the liberal, social gospel message of traditional Afro-American churches in America.

Other broadcasters with similar politico-theological positions, complementing TBN's promotion of Christian Right teaching and news coverage, include Daystar Television Network. Established by Marcus Lamb in 1985 and based in Fort Worth/Dallas, Texas, the network is one of the fastest growing Christian television networks in the world, and is already the second largest Christian broadcaster with satellite broadcasts into 200 countries.[9] CBN was the first Christian television station in America in the 1960s and has grown to such an extent that its coverage is worldwide, providing an unrivalled platform for Pat Robertson and his son Gordon to propagate their political views to an international audience of many millions. As CBN broadcasts have been aired in different countries, so outreaches and church planting programmes have supported them.

In 1982, CBN launched Middle East Television (METV), broadcasting from Israeli-occupied southern Lebanon to fifteen nations in the region including Israel, Jordan, Syria and Egypt.[10] With the withdrawal of Israeli troops from southern Lebanon and the increased risk of violence from Lebanese Muslim militias, resentful of its support for Israel, METV relocated to Cyprus, with broadcasts reaching Iran, Turkey and Libya in 2000. A year later LeSEA acquired METV to add to its World Harvest Television ministry and radio broadcasts, and has continued to disseminate renewalist teaching across the Middle East. LeSEA was founded in 1957 by Lester Sumrall, prolific author of over one hundred books and an evangelist who has visited Israel some one hundred times. Dr Sumrall's son Peter has succeeded him in the ministry, and LeSEA support for Israel continues by providing regular tours to Israel for around 800 people a year.[11] The ministry's television broadcasting was further extended in 2003 with the addition of Far East Television (FETV), broadcasting twenty-four hours a day to Asia, Africa and Australia from its centre in Limassol, Cyprus.[12]

The extent to which television influences the political beliefs of viewers has been the subject of considerable academic debate. While there has been a reluctance to attribute too much influence to television as opposed to the press (Norris, 1996), cultural studies has broadened understanding to include the context in which people relate to the media. As Street (2001: 93, 99) argues, more emphasis needs to be given to the conditions under which viewers view, how they watch and interpret television, and what interests are shaping and creating audiences. This would require greater ethnographical study of audiences, something that has been neglected, particularly in examining viewers of Christian television.

What is certain is that the Christian Right attach considerable importance to television as a medium to transmit their message, and see secular media as having the potential to corrupt and undermine their conception of the moral fabric of the country. Philo explains that television, especially in news production, is able to define what 'acceptable' behaviour is. He argues that 'Messages are situated within political and cultural assumptions about what is normal and acceptable within society' (Philo, 1990: 5). For viewers of TBN, and other Christian Right broadcasters, the celebrity preacher defines acceptable behaviour. This includes images of financial success, conservative moral values including the denigration of alternative lifestyles and prohibiting sexual activity outside of marriage, abstinence rather than sex education in order to combat AIDS/HIV, the subordinate role of women, antagonism and suspicion towards Islam and socialism, and support for Israel.

Christian Right regular viewing audiences, domestically and internationally, tuning into renewalist programming are predisposed to believe the televangelists, who both reinforce and develop viewers' convictions and world-view. Occasional viewers are presented with an image of success that equates Christianity with an American gospel. Notwithstanding debate as to the effects of media content, the extent to which audiences can be observed empirically to respond, for example in terms of financial contributions, would suggest some correlation between views propagated and corresponding beliefs of the audience. The implications – for the security of traditional Christian missions, aid workers and US foreign policy more generally – of Pat Robertson and Benny Hinn proclaiming pro-Israel and anti-Islamic rhetoric throughout the 10/40 window on over fifty occasions over the course of the week studied, and presumably every week have still to be measured.

Missions

Alongside evangelistic crusades and the use of the broadcast media, the Christian Right provide missions as a means of disseminating their ideas. The vast wealth accumulated by the most prominent Christian Right groups claiming tax-exempt (501(c)(3)) status enables them to develop lavish mission programmes as a further evangelistic outreach. CBN founded Operation Blessing in 1978 to distribute relief in various projects throughout America, expanding internationally through Operation Blessing International (OBI), which became a separate entity from CBN in 1991. OBI has systematic and crisis evangelistic relief programmes throughout he world, which distribute food, drill wells, provide medical services, build homeless shelters and administer disaster relief. OBI was actively involved in helping in the aftermath of the 2005 tsunami and Hurricane Katrina in New Orleans.[13] Joyce Meyer Ministries has fifty-two missions around the world distributing food, providing medical and dental care, orphanages and prison outreach.[14] Almost all the leading ministries featured on Christian broadcasting run mission programmes to supplement their teaching and provide further opportunities to spread their message.

For the Christian Right missions are not altruistic endeavours but have a specific agenda to win converts in their own image. Favourite evangelical biblical verses adorn packages supplying food and medicines, and for the recipients there can be no misunderstanding that the price of assistance is their own conversion. There is a close identification of conservative evangelical missions, recipients of federal funding and US foreign policy assistance. The real demarcation between missions and US government under George Bush becomes increasingly blurred under the faith-based initiative, which awards mainly Christian organizations contracts to deliver US assistance through United States Agency for International Development (USAID). Many Christian Right organizations such as Operation Blessing and Samaritan's Purse have received tens of millions of taxpayer dollars to sustain and increase their missions as active participants in US foreign policy.

A close connection between US foreign policy, under Reagan and both Bush administrations, and Christian Right missionary activity has developed. The Christian Right when operating abroad carry forward their support of a partisan Republican agenda. Christian ministries that are obliged to justify their own extravagant lifestyles do so by appealing to selective biblical passages that chime with the

American Dream. It is not too large a leap to suggest that biblical prosperity implies individualism, competition, property ownership, investments, consumerism, free trade, in short American capitalism. This is certainly a connection drawn by Latin American countries, over the past few decades, concerned by missionary collusion with US corporations or secret services, which have sought to expropriate natural resources for corporate interests.

Gerard Colby and Charlotte Dennett (1995) in a huge volume traced the history of seven decades of collusion between evangelism, US capitalism and the CIA. In the book, they implicate Wycliffe Bible Translators and the Summer Institute of Linguistics in the destruction of traditional ways of life through evangelism and introducing Western culture to indigenous peoples, enabling US corporations to exploit the resources of the Amazonian rainforest. These claims followed those of Peter Aaby and Soren Hvalkof's (1982) *Is God an American?*, which also points to a link between the CIA and SIL, a claim repeated by Perkins (2006). Hvalkof (1984: 124), defending his proposition, considers the connection with the CIA of less importance than the 'unquestionable affinity between SIL and U.S. imperialism with respect to ideology'.

Similar problems have emerged more recently in Venezuela, with President Hugo Chávez calling for the expulsion of the New Tribes Mission (NTM) on charges similar to that levelled against SIL during the 1970s and 1980s. Like SIL, NTM translate the Bible into indigenous languages and attempt to convert traditional peoples to evangelical Christianity. In the context of Chávez's Bolivarian revolution, which has restored the dignity of indigenous peoples throughout much of Latin America, attempts over decades by American missionaries, often working under contract from the host government, to convert native peoples undermines such efforts. When Pat Robertson calls for the Venezuelan president's assassination and America is implicated in an abortive coup to topple him, it is hardly surprising that Christian Right organizations working in the region are viewed with suspicion. The Christian Right have consistently supported anti-socialist and anti-communist US foreign policy measures in Latin America, promoting a capitalist version of Christianity (Martin, 1999: 71; Diamond, 1989: 16–17). The close connection between conservative evangelicals and US foreign policy objectives, particularly under Republican administrations, means that conversions offer the possibility of another means of subverting regimes antithetical to US interests.

Impact of the American Gospel

In October 2006 the Pew Forum on Religion & Public Life published a ten-country survey of Pentecostals, entitled *Spirit and Power*. The report was the most exhaustive survey yet carried out of the fastest growing religious movement in the world. According to the *World Christian Database*, Pentecostals now represent a quarter of all Christians, approximately 500 million. The survey has its faults in that it has a narrow definition of Pentecostal churches as belonging to major Pentecostal denominations; it is unclear whether Word of Faith churches are included within this definition. Charismatics are also considered and are defined as being self-proclaimed or tongue-talking Christians who are not from Pentecostal churches but include those of mainstream denominations. The term 'renewalist' is used as an umbrella term referring to both groups (Pew Forum, 2006a: 1). The report considered countries in four continents: the United States, Brazil, Chile, Guatemala, Kenya, Nigeria, South Africa, India, the Philippines and South Korea. Apart from India, all the countries have at least 10 per cent of their populations that can be regarded as renewalist, while Brazil, Guatemala and Kenya have between 49 and 60 per cent (Pew Forum, 2006a: 2).

The survey is particularly useful in attempting to discern the influence of Christian Right renewalist preachers and missions. In doing so, it is as well to bear in mind that although Pentecostalism has its modern roots in Charles Parham's Topeka, Kansas Bible school in 1901 and the Azusa Street revival of 1906, Pentecostal churches throughout much of the global South can be traced back to the early part of the twentieth century. Indigenous Pentecostal churches are well established throughout the world and there is a reverse trend of African, Latin American and Asian renewalist evangelists preaching and seeking converts in America. US Pentecostal and Word of Faith ministries have complemented and reinforced much of what has already been taking place at the local level. Similarly, claims made by celebrity preachers involve considerable overestimates of their scorecard of conversions, baptisms in the Holy Spirit, and supernatural healings, as they compete with other ministries for financial support and reputation.

The survey estimates that 15 per cent of the Brazilian population and 20 per cent of the Guatemalan population are Pentecostals. Some 33 per cent of Kenyans, 18 per cent of Nigerians and 10 per cent of South Africans are Pentecostal (Pew Forum, 2006a: 2). The survey reveals that in all ten countries, Pentecostals feel more strongly than other Christians or the general population do that religious movements should be politically involved (Pew Forum, 2006a: 7). Pentecostals watch or listen to religious programming more than other Christians and the general population. In Brazil, Guatemala, Kenya, Nigeria and South Africa at least 75 per cent of Pentecostals watch or listen to religious broadcasting at least once a week (Pew Forum, 2006a: 20). Pentecostals overwhelmingly (80 per cent or higher) believe that if they have enough faith then God prospers and gives health to believers. Over 90 per cent of Pentecostals in Nigeria, South Africa, India and the Philippines bought into the health and wealth gospel (Pew Forum, 2006a: 29).

On moral questions Pentecostals overwhelmingly consider that homosexuality could never be justified. In America 80 per cent oppose homosexuality, while in Nigeria and Kenya opposition is only marginally under 100 per cent (Pew Forum, 2006a: 36). Between one-third and three-quarters consider AIDS to be a punishment from God, while they overwhelmingly consider that abortion is never justified (Pew Forum, 2006a: 37–8). In every country apart from the United States and South Korea, over half of Pentecostals believe that a wife must always obey her husband (Pew Forum, 2006a: 42).

Pentecostals overwhelmingly endorse the view that most people are better off in a free-market economy despite economic disparities (Pew Forum, 2006a: 52). They believe that faith in God, hard work and education are vital to people's economic success (Pew Forum, 2006a: 54). On matters of foreign policy, Pentecostals are significantly more likely to sympathize with Israel rather than Palestine (Pew Forum, 2006a: 67). Pentecostal support for American leadership in the War on Terror is limited to the United States and those states with a substantial Muslim presence, including Nigeria, Kenya, the Philippines and India (Pew Forum, 2006a: 68).

The growth of Christianity throughout Africa has been phenomenal, increasing from 144 million in 1970 to 411 million by 2005, approximately 46 per cent of the continent's population. During this same period renewalist numbers have grown from 17 million to 147 million, and now account for 17 per cent of the population, mainly located in sub-Saharan Africa. The group represents more than 20 per cent of the populations of Zimbabwe, South Africa, Ghana, Congo (Zaire), Nigeria, Kenya, Angola, Zambia and Uganda. Increasingly Pentecostals are politically active, contesting elections in Kenya and Nigeria and opposing the introduction of Islamic courts covering Muslim areas of the countries. Kenyan, Nigerian, Zambian and Ugandan Pentecostals have held large evangelistic crusades to challenge the perceived ascendancy of Muslims (Pew Forum, 2006b).

The numerical and political growth of the renewalist movement in sub-Saharan Africa has great significance for US foreign policy as the area becomes of increased strategic importance because of the interface with Islamic countries, the War on Terror and natural resources. After having neglected the continent for most of the previous century, including the Rwandan genocide in 1994, the United States, under George W. Bush, has become increasingly concerned and involved with African countries. This has come about in no small measure because of pressure from the Christian Right and other evangelicals in bringing the issues of religious persecution, AIDS/HIV, debt cancellation and poverty relief to the attention of the president and the public. The events of 11 September 2001 have also helped to focus attention on a region that provides more than 10 per cent of America's oil and is a potential recruiting and training ground for Islamic extremists. The potential rise of militant Islam in Somalia and elsewhere, the preponderance of failed states, the history of terrorist acts in East Africa, and humanitarian abuses throughout the continent are all of immediate concern to the Bush administration. The perceived need to counter increased Chinese influence in the continent and competition for raw materials and natural resources has also assumed increased importance to the Bush administration. As a reflection of this, a US military Africa Command (Africom) is being established by the end of September 2008.[15]

African renewalist and especially Pentecostal and Word of Faith Christians tend to be more favourably disposed towards the moral and political values of the US Christian Right and Bush foreign policy. In Nigeria, support for Israel over the Palestinians among Pentecostals was 46 per cent to 7 per cent, the rest expressing no clear preference, and support for US-led efforts to fight terrorism was 71 per cent (Pew Forum, 2006a: 204–5). In Kenya and Nigeria, Pentecostals were even more enthusiastic supporters of touchstone moral issues than their American counterparts. Opposition to homosexuality, prostitution, euthanasia, suicide, sex outside of marriage, and abortion was expressed by over 88 per cent of respondents. As African Pentecostalism grows, then support for Christian Right foreign policy positions at the UN and in the Middle East will also increase. These may well include making abortion more difficult or impossible for women, discrimination against homosexuals and same-gender relationships, and encouraging abstinence rather than sex-education programmes to combat HIV/AIDS.

Vinson Synan, emeritus professor of theology at Regent University, suggests that the growth of Pentecostal and Word of Faith churches in Nigeria can be attributed to prosperity-teaching visits in the early 1990s by Kenneth Hagin and Kenneth Copeland, leading to church growth measures in the millions (Phiri and Maxwell, 2007). Mega-churches have become commonplace in sub-Saharan Africa as the health and wealth gospel resonates with the poor and aspiring middle class. In Lagos, Nigeria, Michael Okonkwo, a graduate of the Morris Cerullo School of Ministry, leads the 4,000-strong Redeemed Evangelical Mission and oversees the annual Kingdom Life World Conference of 150 prosperity gospel churches. David Oyedepo's Winners Chapel International has a 54,000-seat auditorium and Christian college. In December 2006, the church hosted the world's largest Christian gathering ever of around 3 million people. In Zambia, Joe Imakando leads the 6,500-strong Bread of Life Church in Lusaka, which has planted fifty-three other branches around Zambia, Democratic Republic of Congo, South Africa, Malawi and Tanzania. Imakando and other African pastors produce their own television programmes, which supplement similar teachings from the celebrity preachers on TBN. In Zambia, TBN is only one of three television stations available and enjoys a huge audience accordingly, which suggests a significantly greater potential to disseminate Christian Right views (Phiri and Maxwell, 2007).

The African Pentecostal and Word of Faith movement not only receives input from Christian Right teachers such as Kenneth Copeland[16] and T.D. Jakes[17] but also develops links with co-religionists in the outside world (Onishi, 2002). McClymond (2005: 167) considers that these links are 'crucial to their sense of identity and give them a powerful sense of participation in an international movement. In the long run, these connections could play a role in socio-political reform within Africa.' The collaboration of African Pentecostals and their Christian Right counterparts may lead to an increasing international conservativism as the United States receives more support in international forums. Such a scenario, under a Republican administration, could lead to the further erosion of women's rights and of toleration of political, religious, moral and lifestyle differences.

Steve Brouwer, Paul Gifford and Susan Rose (1996) have powerfully argued that American evangelicals have exported an American gospel throughout much of the world to help justify America's cultural and economic imperialism. Although they acknowledge that indigenous ministries have long since replaced American missionaries, these ministries have assimilated American styles of worship and encourage patriarchy by establishing male leadership and emphasizing traditional gender roles. Those churches influenced by US evangelistic efforts by mission or media broadcast encourage 'the kind of civic and psychic orderliness that does not question the rule of the powerful' (Brouwer, Gifford and Rose, 1996: 127). As we have seen, Pentecostals and renewalists seem more favourably disposed towards American foreign policy, conservative morality and capitalism than other Christians or the wider society. In the intervening years, since *Exporting the American Gospel* appeared, these churches have become far more likely to engage politically and, rather than questioning the rule of the powerful, actually to *become* the powerful.

This assimilation of an American gospel is evident in South Korea, which has become a leading capitalist economy since the Vietnam War. In 2006, renewalists accounted for 10 per cent of the country's urban population, and had nine out of the fifteen largest mega-churches. The largest church in the world is the 750,000-strong Yoido Full Gospel Church, led by Paul Yonggi Cho. Cho, who has an honorary doctorate from Oral Roberts University, has been actively engaged in Korean politics over the past few decades, and his church has fielded numerous candidates for political office. After 11 September 2001, Cho led national prayer services for the victims and, following anti-American demonstrations in the capital in 2003, organized counter-demonstrations supporting the US military presence in Korea. Cho and other Pentecostal leaders have led calls for greater freedom in and tougher sanctions to be enforced against North Korea, consistently adopting an American position rather than supporting South Korea's less confrontational approach with their northern neighbour (Pew Forum, 2006d). In 2005, Cho hosted a pro-Israel summit in Seoul with the mayor further demonstrating the similarity of many renewalist churches worldwide to the approach of America's Christian Right.

Conclusion

In spreading the word, the Christian Right have used a variety of measures with varying degrees of success. Traditional approaches of evangelistic crusades have proved successful over the years in gaining converts and establishing churches. Although this method has largely given way to the televised church meeting or motivational Bible study, it has proved effective when accompanied by 'signs and wonders' of supernatural healings (imagined or otherwise), exuberant worship, exciting preaching and charismatic showmanship. The Pentecostal and 'Word of Faith' section of the Christian Right, due to the phenomenal success of TBN and CBN, has dominated the effective use of radio and television to propagate the Christian message. The message delivered is an American gospel that encourages individualism and an image of success that equates to material prosperity. This gospel, delivered by satellites around the world, teaches that salvation is the first step to fulfilling the American Dream, which is evidence of God's favour.

The enormous wealth generated by televangelism helps provide lavish lifestyles for celebrity preachers as well as financing evangelistic missions, which provide significant material and physical help in developing countries in attempting to convert citizens to Christianity. The Christian Right in pursuing evangelistic outreach abroad are not simply seeking converts in fulfilment of the Great Commission but are also advancing political objectives in implicit support of US foreign policy positions on family, sexual and reproductive health, and free-market capitalism. Celebrity preachers endorse a world-view in which capitalism and market democracy are the only godly form of governance, where possessions are next to godliness. They project domestic social and moral conservatism onto an international stage, seeking to promote abstinence, end abortion and outlaw homosexuality by encouraging and legitimating prejudice and discrimination. Through their evangelistic and 'Christian' lifestyle message endeavours, the Christian Right advocate unquestioning support for Israel, heighten tensions with Islam, and seek to undermine socialist and communist governments. Although not setting out to advocate openly for US foreign policy, the similarities between their world-view and US foreign policy under Bush is so close as to be but two sides of the same coin.

The Christian Right have been able to export successfully their American gospel throughout the world, especially through their influence on Pentecostal and renewalist churches, which constitute the fastest growing religious movement in the world. Renewalist churches are far more likely than mainstream Christian denominations to identify with the Christian Right agenda, and the changing religious demography in sub-Saharan Africa, Latin America and Asia is likely to lead to greater interfaith competition and less tolerance of diversity. Indigenous renewalist churches have long assimilated the American gospel, repackaged it for domestic consumption, and developed their identity as part of a global Pentecostal movement. In the next chapter, we consider how the Christian Right continue to be instrumental in promoting and influencing US foreign policy, as an unofficial adjunct to the Bush administration, this time considering Bush's democracy-promotion strategy.

PART II

3

Promoting Democracy or the Gospel?

> The most powerful weapon in the struggle against extremism is not bullets or bombs – it is the universal appeal of freedom. Freedom is the design of our Maker, and the longing of every soul. Freedom is the best way to unleash the creativity and economic potential of a nation. Freedom is the only ordering of a society that leads to justice. And human freedom is the only way to achieve human rights. (George W. Bush)[1]

George W. Bush came to power anxious not to repeat what he saw as the mistakes of his predecessor. He determined that America would not embark on foreign adventures unless the national interests of the country were at stake. The events of 11 September, however, dramatically changed Bush foreign policy from one of realism, acting in defence of the national interest, to a neoconservative version of liberal internationalism's focus on international institutions, cooperation, interdependence and democracy promotion. Rather than regarding international cooperation as a prerequisite for this internationalism, the neoconservative version sought to use American military power to impose its preferred solutions on the world. Multilateral cooperation was desirable but not essential as the United States had the military capability to achieve its objectives unilaterally. Rather than seeking to work through international institutions to achieve military and strategic objectives, the United States, under Bush, seemed happier working with coalitions of the willing. The Bush administration, heavily influenced by neoconservatives in the Pentagon and vice president's office, sought to pursue a dual strategy of power projection and democracy promotion, in the Middle East in particular.

Democracy promotion is deeply engrained within the American psyche and has become an essential component of US foreign policy, albeit with varying degrees of success. As far back as the nineteenth century, Alexis de Tocqueville (1998) portrayed America as an established democracy, and subsequent generations have felt not just contented with their democracy but genuinely believing it to be the best political system imaginable. This polity has a resilience and confidence that finds expression in a desire, though not always the resolve, to export a similar system around the world. American liberal internationalists have long subscribed to the democratic peace thesis endorsing Kant's 'Perpetual Peace' (1970), arguing that America needs to be involved in international affairs and actively promoting its ideas and values. Kant suggested that republican states were less likely to go to war with one another and that only these states could bring about a peaceful international order. Michael Doyle in two seminal articles in the early 1980s substituted the term 'democratic' for 'republican', arguing that liberal democracies do not go to war with one another, but were likely to do so with non-democratic ones (Doyle, 1983a, 1983b). Doyle was echoing the thoughts of Protestant evangelical Woodrow Wilson, Franklin Roosevelt and Harry Truman, each of whom sought to export American democratic values. Truman in particular had the satisfaction of witnessing the most successful democracy-promotion strategy ever with the reconstruction of post-war Italy, Japan and Germany.

After the Second World War, a realist approach dominated US foreign policy, which was to remain throughout the Cold War, subordinating democracy-promotion strategies to the more immediate imperative of national security. The Cold War revealed tensions in US foreign policy between the desire to export American values, including democracy, and the pragmatic decision to make alliances on the basis of a shared commitment not to democracy but to anti-communism. Democracy promotion was covert and just one of a raft of measures designed to undermine the Soviet Union, its allies and client states. The end of the Cold War and the defeat of the 'Evil Empire' left the United States as the sole remaining superpower. Krauthammer's 'unipolar moment' represented for Fukuyama the triumph of liberal democracy and the end of ideological rivalry (Krauthammer, 1991; Fukuyama, 1989, 1992). For George H.W. Bush, this was an opportunity for a new world order based on pragmatic liberal internationalism. Old rivalries were at an end and the international community could cooperate to bring about a pacific international order. The largely peaceful democratic revolutions throughout the former Warsaw Pact and international cooperation surrounding the first Gulf War all created an optimism that continued as the Soviet Union imploded. Samuel Huntington (1993, 1997), who was later to rail against the triumphalism of Fukuyama predicting a clash of civilizations, joined in with this new optimism, urging the United States to promote democracy around the world:

> The United States is the premier democratic country of the modern world, and its identity as a nation is inseparable from its commitment to liberal and democratic values ... Americans have a special interest in the development of a global environment congenial to democracy. (Huntington, 1991: 29–30)

The Bush Senior administration responded cautiously, wary of risking substantial US resources on democracy-promotion initiatives that disappeared into the bank accounts of corrupt officials. Secretary of State James Baker (1992) and Chairman of the Joint Chief of Staffs Colin Powell (1992) provided much of the rhetoric in support of US leadership in promoting democracy, but there was to be no new

Marshall Plan. Under Bush Senior, and his successor Bill Clinton, democracy promotion was to be achieved through expending minimal US resources and seeking to leverage support from allies and the international financial institutions. Herein lies a problem of state-sponsored democracy promotion: the population need to be convinced that assisting people in other countries best serves their own interests, a lesson that, as we shall see, the Christian Right have certainly learned. In weighing up how much US beneficence can be extended to countries, previous administrations have shown considerable caution, except when considering the needs of their key ally Israel, which will be discussed in more detail in a later chapter. The long-term benefits of democratic expansion, in terms of economic opportunities and international security, almost inevitably give way to the exigencies of the immediate. I have argued elsewhere that short-term national security gains, such as the eastwards expansion of NATO and reduced Russian military capacity, during the Clinton administration trumped long-term democratic objectives (Marsden, 2005).

Clinton pursued a policy of engagement and enlargement, seeking to incrrease the number of democracies in the world while strengthening relationships with existing democracies. In doing so, he sought to raise the debate above partisan politics and secure a consensus for promoting democracy in order to strengthen America's national interests. The consensus centred on the efficacy of the democratic peace thesis posited by Michael Doyle (1983a, 1983b) and Bruce Russett (1993), among others. The number of democracies has grown considerably over the past few decades from 45 at the beginning of Reagan's presidency to more than 120 today. America's influence in assisting in this more recent transition is difficult to establish other than in an inspirational capacity.

While members of the Christian Right are for the most part enthusiastic supporters of the principle of democracy their primary motivation is the fulfilment of the Great Commission, and democracy, or the promotion of it at least, presents more opportunities for proselytizing. The benefit of any form of democratization and liberalization to the Christian Right is that it opens up countries, in particular in Muslim, Communist and authoritarian countries, for evangelism that would otherwise be more dangerous and difficult to access. In undermining the political and societal foundations of targeted countries, political and religious dissidents and pro-democracy reformers are encouraged and authoritarian regimes helped to collapse. In enshrining religious freedom in new constitutions, Christians would be free to worship and proselytize confident in their ability to gain more converts than competing religions or secularization. The Christian Right embraced the benefits of democracy promotion by increasing missions and broadcasts to the former Communist bloc exponentially in the 1990s.

Republican presidential candidate Mike Huckabee, a former Baptist minister and governor of Arkansas, who emerged in 2008 as a champion of the Christian Right grassroots, described not only his pragmatic approach to democracy promotion but also the views of many fellow evangelicals in *Foreign Affairs*:

> Although we cannot export democracy as if it were Coca-Cola or KFC, we can nurture moderate forces in places where al-Qaeda is seeking to replace modern evil with medieval evil. Such moderation may not look or function like our system – it may be a benevolent oligarchy or more tribal than individualistic – but both for us and for the peoples of those countries, it will be better than the dictatorships they have now or the theocracy they would have under radical Islamists. (Huckabee, 2008)

When considering democracy promotion the Christian Right share the same generalized conception of democracy as being the equivalent of the American model. Throughout the 1990s, assumptions made by both administrations held that the US system was ideal and that democracy could develop through institutional modelling. Emerging democracies were encouraged to develop institutions that resembled their American counterparts (Carothers, 1999: 86–90). Dahl's model of polyarchy best describes the US system and the model democracy practitioners sought to encourage and export. Polyarchy incorporates free and fair elections between competing political parties with all adults having the right to vote for the candidate who has successfully competed for their support. It includes the freedom to form and join organizations and eligibility to compete for public office. Under this model the institutions for making government policies depend on the votes and other expressions of preferences of the electorate. In terms of civil society, Dahl emphasizes the freedom to form and join organizations, the right to freedom of expression, and the need for alternative sources of information to make informed choices (Dahl, 1971: 3; Marsden, 2005: 136).

For the Christian Right, free and fair elections in foreign countries brought with them possibilities of pro-American, pro-free market democrats, and even Christians, being elected. Freedom to form and join organizations opens up the potential for Christian involvement in the political process being able to exert influence in political parties, in much the same way as they have come to dominate the Republican Party. The ability to form and join churches and parachurch organizations helps with spreading the gospel and mobilizes Values Voters to influence the political process. Polyarchy provides Christians with the opportunity to stand for political office. Freedom of expression and alternative sources of information enable Christians in the democratizing state to proselytize and receive input from fellow Christians in America. In addition, the acceptance of alternative sources of information provides the Christian Right with greater opportunities to broadcast theological and political programmes through broadcasters such as TBN, CBN and God TV.

Democracy Promotion under George W. Bush

George Bush Junior did not enter the White House with a particular agenda on democracy promotion; rather, existing programmes continued and in the former Soviet Union continued being scaled down. 11 September 2001 fundamentally altered Bush's approach to foreign policy with the realization that the United States was in direct conflict with radical Islam. When considering the question 'Why do they hate us?' following al-Qaeda's attack on the Twin Towers and the Pentagon, Bush's retort was that 'they' hate America's freedom and success. In order to defeat the terrorists Bush determined on a dual strategy of military conflict and a campaign to 'drain the swamp' by encouraging democracy throughout the Middle East. Both strategies would provide opportunities for evangelicals of every hue to gain access to formerly restricted territory. Over previous decades, successive US administrations had supported corrupt and authoritarian regimes in order to resist Soviet influence in the region and secure oil resources to fuel the American economy. The War on Terror now involved revisiting the Clinton administration's democratization strategy and directing the attention of democracy-promotion practitioners towards the Muslim world.

The strategy would require a balancing of the idealism of democracy promotion with the pragmatic realism of requiring allies in America's War on Terror, many of which are despotic and undemocratic, to cooperate in both reforming and participating in anti-terrorist measures. There exist the added complications of oil resources, a history of US hypocrisy in the region for supporting regimes known to be human rights abusers, and the stability of such regimes in the face of increasing support for radical Islam. Further complicating factors include a Christian president seeking to promote Western democracy in Muslim countries, and America's support for Israel.

The overthrow of the Taliban in Afghanistan in the aftermath of 11 September provided an opportunity to create a democracy in what the administration began to call the Broader Middle East. In 2002, Bush launched The Middle East Partnership Initiative (MEPI), designed to promote political, economic, educational reform and women's empowerment. During the first five years, about $430 million was spent on more than 350 projects in fifteen countries and the Occupied Territories. The initiative receives bipartisan support in Congress and works in the Broader Middle East and North Africa encouraging democracy, enterprise, the English language, and women's empowerment (MEPI, 2005). MEPI's work complements multilateral initiatives, including the Partnership for Progress and a Common Future with the Region of the Broader Middle East and North Africa/ Broader Middle East and North Africa (BMENA) Initiative, involving twenty countries in BMENA and the G8.

Such initiatives are long-term strategies to shape the region and gradually ease it towards democracy, or more accurately market democracy, where capitalism, privatization and free trade are as important as developing civil society. The president has consistently argued that Middle Eastern countries will not necessarily resemble an American-style democracy, but there will be certain prerequisites for effective democracies, which must:

- Honour and uphold basic human rights, including freedom of religion, conscience, speech, assembly, association, and press.
- [Be] responsive to their citizens, submitting to the will of the people, especially when people vote to change their government.
- Exercise effective sovereignty and maintain order within their own borders, protect independent and impartial systems of justice, punish crime, embrace the rule of law, and resist corruption.
- Limit the reach of government, protecting the institutions of civil society, including the family, religious communities, voluntary association, private property, independent business, and a market economy. (NSC, 2006: 4)

These defining characteristics also serve to tick all the right boxes for the Christian Right. The emphasis given to freedom of religion and religious communities being an essential component of civil society are particularly resonant. Bush and Rice often refer to one of Christian Zionism's heroes, Nathan Sharansky. In *The Case for Democracy* Sharansky argues that the test for democracy is the right to walk into the town square and declare your views without fear of punishment or reprisal (Sharansky, 2004: 40–41). The Christian Right are eager to take advantage of the opportunities this openness would give them to promote their own message of salvation.

The Bush conversion to democracy promotion as a national security strategy has also seen a change in democratization rhetoric. The term 'democracy' has connotations of western values rather than universal values. Bush and his administration have stressed instead the universality of freedom and liberty. Operation Infinite Justice in Afghanistan quickly became Operation Enduring Freedom, and the war to topple Saddam Hussein and establish democracy in Iraq, Operation Iraqi Freedom. Bush's speechwriters have developed the contagious hyperbole of grand-style narrative incorporating biblical imagery with eighteenth-century constitutional notions of freedom, liberty and democracy that Americans, if not the rest of the world, hold to be true and self-evident. Bush has a Manichaean world-view in which the world consists of good and evil, those who love freedom and those who hate it; it is a view shared with fellow members of the Christian Right. Democracy, freedom and liberty are non-negotiable, dividing the world into those 'with us' and those 'against us'. America, in such thinking, is inevitably on the side of good and has a unique historical role to defend and advance freedom and democracy (Bush, 2005b).

Bush has exercised the same dichotomous thinking employed by the Reagan presidency. Reagan is considered by the Christian Right and conservatives to have 'won' the Cold War by not compromising, and rejecting detente in favour of a moral authority that portrayed the United States as 'the city on a hill' and the Soviet Union as 'the Evil Empire'. Radical Islam simply replaces this communist threat. In order to defeat the new threat it is unnecessary to appease or engage with this new enemy. Instead, radical Islam is to be resisted at every turn and defeated in the war against terrorism. The administration considers authoritarian states in the Middle East a breeding ground for radical Islamic terrorism. This, it is suggested, can only be altered over the long term via a democratization strategy, with inducements and penalties being applied to reward progress or punish recalcitrance. In such a programme Iraq becomes the catalyst for a campaign to bring democracy to the whole region.

The Bush approach to democratization owes much to the influence of neoconservatives and support from Christian Right leaders such as Richard Land, who enthusiastically endorses Bush's approach,[2] which believes that invasion and regime change can promote the democratic peace. This is a view that has been strongly criticized by liberal internationalists, who overwhelmingly opposed the Iraq War, including Bruce Russett:

> To justify the Iraq war that way, in retrospect after previous justifications proved wrong, is yet one more distortion to cover a disastrous act. As a general principle, democratization by force is full of practical and moral dangers, depending on many highly unpredictable contingencies, and not to be undertaken as the purpose in a war of choice. (Russett, 2005: 405)

Realists have also criticized the Bush strategy, arguing that democracy promotion must not obscure US vital economic and security interests, which require a more pragmatic and realistic approach in order to maintain and project American power (Mearsheimer and Walt, 2003; Simes, 2003). For realists, the reason for overthrowing Saddam Hussein was not to bring democracy to Iraq but to remove a challenge to American hegemony. The idea of using regime change in order to promote democracy is anathema to those realists who are more comfortable with an international diplomacy that is less idealistic and more concerned with securing national interests base and power maximization.

Nonetheless, Bush's policy of regime change and democracy promotion enjoyed some initial success with well-supported elections in Afghanistan and Iraq, apart from a boycott by most Sunni Arabs. Voting in Iraq was on ethnic lines and significantly affected by sectarian militia instructions on which candidates to support. The benchmarks for a democratic polity five years after the declaration of 'mission accomplished' have still to be met, with inter- and intra-sectarian fighting and over two million fleeing the civil war to neighbouring Jordan and Syria. Despite regime change and elections in Iraq and Afghanistan, the prospects for democracy in both countries are bleak. In Afghanistan, the democratically elected government's remit extends little beyond Kabul. Large swathes of the country have reverted to control by local warlords. The Taliban have regrouped and there seems little prospect of any Afghan government being able to control the country for decades to come.

The failure of democratic imposition by military means has obliged the administration to become far more pragmatic in its approach. The example of parliamentary elections in the Palestinian Authority resulting in a clear victory for Hamas in January 2006 has caused the administration and the Christian Right to rethink its strategy. They will be aided in this rethinking by Dr Paul Bonicelli, the former Dean for Academic Affairs at Patrick Henry College, who was appointed deputy assistant administrator for democracy programmes at USAID in 2006 (Croft, 2007: 699). Christian Zionists within the Christian Right are concerned more with using their influence to protect Israel's interests than with a democratic Middle East. When the two goals are complementary their support for democratization initiatives is resolute, but if democracy promotion leads to a weakening of Israel's security then that support will dissipate. Radical Islamic parties have made a strong showing whenever elections have taken place in Broader Middle Eastern countries. The very process of democratization enables the Arab street to vote in favour of radical Islamic parties, which have developed reputations for welfare programmes and a lack of corruption. After initial pressure for political reform, the administration has recommended, rather than insisted on, democratization among its allies in the Broader Middle East and North Africa. Authoritarian, friendly governments in Azerbaijan, Egypt, Ethiopia, Kazakhstan, Pakistan and Saudi Arabia have little incentive to liberalize their polity, confident of US support as they resist domestic radical Islamists. The Bush administration's opposition to Iran trumps any desire for democracy, as demonstrated by a $63 billion arms package for Saudi Arabia and the Gulf States, Egypt and Israel announced by Secretary of State Rice in the summer of 2007, and reconfirmed during Bush's visit to the Middle East in January 2008, which makes no mention of democratization (MacAskill, 2007).

American efforts to overturn the democratic mandate of Hamas in the Palestinian Authority through the coordination of sanctions, intended to lead to the overthrow of the Haniyeh-led government, has called into question the Bush administration's commitment to democracy. In the *47-Nation Pew Global Attitudes Survey* of the thirteen Muslim countries surveyed, in all but two (Mali and Senegal) a majority of those surveyed disliked 'American ideas about democracy'. Those most hostile to American democratic ideals were Palestinians, whose parliamentary election results the USA refused to accept (71 per cent); Pakistanis, in whose country the USA has supported the undemocratic Musharraf regime (72 per cent); and the population of NATO member Turkey as the most hostile of all 47 countries (82 per cent) (Pew Research Center, 2007: 100). In all, a majority in 43 out of the 47 nations – including all the Muslim countries, and indeed 63 per cent of Americans – believed that the USA 'promotes democracy mostly where it serves its interests', a far more cynical view than the altruistic desire to promote democracy that has become standard rhetorical fare (Pew Research Center, 2007: 106). Tom Carothers considers that by the beginning of 2007, Bush's democracy-promotion strategy in the Middle East was 'effectively over' (Carothers, 2007: 7). The policy exists as an aspiration, and it is to this rhetorical level that we now turn by examining what has been possibly Bush's most important speech advocating democracy promotion, the Second Inaugural Address.

The Language of Freedom, Liberty and Democracy

US democracy-promotion strategy has three main components: major speeches, diplomacy and democracy-assistance programmes. Diplomacy is used to exhort and encourage, reward and punish states that cooperate in the democratization agenda. Democracy-assistance programmes are delivered at the micro-level by NGOs funded by the State Department, USAID and NED. The major speeches of presidents, vice presidents, secretaries of state and national security advisers have influence at the macro-level, setting agendas which have an impact on foreign relations and prepare domestic audiences to cede tax dollars to support the strategy, while reinforcing American exceptionalism and sense of international responsibility. Bush, Cheney, Rice and Hadley have delivered numerous speeches on democracy promotion, which have become almost a freedom mantra.

Here we focus on the Second Inaugural address, one of Bush's most effective speeches on democracy promotion, in order to analyse the rhetoric and discover its appeal to the Christian Right. The Second Inaugural Address is the most important speech given during a president's period in office. He or she has received recognition by the American people for the achievements of the previous four years and their confidence in the president's ability to lead them for another four. The speech will have one eye on the challenges and opportunities that lie ahead and another on the legacy the president wishes to bequeath. Bush's speech was one of the most idealistic ever delivered by a US president and went through twenty-one drafts. Michael Gerson, Bush's senior speechwriter and conservative evangelical, is credited with crafting the speech, although the president had considerable input.[3]

Throughout the speech, the president addresses different audiences at home and abroad. For his Christian Right base there are themes that are almost subliminal rallying calls to the cause:

> At this second gathering, our duties are defined not by the words I use, but by the history we have seen together. For a half century, America defended our own freedom by standing watch on distant borders. After the shipwreck of communism came years of relative quiet, years of repose, years of sabbatical – and then there came a day of fire.

Bush develops his theme of being at a crucial and providential point in America's history. The idea of freedom is introduced early, and either 'freedom' or 'free' is repeated on a further thirty-three occasions during the course of the speech. Freedom, in this speech, is a catch-all concept, which everyone, Bush assumes, supports in principle; Bush is able to connect with his audience at home and abroad by talking about but never actually defining what he means by freedom. The audience are invited to assume that he is referring to those American values that he claims in other speeches to be the envy of the world. Having avoided an attack on home soil throughout the Cold War through fighting and resisting Communism abroad, the post-Cold War period is portrayed as a sabbatical, a period of rest and preparation for what lies ahead. Bush alludes here to the biblical concept of the Sabbath, a rest before the al-Qaeda attacks of 2001, which are described in apocryphal terms: the 'day of fire' – terrifying and yet at the same time purging and purifying, removing the dross of complacency and preparing America to fulfil its God-given role to combat evil. He continues:

> We have seen our vulnerability – and we have seen its deepest source. For as long as whole regions of the world simmer in resentment and tyranny – prone to ideologies that feed hatred and excuse murder – violence will gather, and multiply in destructive power, and cross the most defended borders, and raise a mortal threat. There is only one force of history that can break the reign of hatred and resentment, and expose the pretensions of tyrants, and reward the hopes of the decent and tolerant, and that is the force of human freedom.

The strongly emotive language here is used to ratchet up the perceived level of threat to create a besieged mentality of America against the world. It asserts that no matter how securely the homeland is protected, evildoers are still capable of inflicting death and destruction in America. This sense of victimization and persecution, alongside the implied assertion that the USA has done nothing wrong, resonates with the Christian Right, who feel doubly besieged by what they see as an Islamic threat and the tide of modernization and secularization. The use of the term 'mortal threat' is used to raise the spectre of a loss of American lives and way of life. The focus is placed on American's own sense of mortality and the need to unite in common cause. Against such odds, there is only one 'force of history' that can prevail. The Christian Right, and indeed evangelical Christians of every hue, know that force is Jesus Christ. For Bush that force is described as 'human freedom'. Bush is seeking to appeal to wider America with the rallying call to freedom, while indicating to his core support in the Christian Right that he is indeed one of them.

For Christians, including Bush and Gerson, Jesus and human 'freedom' can be used interchangeably. Indeed, they would claim that true freedom is only found in Jesus. 'If the Son therefore shall make you free, ye shall be free indeed' (John 8:36). The answer to how the Son shall make them free is discovered a few verses earlier: 'And ye shall know the truth, and the truth shall make you free' (John 8:32). The truth is actually the realization that Jesus is the Messiah, the Son of God, and the means of access to a relationship with God: 'Jesus saith unto him, I am the way, the truth, and the life: no man cometh unto the Father, but by me' (John 14:6). Freedom, for the president and the Christian Right alike, is intimately connected with the belief that America's values are essentially Judeo-Christian.

Bush explains clearly that he is endorsing a democratization agenda, exporting American values and – the subtext for the Christian Right – Christianity throughout the world. When he says 'We are led, by events and common sense, to one conclusion: The survival of liberty in our land increasingly depends on the success of liberty in other lands. The best hope for peace in our world is the expansion of freedom in all the world', the statements represent a classic presentation of the democratic peace thesis, except for the replacement of 'democracy' with 'freedom'. Again, the subtext for conservative evangelicals is the linkage of liberty and freedom to their faith: 'Stand fast in the liberty wherewith Christ hath made us free, and be not entangled again with the yoke of bondage' (Galatians 5:1). The link is made more explicit when Bush goes on to say that

> America's vital interests and our deepest beliefs are now one. From the day of our Founding, we have proclaimed that every man and woman on this earth has rights, and dignity, and matchless value, because they bear the image of the Maker of Heaven and earth. Across the generations we have proclaimed the imperative of self-government, because no one is fit to be a master, and no one deserves to be a slave. Advancing these ideals is the mission that created our Nation. It is the honorable

> achievement of our fathers. Now it is the urgent requirement of our nation's security, and the calling of our time.

This section of the speech clearly sets out Bush's religious faith, linking this to the same beliefs of the Founding Fathers. It is upon this Judeo-Christian foundation that America's commitment to human rights, democracy and emancipation have been built. These beliefs also involve an urgent responsibility to share these values with the rest of the world as a divine mission. Here, Bush appeals to American exceptionalism and the sense that there is a divine plan and requirement to fulfil that calling. The 'calling of our time' is full of religious symbolism and reminds the listener of Bush's and fellow evangelicals' sense of God's calling through salvation and sense of destiny. Listeners are presented with his strategy of force and persuasion:

> This is not primarily the task of arms, though we will defend ourselves and our friends by force of arms when necessary. Freedom, by its nature, must be chosen, and defended by citizens, and sustained by the rule of law and the protection of minorities. And when the soul of a nation finally speaks, the institutions that arise may reflect customs and traditions very different from our own. America will not impose our own style of government on the unwilling. Our goal instead is to help others find their own voice, attain their own freedom, and make their own way.

Freedom is portrayed as a free choice; in just the same way as acceptance of Jesus as the saviour is also a matter of free choice. Evangelicals consider that there is a yearning within each person to have a relationship with his or her maker, a longing that can only be satisfied by conversion. In the same way, Bush presents non-democratic nations coming to salvation through a realization of their democratic longing. The new democracies that emerge will not necessarily resemble the US model but, as seen earlier in the chapter, they will inevitably have similar indispensable characteristics.

A Manichaean theme of good and evil runs throughout the text, with tyranny contrasted with freedom. For Bush, America must play its part in a crusade over the long term to end tyranny and liberate the oppressed. He declares that his 'most solemn duty is to protect this nation and its people against further attacks and emerging threats. Some have unwisely chosen to test America's resolve, and have found it firm.' This invokes a responsibility before the American people and God to win the War on Terror while preventing attacks on Americans. The testing of America's resolve has parallels in the testing of Christians' resolution, as they pray in the Lord's Prayer not to be led into temptation and are instructed elsewhere to 'Submit yourselves to God. Resist the devil and he will flee from you' (James 4:7). Bush goes on to present further dichotomous choices between oppression, gaol, humiliation, servitude, bullying and 'freedom which is eternally right'. The use of words such as 'moral', 'eternally right', and 'aspiration' are idealistic trigger words for the Christian Right equating Bush foreign policy with a divine plan.

> Some, I know, have questioned the global appeal of liberty – though this time in history, four decades defined by the swiftest advance of freedom ever seen, is an odd time for doubt. Americans, of all people, should never be surprised by the power of our ideals. Eventually, the call of freedom comes to every mind and every soul. We do not accept the existence of permanent tyranny because we do not accept the possibility of permanent slavery. Liberty will come to those who love it.

Bush returns to the theme of the universal applicability of American values, presented as the 'global appeal of liberty'. The language juxtaposes political concepts with religious metaphor. Freedom/democracy, just like 'saving faith', calls to nations and individuals, a force that demands a response. The call of freedom/Jesus becomes apparent at the intellectual level of 'every mind' and at the spiritual level with 'every soul': 'Behold, I stand at the door, and knock: if any man hear my voice, and open the door, I will come in to him, and sup with him, and he will be with me' (Revelation 3:20). For Americans, and humanity in general, tyranny is portrayed as something that exists and has to be overcome. In responding to the call of freedom/Jesus, the individual/nation is able to escape from the slavery of tyranny, doubt and unbelief: 'He answered and said, Whether he be a sinner [or no], I know not: one thing I know, that, whereas I was blind, now I see' (John 9:25). Just as with Christian faith, where Jesus is said to find the lost, so liberty/democracy will find those who will accept it: 'Ye have not chosen me, but I have chosen you, and ordained you, that ye should go and bring forth fruit' (John 15:16a).

> Today, America speaks anew to the peoples of the world:
>
> All who live in tyranny and hopelessness can know: the United States will not ignore your oppression, or excuse your oppressors. When you stand for your liberty, we will stand with you.

The semi-religious terminology of the above passage echoes the church-speak of so many of Bush's supporters. He does not speak again to the states or nations of the world but rather 'anew' to the 'peoples of the world' as with a divine mandate. The promise is that as they stand up for liberty, America will stand with them in the same way as Christians theoretically support one another. This sense of purpose reminds an evangelical audience of their special status and responsibility to others: 'But ye [are] a chosen generation, a royal priesthood, an holy nation, a peculiar people; that ye should shew forth the praises of him who hath called you out of darkness into his marvellous light' (1 Peter 2:9).

Bush aligns himself with the great and good in American history to demonstrate continuity with American values and ideals when he says, 'the rulers of outlaw regimes can know that we still believe as Abraham Lincoln did: "Those who deny freedom to others deserve it not for themselves; and, under the rule of a just God, cannot long retain it."' At the same time God is invoked to align Bush's idealist aspirations with divine justice and America's role in dispensing that justice.

> From all of you, I have asked patience in the hard task of securing America, which you have granted in good measure. Our country has accepted obligations that are difficult to fulfill, and would be dishonorable to abandon. Yet because we have acted in the great liberating tradition of this nation, tens of millions have achieved their freedom. And as

> hope kindles hope, millions more will find it. By our efforts, we have lit a fire as well – a fire in the minds of men. It warms those who feel its power, it burns those who fight its progress, and one day this untamed fire of freedom will reach the darkest corners of our world.

As with all divine missions, Bush invokes images of hardship, struggle, fortitude and patience in fulfilling an honourable commission. The struggle for Bush and, he assumes, for his audience, is difficult but worth it because it appeals to a higher motivation and calling. The fire of destruction visited on the World Trade Center is contrasted with the inspirational fire that compels action in advancing democracy, which becomes irresistible and will consume the whole world. Here, Bush employs pure biblical symbolism that speaks directly to conservative evangelicals. Fire is synonymous with the presence of God, who revealed himself to Moses in the burning bush (Exodus 3:2), led the Israelites through Sinai by night as a pillar of fire (Exodus 13:21), and is found in the fiery furnace in the book of Daniel (Daniel 3:25). God is described as a consuming fire (Deuteronomy 4:24; Hebrews 12:29). Believers are purged and purified by fire (Zechariah 13:9; Matthew 3:12; Luke 3:17) and baptized with the Holy Ghost and fire (Matthew 3:11; Luke 3:16; Acts 2:3). The other analogy involves punishment for wrongdoers and unbelievers, beginning with Sodom and Gomorrah being destroyed by fire (Genesis 19:24) and ending with unbelievers being cast into the lake of fire (Revelation 21:15–16). For Bush's fellow conservative evangelicals, hellfire (Matthew 5:22; Luke 3:9; Mark 9:43–49) is a very real concept, and the dual aspect of God's presence and judgement through the analogy of fire links their religious beliefs with the political imperative to promote democracy.

> A few Americans have accepted the hardest duties in this cause – in the quiet work of intelligence and diplomacy … the idealistic work of helping raise up free governments … the dangerous and necessary work of fighting our enemies. Some have shown their devotion to our country in deaths that honored their whole lives – and we will always honor their names and their sacrifice.

The subtext reads: such a high calling will take sacrifice; many have made such a sacrifice – are you willing to do likewise? God will work through the United States in destroying the enemies of freedom.

> All Americans have witnessed this idealism, and some for the first time. I ask our youngest citizens to believe the evidence of your eyes. You have seen duty and allegiance in the determined faces of our soldiers. You have seen that life is fragile, and evil is real, and courage triumphs. Make the choice to serve in a cause larger than your wants, larger than yourself – and in your days you will add not just to the wealth of our country, but to its character.

Bush appeals not just for this generation of soldiers to be prepared to die for their country and the ideal of democracy but for the next generation to do so as well. Americans are asked to sign up for a crusade in which whoever Bush determines to be the enemy becomes the embodiment of evil – sometimes Osama bin Laden or Saddam Hussein; at other times Mahmoud Ahmadinejad or Hassan Nasrallah. Again, the triumph of good over evil employs biblical imagery and seems to have particular resonance with young men and women among conservative evangelicals, who disproportionately volunteer for the military. Bush continues to reinforce his emphasis on idealism and courage, reaffirming American leadership as an exemplar to the rest of the world: 'America has need of idealism and courage, because we have essential work at home – the unfinished work of American freedom. In a world moving toward liberty, we are determined to show the meaning and promise of liberty.' Religious symbolism and imagery persist throughout the largely domestic sections of the speech, with references to the 'truths of Sinai, the Sermon on the Mount', the 'ideals of justice' as being implicitly the same as Jesus 'yesterday, today, and forever'.

For George Bush the legacy question is not about triumph in the war in Iraq but, rather, whether he and his supporters have remained true to their beliefs and advanced the cause of Judeo-Christian values and democracy.

> We felt the unity and fellowship of our nation when freedom came under attack, and our response came like a single hand over a single heart. And we can feel that same unity and pride whenever America acts for good, and the victims of disaster are given hope, and the unjust encounter justice.

The events of 9/11 provided a temporary unity across political divides, which Bush intimates he wishes to return to. For Bush, this can be achieved by uniting around the democracy-promotion agenda, which he presents using messianic terminology. America/Jesus gives hope to victims of disasters, punishes the unjust (Psalm 28:4; 2 Peter 2:19), and sets those captives of socialism, communism, atheism and radical Islam free (Isaiah 61:1; Luke 4:18).

> We go forward with complete confidence in the eventual triumph of freedom. Not because history runs on the wheels of inevitability; it is human choices that move events. Not because we consider ourselves a chosen nation; God moves and chooses as He wills. We have confidence because freedom is the permanent hope of mankind, the hunger in dark places, the longing of the soul. When our Founders declared a new order of the ages; when soldiers died in wave upon wave for a union based on liberty; when citizens marched in peaceful outrage under the banner 'Freedom Now' – they were acting on an ancient hope that is meant to be fulfilled. History has an ebb and flow of justice, but history also has a visible direction, set by liberty and the Author of Liberty.

As the speech moves towards its climax, the intermingling of religious imagery and political agenda is intended to draw the listener to the inevitable conclusion that God and the Founding Fathers inspire Bush's strategy of democracy promotion abroad, and underpin conservative social values at home. Bush is suggesting a grand narrative with a linear directional history that does not emphasize the inevitable triumph of capitalist liberal democracy, unlike Francis Fukuyama (1989, 1992). Instead, Bush conceives of history directed by God, 'the Author of Liberty', in which Bush and America are in God's plan. Only America/Jesus can provide a 'permanent hope for mankind', the envy and desire of the rest of the world. Bush recoils from publicly describing America as 'a chosen nation', to avoid alienating Christian Zionists (who consider only Israel to be God's chosen nation) and foreign allies, and provoking a terrorist attack. This passage could have been written by leading Southern Baptist Richard Land, who argues that America is not a chosen nation but has been providentially blessed by God and therefore has an obligation and responsibility to share this with the rest of the world.[4]

The speech ends with a further appeal to American historical tradition and mission to proclaim liberty to the rest of the world. The final line is 'May God bless you, and may He watch over the United States of America.' The inference is that God is more likely to bless you if you accept Bush's 'divinely inspired' call to promote freedom and liberty. This also suggests that 'He' may also be more inclined to watch over the United States of America, and enable it to prevent another devastating attack.

Democracy Promotion and the Christian Right

The religious symbolism that has become a regular feature of Bush's most significant speeches owes much to the sensibilities of Michael Gerson, who probably enjoyed greater influence than previous presidential speechwriters did. Gerson was able to articulate the thoughts of Bush with powerful effect; however, they remained the president's thoughts and reflected his world-view. When Bush speaks, he identifies himself as being a conservative evangelical and member of the Christian Right. The White House, despite the protestations of David Kuo (2006), former deputy director of the Office of Faith-Based and Community Initiatives, has been overwhelmingly supportive of Christian Right interests and appreciative of their backing for the president. In the area of foreign policy and particularly the strategy of democracy promotion, Bush has received approval from his core support. *Christianity Today* recounts a description of US foreign policy under Bush as being 'morality-based' (*Weekly Standard*) and 'faith-based' (Howard Fineman of *Newsweek*) (Carnes, 2003).

In championing and promoting religious freedom, through the US Commission on International Religious Freedom, and democracy as a national security strategy, the president has made conservative evangelicals in particular feel good about themselves and the new influence they have been able to exercise. All the more so because they perceive that Bush is not making concessions to them but rather is pursuing such policies because he is one of them. Don Evans, Bush's first-term commerce secretary, told *Christianity Today* that Bush foreign policy was 'Love your neighbor like yourself. The neighbors happen to be everyone on the planet' (Carnes, 2003). That such a concept exists at any level other than the rhetorical is clearly fanciful, but the power of rhetoric to motivate and maintain the support of the Christian Right has been an important element of Bush's political strategy.

Bush's foreign policy, when stripped of the realist pragmatism necessary to protect its economic, political and strategic interests, is an extension of his religious faith. He confessed to journalists in July 2007 that he approached his democracy/freedom promotion agenda

> Really not primarily from a political science perspective, frankly, it's more of a theological perspective. I do believe there is an Almighty, and I believe a gift of that Almighty to all is freedom. And I will tell you that is a principle that no one can convince me doesn't exist. (Carothers, 2007: 4; Brooks, 2007)

The Christian Right warmly receive this personal faith, projected in the name of US foreign policy. Bush has a unique ability to reach out to this core support, to involve and enlist them in US foreign policy. At the National Religious Broadcasters' Convention in February 2003, Bush specifically enlisted the support of Christian media to garner support for war against Iraq, telling them that they 'bring words of truth, and comfort, and encouragement into millions of homes. Broadcasting is more than a job for you. It is a great commission. You serve with all your heart and soul and America is grateful.'[5]

In a meeting with nine Christian editors and writers in May 2004, Bush spoke frankly about his desire to build a free Iraq, and to change

American culture through faith-based initiatives, and about the importance of prayer in his own life and of valuing the prayers of others for his and his family. He discussed the books he was reading at that time, staple evangelical fare including Oswald Chambers, Lloyd Ogilvie and the One-Year Bible, which he reads every other year and a half. He also mentioned on two occasions his reliance on the advice given to him by Christian Right leader Father Richard Neuhaus. The impression conveyed to the immediate audience, and further disseminated by the Christian media, is that this is a Christian president, leading a Christian country in a mission to change America and the world to reflect their Christian/American values.[6]

Richard Land, the most articulate of the Christian Right leaders, explains the depth of conservative evangelical support for Bush's freedom strategy: 'I do think the President's policies regarding the promotion of democracy and the promotion of freedom resonate with the evangelical community, probably more than with any other community in the United States.'[7] Democracies allow their citizens to worship freely and to practise their religion. They allow religions as well as political parties and myriad organizations to proselytize and compete in the marketplace of ideas. Conservative evangelicals respond favourably to a foreign policy that provides opportunities to spread their gospel and protect the religious freedom of converts. In his Inaugural Addresses, State of the Union addresses and major speeches on the freedom agenda Bush is not only speaking to conservative evangelicals but also on their behalf. The following comments could have come straight from the lips of George Bush but in fact come from Richard Land:

> For whatever reason this country has been uniquely blessed, and most evangelical Christians will argue that it is not fortuitous, it's providential – that, for whatever reason, God uniquely blessed this country and that imposes certain obligations and responsibilities: 'to whom much is given, much is required'. And so, while we don't believe that America has a special claim on God, we do believe that God has a special claim on us to be the friend of freedom, to be the defender of freedom, and

> that, while we don't have the right to impose freedom on others, we do have an obligation and a responsibility based upon the blessings we've received, to assist and help others who desire freedom. And we also believe that freedom is the universal desire of the human heart. I mean, evangelicals agree with George Bush in sort of betting the farm that no matter what culture you've grown up in, no matter what religion you espouse, that all men are created equal and they have the right to life, liberty and the pursuit of happiness; that those are not American ideals, that those are universal deals. And, of course, some of us would point to Japan and Germany as good examples of that.[8]

Land has some justification in claiming to speak on behalf of most conservative evangelicals, if not evangelicals as a whole, as the most prominent voice, representing as he does 17 million Southern Baptists, the largest evangelical denomination in America. There has been some discontent, however, with Bush's democracy-promotion strategy. This is rooted in the disconnection between democratization and religious freedom in the Broader Middle East. The democratic imposition in Afghanistan and Iraq has failed to guarantee religious freedom for missionaries, converts and established Christians in these countries. The case of Abdul Rahman, an Afghan convert to Christianity given asylum in Italy after being arrested for apostasy, highlighted the dangers facing converts from Islam. Sunni and Shia militias and the Taliban have targeted Christians, their churches and converts, while faction-dominated Iraqi and Afghan governments have not attempted to protect Christian minorities in either country.

Chuck Colson expressed the thoughts of many evangelicals:

> I have supported the Bush administration's foreign policy because I came to believe that the best way to stop Islamo-fascism was by promoting democracy. But if we can't guarantee fundamental religious freedoms in the countries where we establish democratic reforms, then the whole credibility of our foreign policy is thrown into question.[9]

Tony Perkins of the Family Research Council expressed similar reservations, asking 'How can we congratulate ourselves for liberating Afghanistan from the rule of jihadists only to be ruled by Islamists who kill Christians? … Americans will *not* give their blood and treasure to prop up *new* Islamic fundamentalist regimes.'[10]

Overall, though, such criticism is muted and not directed at Bush personally. Bill Saunders, an articulate Harvard-educated lawyer and senior fellow and director of the FRC's Center for Human Life and Bioethics, was a leading advocate for Sudanese Christians and in the campaign to introduce the Religious Freedom Act. He believes that the problem lies not with the Bush administration itself but rather with the State Department, which is in need of further reform,

> so that they understand the importance of religious freedom as a human right and the importance of religion to communities in countries where they have relations. A lot of people at the State Department don't understand Islam, or they look at Islamic people as interest groups.… They don't have a proper understanding, I think, of the importance of religion to people and they try to ignore it most of the time; and when it becomes a problem they try and manage it in ways that are not really, deeply, respectful.… So, I think there's a huge opportunity to continue to reform the State Department or to begin to reform the State Department so that they take religion into account.[11]

The Christian Right tend to be supportive of the principles of Bush foreign policy but are troubled by the lack of tangible results of the democracy-promotion strategy. They will continue to support such an approach because it is the outworking of their faith and religious conviction, taking the gospel into the entire world. Richard Land, as usual, expresses this view most succinctly:

> America is not just a country with national interests. It is a cause, and that cause is freedom. If freedom is a God-given, undeniable right of every human being on the planet, then it is a God-given right not just for ourselves, but also for others. Therefore, it should be part of the foreign policy of the United States of America to promote freedom, to expand freedom, and whenever possible to protect and enlarge the realm of freedom in the world. And that freedom includes the choice either to acknowledge God or not to acknowledge God's *soul freedom*. (Land, 2007: 210)

Conclusion

The Bush administration strategy of promoting freedom, liberty and democracy around the world is part of a long tradition of US administrations seeking to export their values abroad. Bush, in common with his predecessors, has sought to present democratization as a universal value rather than being culturally specific. In doing so, he has enlisted the support of the Christian Right to secure the support of core voters for an idealist strategy that becomes increasingly realist as it encounters the realities of circumstances on the ground. The strategy, inspired by the events of 9/11, marked a departure from the administration's initial commitment to pragmatic realism, but once entered into was pursued with great zeal until setbacks in Iraq, Afghanistan and Palestine forced the administration to rethink its policy.

The democracy-promotion agenda resonates with the Christian Right because it coincides with their agenda to evangelize the world and the idea of a Democratic Peace, which superficially promises a more pacific international order, including religious freedom. Throughout the Bush presidency the Christian Right have remained the most fervent and vocal supporters of democracy promotion. This is not merely a reflection of the convergence of US national security interests and the worldwide evangelistic mission; it is because US foreign policy is led by a conservative evangelical commander-in-chief who is able to inspire evangelicals with a sense of mission and purpose through religious speeches, such as the Second Inaugural Address, that connect with their own sense of divine purpose.

Overall, however, Christian Right support for democracy promotion has made little difference to the success of attempts at making the policy popular among the America people or in the Broader Middle East. The Christian Right have provided justification and theological support for a policy that had already become an integral part of US foreign policy during the past quarter of a century. Democracy promotion under George Bush has proved an abject failure, especially in those areas of North Africa and the Middle East singled out for special attention. As the War on Terror continues, without clear parameters by which to establish victory or defeat, pressure on allies to democratize and reform is maintained only at the rhetorical level. In occupied Iraq and Afghanistan, the governments retain nominal power, entirely dependent on US military support, and religious freedom comes low down the list of concerns. The Christian Right, who have been the administration's main supporters, share culpability by providing support for a policy that has failed to progress beyond the merely rhetorical. The chapter is headed 'Promoting Democracy or the Gospel?' As we have seen, for Bush and the Christian Right the answer is that they are indivisible and interchangeable concepts, and both have failed to make the impression that advocates from the political and religious spectrums would have liked. In the next chapter we move from considering democracy to those other pillars of global civil society, human rights and humanitarian assistance.

4

Hijacking the Human Rights and Humanitarian Assistance Agenda

Following their re-emergence as a potent political force in the late 1970s, the Christian Right tended to concentrate their political efforts on a domestic moral agenda and facing down the forces of liberalism within the United States. Missionary organizations sought to fulfil the Great Commission by evangelizing worldwide within the constraints of a Cold War system that polarized much of the world into the ideological camps of atheistic communism and secular capitalism. Pleas were made for fellow believers to remember the 'persecuted church' behind the iron curtain, and televangelists including Jimmy Swaggart, Morris Cerullo, Oral Roberts, Kenneth Copeland, Pat Robertson, Jerry Falwell and Benny Hinn made converts and money spreading an America gospel of healing and prosperity to Latin America, Asia and Africa. The CIA was able to recruit evangelical organizations to help undermine Communist influence in areas of US strategic interest, but such covert action went largely unnoticed. Such activities took place beneath the political radar and occurred in an ad hoc manner dependent upon the vision of individual organizations. As a movement, the

Christian Right under the careful nurturing of Jerry Falwell and Paul Weyrich were more concerned with taking over the Republican Party and promoting a conservative domestic agenda.

It is only with the end of the Cold War that we start to see Christian Right organizations taking more of an interest in international affairs. The fall of the Berlin Wall and the collapse of Communism were greeted by triumphalism not only in political and academic circles but also in religious ones. Fukuyama (1989, 1992) may have proclaimed the end of history and the triumph of liberal democratic capitalism, but the Christian Right considered the West's ideological victory to be divinely inspired. If the power of prayer and Christian witness combined with Reagan's leadership and resolution could bring down the godless or even 'satanic' forces of atheistic communism then there were no limits to what could be achieved by concerted Christian action. In a unipolar world, the ability of American Christians to influence their own government could have a profound impact on world as well as domestic politics. With the election of George W. Bush new possibilities opened up for the Christian Right to extend their influence on the world stage.

In this chapter, we consider how the Christian Right have organized around issues of human rights and religious persecution to persuade the administration to protect the interests of Christians worldwide. The chapter goes on to examine how the movement has managed to break down the wall of separation between church and state by acquiring USAID funds to deliver humanitarian assistance programmes while propagating an American gospel. In the final section, we explore how the Christian Right have used their ideas on family values and morality to affect humanitarian assistance adversely in the fight against HIV/AIDS and disadvantage women in both the North and the South. Gender aspects are analysed, revealing how the Bush administration has granted Christian Right groups privileged NGO delegate and observer status at the United Nations, and in international forums, which has been used to undermine women's right to choose an abortion and to discriminate against homosexuals.

The chapter concludes by appraising the movement's effectiveness in shaping the US foreign policy agenda in these areas.

The Persecuted Church

Given that the movement began with the torture and death of its founder it is perhaps unsurprising that persecution has continued to play a prominent role in the Christian psyche over the past two millennia. Jesus warned his disciples that 'if they persecuted me, they will also persecute you' (John 15:20). Such persecution was inevitable and represented a communion with Jesus' own suffering:

> Blessed are ye, when *men* shall revile you, and persecute *you*, and shall say all manner of evil against you falsely, for my sake. Rejoice, and be exceeding glad: for so persecuted they the prophets which were before you. (Matthew 5:11–12)

Persecution has been a recurring theme throughout Christian history. Indeed, for St Paul no turn was left unstoned. The idea of a suffering church has been conveyed through a combination of centuries of real persecution, much of it inflicted at the hands of fellow believers, and the mythologizing of suffering through literature and oral tradition. Followers identify with Christ's suffering through the rites of communion (drinking his blood and eating his broken body) and baptism (dying to the old self before rebirth as a Christian). Persecution led the Pilgrim Fathers to seek a new life in America where they would be free to practise their religion. The early settlers for the most part were religious dissenters from Europe and this inheritance is utilized at various times to develop empathy with persecuted Christians elsewhere in the world.

During the Cold War, the combination of evangelicalism and American exceptionalism meeting in Christian nationalism led to support for fellow Christians under Communist systems. Magazines, films and videos kept the church aware of the plight of fellow believers in the Soviet bloc. Organizations such as Open Doors with Brother Andrew and Brother David kept Western Christians enthralled with their adventures in smuggling Bibles behind the Iron Curtain. Richard Wurmbrand, a Romanian pastor imprisoned by the Soviet authorities in the 1950s and 1960s, following his release from prison and exile from Romania established the Voice of Martyrs organization to increase awareness of the underground church in Eastern Europe and the Soviet Union. Christian Solidarity International (CSI) – USA also emphasized Communist oppression. However, these and similar organizations made little impression on US foreign policy other than providing successive presidents with the opportunity to castigate their Communist adversaries.

The post-Cold War era invoked much contemplation of new world orders politically and religiously. For conservatives, the collapse of Communism represented the triumph of American values of freedom, liberty and markets. In America, however, conservative evangelicals considered those same values under threat by liberal, secularizing forces that sought to undermine traditional moral values. Church leaders emphasized that it was only through coordinated action and engagement with the political process that conservative Christians could recover some of the influence they enjoyed during Reagan's presidency. Initially the emphasis was on involvement with domestic issues with little concern about advancing that political agenda abroad. The GOP capture of both houses of Congress in 1994 provided the opportunity for increased political activity by the Christian Right. Christian Right leaders in the Republican Party were promoted to key foreign policy positions on Capitol Hill, with Senator Jesse Helms chairing the Senate Foreign Relations Committee and Senator Sam Brownback subcommittee chair on Near Eastern and South Asia Affairs (Castelli, 2005: 329).

Outside Congress, the notion of promoting American/Judaeo-Christian values internationally grew in resonance. Nina Shea, a campaigner against liberation theology and communism in Latin America and director of the Center for Religious Freedom at Freedom House, was one of the few people actively campaigning to increase awareness of Christian persecution abroad.[1] By 1995, however, a neo-conservative, Michael Horowitz at the Hudson Institute, added his support to a campaign that sought to put Christian persecution at the centre of US foreign policy. Horowitz wrote an editorial in the *Wall Street Journal* entitled 'New Intolerance between the Crescent and the Cross'; the piece drew attention to the persecution of Christians in Africa and the Middle East and called for a foreign policy that intervenes in such circumstances (Horowitz, 1995). He followed up the editorial by writing to 150 mission boards to urge on them the severity of the challenge facing the church. Nina Shea and Horowitz began coordinating their strategy and working together to raise the issue's profile. In January 1996 they hosted a conference in Washington DC for religious leaders on the theme 'Global Persecution of Christians'. The conference raised tremendous interest and was instrumental in the National Association of Evangelicals, Episcopalians, Presbyterians and Southern Baptists pledging their support and commitment to the persecuted church. Horowitz also helped establish an International Day of Prayer for the Persecuted Church, which continues to focus the attention of churches and politicians on the plight of Christians facing hardship abroad (Green, 2001).

Horowitz's and Shea's efforts began to gather support from evangelicals, conservative Jews and Catholics. Although the main impetus lay with the Christian Right and their developing alliance with neo-conservatives, including Elliott Abrams, then head of the Ethics and Public Policy Center, Christian Right leaders including Chuck Colson, James Dobson and William Bennett mobilized their supporters around the issue using the Christian media, which in turn raised persecution as an issue with their congressional representatives (Green, 2001). On Capitol Hill, congressional representatives Frank Wolf (R–Va), Chris Smith (R–NJ) and senator Arlen Specter (R–Pa) took the initiative in proposing legislation to ensure that action to prevent the persecution of Christians would become enshrined in US foreign policy. In 1997, Wolf and Specter introduced the Freedom from Religious Persecution Act, which obliged the State Department to produce an annual International Religious Freedom Report, detailing the state of religious persecution around the world. The Act compelled the president to take specific action to punish states committing abuses by affording a range of sanctions. Business interests in Congress, however, managed to insert the right of presidential waiver if considered in the US national interest. The Act established a permanent position of Ambassador-at-Large for International Religious Freedom at the Department of State and an independent US Commission on International Religious Freedom, and was passed into law in 1998 (Green, 2001; Saunders, 2007). In the final wording of the Act, the value-laden and rhetoric-driven terminology of persecution was replaced by 'particularly severe violations of religious freedom' and 'violations of religious freedom' (Castelli, 2005: 327).

The Christian Right and their neoconservative allies turned the plight of Christians in the Sudanese civil war into a cause célèbre. With Communism seemingly defeated, Sudan provided an opportunity for comfortable Christians in the West to identify and empathize with the suffering church in Africa. An added benefit was that Islam could replace Communism as a unifying force to rally Christians against an ideological and spiritual rival. The new expression of Christian solidarity was reinforced by the publication of Nina Shea's seminal text, *In The Lion's Den*, and the continuation of her efforts with Horowitz (Shea, 1997). Christian Right church and parachurch groups and politicians campaigned actively for the Clinton administration to act on reported human rights abuses inflicted by Muslims against Christians in Sudan. International Christian Concern organized a letter-writing campaign to inform Congress of their concerns and calling for action.[2]

In preparation for the Freedom from Religious Persecution Act, the State Department's Advisory Committee on Religious Freedom Abroad investigated Sudan and Pakistan, increasing the momentum for the United States to act. Senator Sam Brownback, following on from his subcommittee hearings in 1997 into religious persecution in the Middle East, which relied heavily on the testimony of Shea and Wolf, introduced the Sudan Peace Bill into the Senate in 1999 (Castelli, 2005: 327–8). The Clinton administration, and State Department in particular, were unhappy about the legislation, which restricted their room for manoeuvre in foreign policy, a challenge the incoming Bush administration would have to deal with.

Bush was initially more interested in pursuing his domestic agenda rather than focusing on Sudan, especially as any action against the Sudanese government would upset the business interests eager to acquire oil rights in the region. The Christian Right and neoconservatives, however, saw Sudan as an ideal test case to assert American power and principle in a continent largely ignored by previous administrations. The FRC, Persecution Project Foundation (PPF), International Christian Concern (ICC), Christian Freedom International (CFI), and Voice of the Martyrs (VOM), among others, lobbied the White House and Congress for the USA to defend Christians in Sudan. They were assisted in this task by neoconservatives who wrote to the president urging him to make religious freedom and human rights a priority or risk alienating religious communities in America (Green, 2001).

The objections of business interests and Bush's reluctance to become ensnared in internal Sudanese affairs were overcome as Karl Rove began to see the benefits of supporting the Christian solidarity position. Bush's core support in the Christian Right had allied themselves with black evangelical churches, traditionally Democratic Party supporters, but potential recruits for an overtly religious president. Prominent neoconservatives occupied key positions within the new administration. Elliott Abrams, former president of the EPPC and chairman of the US Commission on International Freedom, was appointed Special Assistant to the President and Senior Director for Democracy, Human Rights and International Operations. Abrams was able to complement the efforts of others, including Michael Horowitz, arrested after chaining himself to railings outside the Sudanese embassy, Franklin Graham (Samaritan's Purse), who appealed to Bush in person, and Frank Wolf, chair of the House Appropriations

Subcommittee (Green, 2001). Such efforts resulted in the appointment of John Danworth as special envoy to Sudan and the passing of the Sudan Peace Act in both Houses of Congress. The administration, however, remained reluctant to approve the Act because of the implications of sanctions for corporate oil interests.

Before a definitive decision could be taken the 11 September 2001 attacks intervened dramatically, altering the administration's foreign policy agenda. Sudan now became strategically important as an ally in the War on Terror providing information on al-Qaeda. The impetus to rein in the Sudanese government to halt abuses against Christians was lost. However, the new alliance of Christian Right, Catholic, Episcopal, Southern Baptist and black organizations determined to continue its pressure on government, targeting the president as well as the Department of State (Green, 2001). The Sudan Peace Act (2002), with accompanying sanctions, helped prepare the way for a ceasefire and peace settlement in January 2005 after twenty years of civil war (Haynes, 2007: 255). The conflict resulted in the deaths of 2 million people and the displacement of a further 5 million. The administration, conscious of the need to maintain good relations with the Sudanese government for oil and cooperation in the War on Terror, has downplayed the role of religion in the civil war, much to the chagrin of the Christian Right. Christian solidarists lean closer to Samuel Huntington's clash of civilizations thesis between Islam and Christianity than to the administration's insistence on the dualism of good and bad Muslims (Huntington, 1997). Nina Shea, in presenting evidence before the House Subcommittee on Africa, Global Human Rights and International Operations in March 2006, castigated the State Department's *Country Report* on Sudan for failing to mention that the conflict had been a religious war (Shea, 2006a).

Despite George Bush's evangelical credentials the administration has sought to expand the theme of violations of religious freedom from a narrow emphasis on the supposed suffering of Christians around the world to include all religions. This has been a source of constant frustration for the Christian Right as Bush has attempted to balance

US national security interests with their demands for him to pursue a foreign policy that safeguards and advances Judaeo-Christian interests. The administration's increased emphasis on religious freedom has provided Christian Right organizations with an opportunity to evangelize in areas previously inaccessible. The Persecution Project Foundation used the Sudanese civil war as an opportunity to launch a radio station proselytizing in Arabic and several African dialects. The founder, Brad Phillips, expresses the thoughts of many similar organizations: 'What's exciting is to see some cultures that are traditionally closed off to the Gospel now having the opportunity to receive the Word of God in the context of their situation that they're in right now' (Mission Network News, 2005).

The concept of religious freedom is used selectively to assail countries hostile to America. These include Chinese treatment of Muslims in Xingjian, Buddhists in Tibet, Falun Gong and Christians in the house church movement (Hehir, 2001: 33–54; Shea 2006a; Thomas, 2005: 214–15). Most Islamic nations are condemned for their treatment of Christians, Jews, Baha'is and minority Muslim sects within their borders. Christian Right organizations concentrate almost exclusively on the sufferings of Christians in Communist and Islamic countries. In doing so they seek to use religious freedom to develop a sense of shared persecution among Christians and highlight their allegations of an Islamic threat to Judaeo-Christian civilization. In an interview with *Christian Monitor*, Kristin Wright from Stand Today, a Christian Right lobbying group on behalf of persecuted Christians worldwide, claimed that the persecution of Christians globally was increasing:

> Yes, I believe it is – because of one main reason: radical Islam. That is the simplest, most direct answer I can give. In the coming years we are going to see an expansion of radical Islam across the world, affecting millions of Middle Eastern and African Christians – unless it is stopped. The Church needs to wake up to the credible threat that radical Islam poses to Christians worldwide. And we need to take action: speaking out on behalf of those who are already in its cruel grasp, and fighting for freedom and democracy in countries that are

> teetering on the brink of Islamization. The Christian community in free nations has the power to affect foreign policy. We should definitely be exercising that power.[3]

ICC has produced a Hall of Shame identifying their list of top ten persecutors of Christians; these include North Korea, Iraq, Ethiopia, Saudi Arabia, Somalia, Iran, Eritrea, China, Vietnam and Pakistan (ICC, 2007). Similarly, CFI compiles its own list of persecutors, also featuring North Korea and China, Eritrea, Iran, Pakistan and Saudi Arabia in common with ICC. Others in the list include Bangladesh, Burma, Indonesia, Laos, Nigeria, and Sudan (CFI, 2006).

The Fund for Peace and *Foreign Policy*'s 'The Failed States Index 2007' reveals that the worst twelve human rights abusers are Sudan, Iraq, Somalia, Zimbabwe, North Korea, Turkmenistan, Equatorial Guinea, Chad, Ivory Coast, Haiti, Uzbekistan and the Democratic Republic of Congo (*Foreign Policy*, 2007). Zimbabwe, Turkmenistan, Equatorial Guinea, Chad, Ivory Coast, Haiti and Uzbekistan fail to make the top dozen human rights abusers in the Christian solidarists' lists. Indeed only one of the six countries in both ICC and CFI lists (North Korea) can be found in the top dozen on the *Foreign Policy* index. Christian Right organizations appear closer to the State Department's *International Religious Freedom* report, which has identified Burma, China, Eritrea, Iran, North Korea, Saudi Arabia, Sudan and Vietnam as being countries of particular concern for violating religious freedom. In 2004, Iraq was taken off the list of countries of particular concern, although by any measure religious persecution remains among the worst in the world. While State Department reports are ostensibly about all violations of religious freedom, there is a surfeit of information on Christian persecution at the hands of Islamic and former Communist states. There are hardly any mentions of violations of Muslim freedom of religion or any criticism of Israel (USDOS, 2007).

In a June 2006 hearing by the House Subcommittee on Africa, Global Human Rights and International Operations, Chair Chris

Smith sought to raise the plight of Palestinian Christians affected by Israel's separation wall. He called on Nina Shea, vice chair of the US Commission on International Religious Freedom, to report his concerns about the negative impact of the wall and the unrealistic level of compensation paid for the loss of Palestinian land. After initially ignoring the request, Shea agreed to report the concerns to her Commission before immediately changing the subject to Christian persecution at the hands of Muslims in Iraq (Shea, 2006c).

ICC and CFI typify the efforts of organizations involved in the Christian solidarist movement. They meet regularly with senators, congressional representatives and White House staff and encourage their supporters to lobby politicians in an attempt to influence policy and legislation. CFI also attend briefings at the State Department and the UN (CFI, 2006; ICC, 2007). Both organizations stress the danger of Islamic states to religious freedom. CFI's annual report claims that 'the worst violators of this most basic human right tend to be Islamic states' and cites thirty-five of them out of list of fifty countries it accuses of persecuting Christians (CFI, 2006). Jeff King, president of ICC, explains that Islam is the 'leading source of Christian persecution' because 'persecution of other faiths is encoded into the Holy Books of Islam'. He makes further unsubstantiated claims that Muslims are warlike, that Saudi oil wealth spreads Wahhabism and armed conflict, and that the situation in Palestine and Iraq is exploited by Muslims to increase resentment against the west (CFI, 2007).

The attempt by many Christian Right organizations to interpret the War on Terror and violations of religious freedom as a clash of civilizations between Islam and Judeo-Christianity has largely been resisted by the Bush administration. Bush and Secretary of State Rice have continually emphasized that Islam is a peaceful religion and that there are good and bad Muslims. In this dichotomous world-view, good Muslims are those who agree with US foreign policy and bad Muslims are 'Islamofascists'. In the War on Terror, Bush has ignored or downplayed democratic requirements for Islamic allies in the War on Terror, such as the Central Asian republics, Saudi Arabia, Egypt,

Sudan and Pakistan. At the same time democratization and religious freedom agendas have been used as a tool to weaken hostile regimes by supporting opposition forces, including pro-western Christian groups within Islamic and Communist countries.

The Christian Right's position has become nuanced, with some organizations supporting the president's position on the grounds of national security while others, as we have seen, continue to press for punitive sanctions and further action against what they perceive to be an Islamic threat, which they suggest is inherent in all strands of Islam. Nina Shea has been at the forefront in highlighting violations of religious freedom by two of America's closest allies, Saudi Arabia and Egypt, and calling for a governmental response (Shea, 2005a, 2005b, 2006b, 2007). This theme, which is regularly reiterated by televangelists on TBN and CBN, calls for a delicate balancing act by the White House and State Department, who are anxious not to lose either the support of their religious base or their strategic allies in the Middle East.

Faith-based Initiatives

In a calculated move to appeal to his core constituency, during his first term, Bush launched domestic and international faith-based initiatives designed to leverage public finance for religious groupings to carry out social and welfare functions formerly carried out by government or secular organizations. In December 2002, the Center for Faith-Based and Community Initiatives (CFBCI) was created within USAID. The Center's declared intention was to 'create a level playing field' for faith-based and community groups to compete for USAID programmes. The organization was tasked with proactively encouraging faith-based and community groups to compete for funding through the organizing of information meetings and supporting a 1,200-strong mailing list (USAID, 2005). As with its domestic equivalent the move was seen as payback for the support of the Christian Right in the 2000 election and advance payment for support in 2004.

A prominent official in USAID informed me that Bush's motivation came from his own experience as governor in Texas witnessing the self-proclaimed success of Christian prison rehabilitation programmes, where the reduced re-offending rate convinced him that faith-based organizations (FBOs) were better equipped than governmental ones to deliver such programmes. If such models could be replicated on the international stage, US assistance could be leveraged through the extensive social networks and infrastructure developed by faith communities. The CFBCI acts as a point of contact between USAID and the faith and community organizations, providing them with details of all programmes for which they can compete. All offices within the State Department are expected to encourage faith-based approaches to assistance delivery. This presidential initiative is problematic and calls into question the First Amendment separation of church and state (Lynn, 2006: 117–19). The administration has sought to get around accusations of constitutional malfeasance by insisting that there is clear separation between the government-funded service delivery and the spiritual activities of the grantee. A senior USAID official informed me that it is unclear how this is monitored, if at all.[4]

USAID manages approximately $10 billion US foreign assistance programmes in eighty-four developing countries, over half of which are countries with a majority Muslim population (USAID, 2007). Despite this, Islamic organizations simply fail to apply for, or find it very difficult to access, funding. A *Boston Globe* survey of prime contractors and grantees revealed that just over 98 per cent of funds to FBOs went to Christian organizations (Kranish, 2006). Similarly, secular organizations, like Planned Parenthood, which partner similar organizations overseas in providing vital health care, sex education, and sexual health information services, find themselves denied USAID funding because they offer an abortion option as part of their advice and guidance on family planning and reproductive health, a stance at odds with the administration's policy. CARE, an organization delivering US assistance since the aftermath of World War II, has seen its USAID grants fall each year from $138 million in FY2001 to

$98 million in FY2005 (Kranish, 2006). This is part of a deliberate attempt to skew assistance in favour of Christian organizations based on political considerations rather than ability or expertise in delivering services.

Faith-based initiatives (the term 'faith and community' is barely used within the administration) are led by members of the Christian Right and provide a direct line of communication with the administration's most active supporters. James Towey, director of the White House Office of Faith-Based and Community Initiatives from 2002 to 2006, saw one of his roles as transferring international assistance from groups and staff members within USAID, who were unsympathetic to Bush's moral majoritarian foreign policy agenda, to FBOs (Krandish, 2006). Andrew Natsios, former vice president of World Vision, the largest Christian Right recipient of USAID funds, was appointed head of USAID.[5] Dr Anne Peterson became global health director; Benjamin Horman, president of the evangelical Food for the Hungry, was appointed chair of USAID's advisory board; and Karen Hughes returned to the administration in the second term as under-secretary of state for public diplomacy and public affairs. More recently, in August 2006 Terri Hasdorff took over as director of the CFBCI at USAID, after running a FBO initiative in Alabama.

In a bid to increase international support in the battle for hearts and minds in the War on Terror, the Bush administration has made increasingly large amounts of money available for foreign assistance. The budget grew from $7 billion to $14 billion per annum from 2002 to 2004, the largest increase in development assistance in forty-five years (Natsios, 2005). Of this budget, an increasing amount has gone to Christian FBOs. *The Boston Globe* investigation revealed that in the five fiscal years from 2001 to 2005, 159 FBOs received over $1.7 billion in USAID prime contracts, grants and agreements.[6] By FY2005, 347 awards totalling over $591 million were made (Hasdorff, 2006). USAID has awarded contracts to a wide range of Christian organizations, including traditional denominations. Indeed, the largest funding recipient is the Catholic Relief Service, which received over $638 million during the same five-year period.[7] Much of the money, however, has gone to evangelical organizations, which combine their assistance work with a strong proselytizing emphasis. CFBCI has actively encouraged Christian organizations at a series of meetings around the country to apply for USAID funding in order to deliver services while still being able to evangelize. In recruiting FBOs, lack of experience or expertise is no impediment to being awarded a contract. The CFBCI simply arranges for the inexperienced organization to team up with a more experienced partner. Senior partners are invariably other faith groups, but secular organizations are also under pressure to subcontract work to FBOs in order to maintain service delivery.

Although the evangelistic impetus of most of the FBOs is not disputed, CFBCI insists that there is a clear separation between proselytizing and service delivery, although there is no monitoring. USAID funding provides evangelical groups with the opportunity to expand their usual range of activities with government money, while presenting this assistance as a demonstration of the benevolence and superiority of the Christian God (see Milligan, 2006). In FY2006, World Vision received over $100 million to distribute food under the food assistance programme for emergency and non-emergency activities in Ethiopia, Southern Africa, Mauritius, Mozambique, Uganda, Indonesia, Haiti, Honduras and Afghanistan, in addition to other activities carried out in Islamic countries (USAID, 2006). World Vision has 18,000 volunteers worldwide. Its senior vice president Bruce Wilkinson claims that 'the controversy over evangelizing in Muslim countries is felt more acutely in the United States than it is in places like Iraq or Afghanistan, where needy citizens are happy to receive aid' (Alter, 2003). Considering the number of attacks on Christians and their infrastructure in Iraq and Afghanistan, this claim seems questionable.

There appears to be little attempt by USAID or the organizations they fund to maintain a separation between church and state activities. This is becoming increasingly problematic, as the War on Terror is seen by many Muslims as an attack on Islam, an impression given added credence when we register that only two Muslim organizations received funding between 2001 and 2005 and note that assistance provision is accompanied by prayer, Bible study, church services and attempts to convert recipients from Islam and other faiths. Food for the Hungry received $10.9 million to deliver training in disease prevention in northern Kenya. Health education classes begin and close with prayer and have been followed by Christian services. The combination of health education and the gospel has, according to field workers, helped convert most of the area to Christianity, and USAID has rewarded such endeavours by increasing the group's funding from $7 million in FY2001 to $20 million in FY2005 (Stockman et al., 2006).

Another organization working in Kenya with US taxpayers' money is Partners Worldwide, formerly known as Partners for Christian Development. Partners works in twenty countries providing loans, mentoring and training for Christian businesses. They received $700,000 USAID funding in FY2005 for training and mentoring programmes, which the White House has lauded as a success (Stockman, 2006). The organization's mission is to promote Christianity and Christian business as a witness to the perceived inadequacies of other faiths. The combination of enterprise and religion wins approval in Washington and promotes an American gospel on the interface between Islam and Christianity in sub-Saharan Africa.

Another method of preaching the gospel, while receiving government funding, is to provide medical facilities in countries identified as being mission fields. World Witness, Evangelistic International Ministries, Operation Blessing and Samaritan's Purse are among scores of conservative evangelical groups that have successfully combined the two functions throughout the Muslim world and sub-Saharan Africa. Christian hospitals and health centres present ideal opportunities to demonstrate the healing power of Jesus' followers, and the well-funded facilities offer a contrast with the cash-strapped resources of municipal hospitals throughout the developing world. Along with medical assistance, patients are subjected to Bible verses, tracts, continuous showing of *The Jesus Film*, and proselytizing from medical practitioners and their staff. Samaritan's Purse, whose founder Franklin Graham is one of President Bush's favourite evangelicals, received around $31 million in USAID funding up to 2006. This included $830,000 for building the Evangelical Medical Center in Lubango, Angola. The staff at the Center are all evangelical and exercise a policy of not employing Catholics; nurses are expected to evangelize. However, because USAID funding provided building finance rather than service delivery, the constitutional requirement of separation is fulfilled. In early 2001, the group demonstrated USAID complicity in using taxpayers' money for evangelistic purposes when Samaritan's Purse would only distribute earthquake relief in El Salvador after evangelistic services, and USAID refused to act (Klein, 2006; Milligan, 2006; Canellos and Baron, 2006).

The War on Terror has provided new opportunities for Christian Right organizations to help in the battle for hearts and minds, with the Bush administration encouraging, through its faith and community-based initiatives, the conversion of Muslims in countries once inaccessible or difficult for missionaries, and the strengthening of Christian witness in front-line countries. Organizations with little proficiency or expertise have commanded significant USAID resources. Out of a total of $390 million awarded to NGOs in the Muslim world (2001–05), $57 million funded FBOs in Pakistan, Indonesia and Afghanistan. No USAID prime contract funding was available for Muslim organizations in the aftermath of the tsunami in Indonesia in 2004.

Conservative evangelicals have been at the forefront of efforts to evangelize the Muslim world using humanitarian aid as the point of access. Voice of the Martyrs, Southern Baptist Convention, Samaritan's Purse, and the Association of Baptists for World Evangelism are all active in Iraq. These organizations are actively seeking to target Muslims for conversion in what they describe as the 10/40 window.[8] Volunteers are encouraged to enter the region by applying to university, teaching, starting up businesses, serving in business

TABLE 4.1 USAID contracts with selected faith-based organizations, FY 2001–2005 ($1,000)[9]

Organization	2001	2002	2003	2004	2005	Total 2001–05
World Vision	47,069	43,333	120,597	109,098	54,691	374,788
Food for the Hungry	7,307	7,059	8,092	6,969	19,837	49,265
Samaritan's Purse	6,782	6,477	2,502	5,720	9,774	31,256
World Witness	370	370	300	325	300	1,665
Partners Worldwide			500	200		700
Operation Blessings		116	116	80	80	392
Voice of the Martyrs		30	30	123	123	306
Evangelistic Int Min.				99	193	292
Total of all FBOs	246,770	260,552	419,683	418,966	375,044	1,721,015

and information technology, or working in health care. An official at USAID informed me that currently there are tens of thousands of American Christian church volunteers delivering assistance throughout Africa seeking to win souls. Unfortunately, fundamentalist leaders like Pat Robertson and Franklin Graham, who make no secret of their contempt for Islam, even in its moderate guise, inspire many of these; a message which is not lost on Muslims in the targeted areas.

The attitude of evangelicals, in particular conservative evangelicals, towards Islam is well summarized by Dr Richard Land:

> I think that Islam is a many-splintered thing and that I disagree with Islam – obviously, fundamentally, as an evangelical Christian. I think it's a wrong religion but I also think Judaism is wrong. Now the distinction that I would make, and I think many other evangelicals would make between Judaism and Islam, is that while we believe Christianity and Judaism worship the same God – we don't have the same faith but we have the same God – most evangelicals would argue that Allah is not the Father of our Lord and Saviour, Jesus Christ.[10]

For the Christian Right, citizens in Muslim countries are candidates for conversion, and America's military and global presence presents new opportunities, funded partly by US tax dollars. Land explains one such opportunity: 'I can't help but imagine that Christianity would be appealing to at least one segment of Muslim society – women. Equality is a powerful attraction!'[11] Richard Land, unlike many of his evangelical peers, believes that there should be a clear separation between assistance paid for by USAID and the FBOs' evangelistic ministry. The blurring of this distinction has concerned members and former members of the administration. Former UN ambassador John Bolton, now working with fellow conservatives in the American Enterprise Institute, expresses such concerns succinctly:

> I think there is always a danger with funding NGOs that are something other than service providers. That even if you're not directly funding their other activities, and even if you're not indirectly funding them such as providing overhead, pro-rata share of overhead, you're at risk internationally that people can't see the difference between the provision of specific services, disaster relief or other humanitarian relief, on [the] one hand, versus their advocacy activities, on the other. It's one reason Planned Parenthood, to take an example on the left, has been cut off funding. Not necessarily because people thought they were ineffective in distributing family planning services [but] because they were also advocating abortion as a policy and that was just unacceptable. ... The possible confusion in the minds of recipients or listeners when a group is being funded by the government for one thing and is also doing something else I think is real.[12]

HIV/AIDS and the Christian Right

The confusion becomes real when FBOs are preferred to long-standing USAID partners in the delivery of HIV/AIDS programmes in the developing world. Until late into Bush's first term the administration and the Christian Right had been largely silent on the issue of HIV/AIDS, variously interpreting it as divine punishment for immorality, the outworking of biblical principles of sowing and reaping, or something that affected mainly non-believers and therefore not of immediate concern to the church. This arrogance and complacency changed dramatically, largely due to the efforts of the US branch of Jubilee 2000, committed to debt relief for the poorest countries in the world, and Bono from the rock band U2. Bono assiduously courted leading members of the Christian Right, including Senator Jesse Helms, chair of the Senate Foreign Relations Committee and notorious xenophobe, who campaigned vigorously against foreign assistance, and Franklin Graham, son of Billy and founder of Samaritan's Purse. Bono reminded Helms of the over two thousand biblical references to poverty and quoted verses from Matthew's gospel that brought the octogenarian to tears (Bunting and Burkeman, 2002).

> Then shall the King say unto them on his right hand, Come, ye blessed of my Father, inherit the kingdom prepared for you from the foundation of the world: For I was an hungred, and ye gave me meat: I was thirsty, and ye gave me drink: I was a stranger, and ye took me in: Naked, and ye clothed me: I was sick, and ye visited me: I was in prison, and ye came unto me. Then shall the righteous answer him, saying, Lord, when saw we thee an hungred, and fed thee? or thirsty, and gave thee drink? When saw we thee a stranger, and took thee in? or naked, and clothed thee? Or when saw we thee sick, or in prison, and came unto thee? And the King shall answer and say unto them, Verily I say unto you, Inasmuch as ye have done it unto one of the least of these my brethren, ye have done it unto me. (Matthew 25: 34–40)

Helms publicly repented of his former attitude, telling Christian AIDS activists that he was ashamed for not acting earlier and committing himself to working to alleviate poverty and suffering. Working with Bill Frist in the Senate, Helms announced that they were planning legislation to commit a further $500 million in AIDS prevention. Helms's conversion provided access for Bono to take the campaign to the White House. Bush had previously only committed $200 million in FY2002 and FY2003, but in June 2002 he announced a new $500 million initiative. This sum was further increased following the State of the Union address, in which the president called for $15 billion AIDS expenditure over five years, including $10 billion in new money for the 'most afflicted nations of Africa and the Caribbean' (Singer,

2004: 121). For the first time generic drugs were to be provided for HIV/AIDS treatment, but multilateral aid projects through the UN Global Fund were replaced by direct bilateral US assistance (Kaplan, 2005: 188). As welcome as this new commitment on behalf of the Christian Right and the president has been, it has come at a tremendous cost.

The Christian Right considered that with the election of George Bush there was an opportunity to roll back the tide of liberalism and immorality they considered a distinguishing feature of Clinton's America. They believed a moral agenda could be pursued that would reinforce the traditional family against the 'creeping tide' of homosexuality, sexual promiscuity, civil unions and same-sex partnerships, pornography, prostitution, abortion and stem-cell research. A new interest in foreign affairs, largely attributable to the campaign against Christian persecution in Sudan, extended this moral agenda to US involvement overseas.

The organizations principally involved in delivering US foreign assistance tended to be secular organizations, politically progressive and more concerned with the effective delivery of services that would help relieve suffering, prevent the spread of disease, including HIV/AIDS, and empower women to control their own fertility. Such organizations represented a challenge to moral majoritarian principles that sought to proscribe sexual behaviour, to encourage sexual abstinence other than for procreative purposes in a marriage between a man and a woman, and to recognize the sanctity of life from the moment of conception. The tone for the administration's policy on foreign assistance in this area was set in an action cable sent by Secretary of State Powell on Christmas Eve 2002:

> All operating units should ensure that USAID-funded programs and publications reflect appropriately the policies of the Bush administration. Careful review of all programs and publications should ensure that USAID is not perceived as using U.S. taxpayers' funds to support activities that contradict our laws or policies, including trafficking of women and girls, legalization of drugs, injecting drug use, and abortion

> ... All operating units should review their own websites and any websites fully or partially funded by USAID to ensure the appropriateness of the material ... You should also review the appropriateness of the messages on the websites of our cooperating partners.[13]

The administration insisted that a global gag rule should apply to all organizations in receipt of family planning grants. This rule prohibits organizations from advising women that abortion is an option or referring them for an abortion. Organizations are also prevented from lobbying for safe abortion access or providing abortions themselves, unless they use their own funds. In response to pressure from Christian Right organizations including Prison Fellowship Ministries (PFM), FRC and CWA, Congress and the administration incorporated measures that diminished the efficacy of the new further caveats. One-third of all HIV/AIDS prevention initiatives were to be reserved for those promoting an abstinence-until-marriage message, forbidding the mention of condoms (Superville, 2003). A conscience clause was inserted, which allowed FBOs to continue receiving government funding even if they rejected prevention strategies that they found morally objectionable, such as working with high-risk client groups including sex workers or homosexuals, or even distributing condoms. They also succeeded in achieving a ban on needle exchange schemes and a ban on endorsing prostitution (Kaplan, 2005: 188–90). Organizations were accused of endorsing prostitution if they handed out condoms to prostitutes and/or their clients and educated them about safe-sex practices, even though condoms are the surest defence against transmission of the disease and alternative choices for sex workers in the developing world are hard to come by.

The Christian Right have essentially driven US policy on HIV/AIDS during the Bush administration, encouraging an increase in funding but strictly controlling those funds in advancing their own moral agenda. Franklin Graham met regularly for discussions with Karl Rove on HIV/Aids and was briefed before Bush's 2003 HIV/AIDS announcement. Andrew Natsios and Senate Majority Leader Bill Frist attended an AIDS conference Graham organized in Washington

DC. Frist also accompanied Samaritan's Purse on trips to Africa on several occasions, while Health Secretary Tommy Thompson went on another occasion with Shepherd Smith, founder of the evangelical Institute for Youth Development (Kaplan, 2005: 190; Baxter, 2003). The National Association of Evangelicals lobbied the administration, adding their weight behind Christian Right congressional representatives and senators, CWA, FRC, FOF and the TVC, to increase funding to FBOs and remove it from traditional family planning agencies. Over the course of the administration, the International Planned Parenthood Fund, UN Population Fund, Reproductive Health for Refugees Consortium, Marie Stopes, CARE, and Advocates for Youth are among the many service deliverers targeted by the Christian Right; they have lost millions of dollars in government funding (Kaplan, 2005; Kranish, 2006; Pizzo, 2004). This has caused the closure of numerous projects throughout Africa, replacing experienced and sensitive service delivery with sectarian moralizing carried out by friends of the administration.

The President's Emergency Plan for AIDS Relief is one of the largest sources of funding for FBOs. This funding has been mainly channelled through USAID. Members of the Christian Right who have been installed in key positions have dominated the allocation and policy direction. These include USAID administrator Natsios, who, although claiming not to be a member of the Christian Right, has nonetheless supported its social and moral agenda internationally; Anita Smith, chair of the Presidential Advisory Council on HIV/AIDS; and Dr Anne Peterson, global health director, who was later forced to resign after James Dobson attacked her for advocating the use of condoms to prevent AIDS (Peterson's replacement was another conservative evangelical, Kent Hill, who although unqualified for the role was nonetheless 'sound' on condom use). Les Munson, a former Helms spokesperson, was appointed chief of staff in USAID's Bureau for Global Health. Another former staffer for Helms, Garrett Grigsby, served as number two in the humanitarian assistance bureau. Dr Alma Golden was appointed Deputy Assistant Secretary of Population

Affairs, and co-chair Tom Coburn and Dr Joseph McIlhaney were appointed to the President's Advisory Council on HIV and AIDS. Conservative evangelicals were also well represented on the Federal Drug Administration's Reproductive Health Drugs Advisory Committee by Dr David Hager, Dr Joseph Stanford and Susan Crockett. These appointments helped ensure that USAID maintained policies in favour of abstinence and against condoms, delivered by like-minded FBOs (Kaplan, 2005: 232; Pizzo, 2004; Kranish, 2006).

The partisan nature of USAID administration of the HIV/AIDS assistance programme can be clearly seen in two incidents in 2004 and 2006. In November 2004, funding to Children's AIDS Fund, a conservative evangelical organization that encourages abstinence, received approval. Although USAID's technical review panel ruled that the group's proposal was 'not suitable for funding', Natsios personally intervened to approve the funding because the group favoured abstinence, awarding them up to $10 million over a five-year period. The group was, coincidently, founded by Shepherd Smith and former chair of the President's Advisory Council on AIDS, Anita Smith (Brown, 2005; Kranish, 2006). Whereas the rules could be broken to provide funding for an evangelical Christian organization, a sustained campaign by Senator Rick Santorum and James Dobson deprived CARE of further funding for its AIDS-prevention programmes, replacing its $50 million contract for one four times larger targeted towards FBOs in 2006. CARE was guilty of subcontracting work to Jewish and Muslim groups, and advocating the use of condoms for sex workers. With encouragement from USAID, CARE awarded a $100,000 grant to one of the administration's favoured evangelical groups, Samaritan's Purse, for work in Mozambique, but it was too little too late to secure continued funding (Kranish, 2006).

The Christian Right and the United Nations

In addition to their attempts to control the distribution of USAID resources, the Christian Right have also sought to extend their domestic influence to the United Nations. Bearing in mind the hostility to the institution reflected in such writings as Pat Robertson's *New World Order* and Tim LaHaye and Jerry Jenkins's *Left Behind* series, it is strange that, rather than concentrating their efforts on pulling America out of the organization, key organizations seek to use the system to advance a conservative agenda. Barry Lynn, when interviewed, summed up the paradox:

> I would say they don't have an answer beyond 'we can manipulate it, we can gain some prestige claiming to be there at the heart of solving problems'. But they don't have a good answer to the fundamental question, which is: 'if you don't like the United Nations, why don't you spend all that time just trying to get out of it?'[14]

The Christian Right tentatively began attending UN meetings in the mid-1990s in order to challenge what they perceived as a liberal bias that sought to introduce legislation into America via the circuitous route of the UN in New York. In acquiring UN delegate and observer status the Christian Right could extend their influence internationally, prevent activist judges from applying international law in US courtrooms, and greatly enhance their kudos with supporters and politicians alike by promoting moral majoritarian values abroad. Lynn again puts this into context:

> It is relatively easy to get you non-governmental organization status ... It sounds pretty prestigious when you go around and they say 'this is the NGO representative of XYZ society' and there really is an opportunity to do considerable damage if your guy is 'in' – that is to say, a person friendly to your theological point of view happens to be the ambassador.[15]

Former Ambassador to the UN John Bolton summarizes why, having acquired their status, the Christian Right have become so active in this forum:

> [At the UN] the NGOs tend to be international and tend to be on the left of the American spectrum dealing with the UN. There, certainly, the family issues are quite important to them domestically and they

> want to make sure that there's no slackening in the international arena. And it's a sound strategy from their point of view since many people on the left in the United States, who can't get what they want through Congress in the past ten or fifteen years, have figured out that an alternative route is to internationalize the question. So, not just family issues but gun control climate issues or a whole range of things people are now trying to resolve internationally. So, the religious groups have seen that their success domestically doesn't necessarily guarantee like success internationally. That's why I think they've become more active.[16]

The fear of foreign legislation affecting US domestic law has meant that the Christian Right have also played a prominent role in opposition to the International Criminal Court (Hurlburt, 2001; Crouse, 2002) and Kyoto protocols. As the Christian Right have grown more experienced in presenting their case in international forums, the movement has grown in confidence and, rather than simply containing the liberal threat, there is increased confidence in attempting to roll back liberal advances in women's, children's and gay rights, gender equality, reproductive health and stem-cell research. The standard-bearers for the Christian Right in advancing this conservative moral agenda have been Concerned Women for America, the Family Research Council and Focus on the Family. Over the past decade, they have sought and acquired consultative status at the United Nations, entitling them to attend many UN meetings and to lobby governments and staff at the UN and in the field (Butler, 2006: 43). During the Bush administration, this influence has grown to include delegate status participation in negotiations on behalf of the US government, dealing with the rights of women, children, families, and reproductive and sexual health.

Christian Right organizations have sought to extend their domestic agenda into the international sphere, which for an organization like Focus on the Family means spreading the 'Gospel of Jesus Christ' by stressing the importance of a traditional understanding of family. Their vision is one of 'redeemed families, communities, and societies worldwide through Christ'. Focus stresses the pre-eminence of evangelism, the permanence of marriage, the value of children, the sanctity of human life, the importance of social responsibility, and the value of stereotypical male and female roles. Sexuality is described as 'a glorious gift from God to be offered back to Him either in marriage for procreation, union and mutual delight or in celibacy for undivided devotion to Christ.'[17] The organization seeks to apply such values to the public arena, to public and international policy, rather than simply being a set of principles for fellow believers to live by. In order to advance this agenda FOF, CWA and FRC have formed strong relationships and working partnerships with Catholic and Mormon organizations to advance their moral agenda. The most prominent of these organizations are the Catholic Family and Human Rights Institute (C–FAM) and the Church of Latter-day Saints' World Family Policy Center (WFPC). Such associations are based around shared values on family, marriage, life and sexual orientation. The relationships are problematic, however, in that association with organizations that many of the Christian Right's members regard as apostate or cultish compromises their evangelical message.

In addition to building close ties with C–FAM and WFPC, Christian Right organizations at the UN have also sought to reach out to Islamic states, Muslim organizations and morally conservative forces in the global South, where Pentecostalism and Islam are both growing exponentially. Again, the shared agenda of traditional family values, abstinence before marriage, and opposition to abortion, stem-cell research, homosexuality and sex working is emphasized. The incongruity of working with Islamic organizations and countries that permit polygamy and whose leaders and Prophet Christian Right leaders are constantly deriding is not lost on evangelical practitioners involved in promoting a moral agenda. A further compromise, or outright hypocrisy, is involved in allying with human rights abusers in order to prevent women controlling their own fertility or homosexuals receiving equal treatment. Janice Crouse, senior fellow at the Beverly LaHaye Institute, the think-tank of CWA, explained the dilemma after being confronted by a Canadian delegate at the Status of Women conference in 2003, when accused of siding with some of the worst human rights violators in the world:

> Which was true, unfortunately, but when you get to the UN, the other people who are pro-life, pro-family and pro-marriage, you can put in one hand just about. And some of them are not people you would necessarily want to be allied with, but you have to take your friends where you can find them at the UN. And that has been one of the major problems we have confronted: that the people who are with us on the crucial issues are not the people whose governments are admirable.[18]

Fortunately for CWA, FRC and FOF, their supporters are not aware or concerned with what is going on at the UN and the unhealthy alliances they are forming in order to prevent gender equality and the ending of discrimination in terms of sexual orientation. A single supporter finances CWA's work at the UN and so their activities do not impinge too much on members' sensitivities. Janice Crouse explained the lack of awareness by the membership. 'I'm not sure our constituency, and people in general, are aware at that level that we are working as closely as we are with people who are undesirable in so many other ways.'[19] The extent of collusion with governments with dubious human rights records, including Sudan, Iraq, Iran and Libya, in opposition to homosexuality and feminism, is kept largely concealed from the membership in order to avoid answering the difficult questions about conflicts of interest.

While the Christian Right were condemning human rights abuses and the persecution of fellow believers in Sudan, their representatives at the UN were developing an alliance against sexual and reproductive autonomy with the Sudanese government. While George Bush railed against the Axis of Evil, Christian Right representatives were engaged in discussions on cooperation with representatives of Saddam Hussein, with Iran's religious leaders and with Gaddafi's Libyan representatives before they had abandoned their weapons-of-mass-destruction programme (Lynch, 2002).

The catalyst for Christian Right involvement in the UN can be traced to 18 December 1979 and the passage of the United Nations Convention on the Elimination of all Forms of Discrimination Against Women (CEDAW). President Carter signed the Convention in 1980 and the Senate Foreign Relations Committee passed it in 1994. It has yet to be ratified by the full Senate but has been by 165 countries around the world. The Christian Right's objection to CEDAW is that they see it as an international Equal Rights Amendment (ERA); similar to the federal ERA they were so active in defeating at home. CWA complains that signing up to CEDAW would undermine the traditional family structure and undercut what they see as the proper role of parents. They also charge the Act with mandating gender re-education, calling for equal pay for unequal work, promoting abortion, seeking to introduce ERA by the back door, and advocating homosexuality, same-sex marriages and the legalization of prostitution (MacLeod and Hurlburt, 2000). Jesse Helms led the attack on CEDAW while chair of the Senate Foreign Relations Committee, and CWA have continued the assault on feminism and equal rights.

The international campaign to enhance equality and the status of women took a step forward with the fourth World Conference on Women in Beijing in 1995. Ambassador to the UN Madeleine Albright and Hillary Clinton led the US delegation. Writing of her experience, Albright describes her mission and the response from a leading member of the Christian Right:

> We sought and obtained support for the rights of women and girls to have equal access to education and healthcare, to participate in the economic life of their societies and to live free from the threat of violence ... I am proud to have led the United States' delegation. James Dobson was less enthusiastic, describing the Platform for Action as 'Satan's trump card'. (Albright, 2007: 86)

The Institute on Religion and Democracy asked Janice Crouse to lead a delegation to the conference to challenge liberal assumptions and values. Crouse called her delegation the Ecumenical Coalition on Women and Society. Through the efforts of Jesse Helms, the UN granted accreditation to the conservative evangelical delegation. The delegation was able to maintain the traditional definition of the family as a social group based on a man and a woman and their children, and gain acceptance that people should be free to worship as they choose.[20] The Clinton administration sought to keep Christian conservatives at bay, considering that they represented a threat to progress on improving the status and life chances of women in a world still characterized by patriarchy.

At the start of the twenty-first century, the incoming Bush administration reversed the Clinton policy and allowed the Christian Right greater access to the UN and international conferences. Ellen Sauerbrey, a staunch social conservative, was appointed US Ambassador to the UN Commission on the Status of Women (CSW) and for family concerns. She led US delegations to the annual CSW conferences and international conferences on the family and children, until her controversial appointment in January 2006 as Assistant Secretary of State for Population, Refugees and Migration. Wade Horn was appointed Assistant Secretary for the Administration of Children, Youth and Families, and the contact point linking US missions at the UN with the Christian Right (Butler, 2006: 109). For the first time conservative evangelicals were regularly invited to be part of US delegations. Jeanne Head, of the National Right to Life Committee, was a delegate in 2001 to the World Health Assembly. The following year Bill Saunders (FRC), Bob Flores (National Law Center for Children and Families), Paul Bonnicelli (Patrick Henry College), Janice Crouse (CWA), John Klink (former representative of the Vatican), congressional representative Chris Smith, and Wade Horn were part of the US delegation to the UN Special Session on Children. Janice Crouse and Sherry Dew were part of the delegation to the 2003 CSW and were invited by Ambassador Sauerbrey to address the NGO delegates (Vineyard, 2003).

Apart from participation as members of government delegations, CWA, FRC and FOF campaign alongside C–FAM and WFPC at the UN providing information for America's and other countries' delegates. They have built strong coalitions with other countries' delegates and have sought to bring others on board, particularly where they know the country has a socially conservative outlook. Focus on the Family uses its twenty associated offices in the developing world, including Costa Rica, to pressure host governments to support US policy and draft supportive UN resolutions. The Christian Right and their allies have tended to fight a rearguard action, attempting to frustrate and hinder progress on reproductive and sexual health and broadening traditional concepts of the family. The main tactic apart from developing alliances has been to obfuscate and frustrate attempts by liberals and progressives to advance a radical social agenda through international law. They have spent inordinate amounts of time arguing over the minutiae of language used in UN documentation and statements in order to try to prevent reproductive health, meaning abortion. They have also used their privileged status as US delegates to insist that State Department officials are attentive to their viewpoint. As Bill Saunders, delegate to the Children's Summit in 2002, explained:

> We were quite straight with the State Department officials – career people and the foreign service people – that, we were just not going to accept language that included things like abortion ... you're not going to put us on a delegation and tell us that we have to accept something because of any consideration that you have at all. We're there to reflect our views and if you go against them then we're going to go above you.[21]

The Christian Right's tactics have been particularly successful, and have succeeded in thwarting a progressive social agenda and implementation of CEDAW. They have become a permanent feature at the UN and other international forums promoting their social conservative agenda. The United States promotes the Mexico City global gag rule on abortion, and promotes an ABC approach to HIV/AIDS of abstinence, being faithful, and using condoms as a last resort. Governmental funding has been restricted to organizations pursuing such strategies based on moral absolutism rather than effectiveness.

The Christian Right have successfully managed to remove government funding for Planned Parenthood and the UN Population Fund, weakening the ability of such organizations to provide essential services. They have successfully thwarted UN attempts to deal effectively with issues of sex trafficking and prostitution by justifiably linking the two areas, but then encouraging the administration to refuse to cooperate in interim measures to protect sex workers and reduce the risk of HIV/AIDS.

At the 2002 UN Convention on the Rights of the Child, along with Somalia the United States refused to sign legislation that was deemed to threaten parental rights and responsibilities. It was largely due to the efforts of the Christian Right, and in particular CWA representatives Wendy Wright and Janice Crouse, that the US delegation was able to frustrate attempts by the majority of other nations to redefine concepts of family. These redefinitions included same-sex partnerships, and they succeeded in removing the term 'reproductive health services', which they understood to mean abortion. They can also point to successes in restricting sex educational programmes and preventing the outlawing of the death penalty for crimes committed by minors, under 18 at the time of their offence (Butler, 2006: 66–9; Kaplan, 2005: 234–8).

The rearguard action taken at successive CSW and Beijing (+5 and +10) meetings resisted action on preventing violence against women in conflict and post-conflict because it was suspected that 'forced pregnancy' was a precursor to abortion rights. The Beijing Platform for Action, approved by 181 nations, is still not operational in the United States, and attempts to introduce customary international law have been largely unsuccessful. A troika of the United States, the Vatican and Costa Rica (encouraged by intensive lobbying in Costa Rica by representatives of Focus on the Family) succeeded in achieving the United Nations Declaration on Human Cloning (2005). The Declaration, which is not legally binding, effectively outlaws both reproductive and therapeutic human cloning. CWA, demonstrating increased tactical awareness, led the campaign on the basis of protecting the rights of women in the developing world who would be obliged to sell their embryos to the developed world at risk to their personal health (Butler, 2006: 118–19; Dobson, 2005).

The Christian Right have formed their alliances with conservative Catholics, Mormons and Muslims at an organizational level, and with small countries including the Vatican, Costa Rica and Qatar. At the national level, the movement receives support from think-tanks, from endowments, and from neoconservatives sharing objectives of promoting conservative American/Judeo-Christian social and fiscal values throughout the world. The Ethics and Public Policy Center, IRD, the Institute on Religion and Public Life, and the Center for Security Policy provide research used by the Christian Right in pursuit of their international objectives. Neoconservative-linked organizations, including the Project for a New American Century, the Federalist Society, Heritage Foundation, Hudson Institute, Free Congress Foundation, and Empower America, in cooperating with the Christian Right have been able to leverage their own influence, particularly with George Bush in the White House (Butler, 2006: 141; Monkerud, 2005).

Success for the Christian Right and Bush administration policy at the United Nations in respect of issues surrounding women, children, gender, abortion, trafficking and prostitution has been the negation of the progress desired by most countries in the world. Although this has infuriated many, the Christian Right's influence has been appreciated within the administration. When reflecting on their contribution at the UN, Ambassador Bolton considers that there are no more opportunities for their agenda now than existed at the start of the administration but they have grown more efficient:

> I think it's essentially defensive action but they're very good at it and certainly very helpful on a number of the efforts that I was involved in because they've learned the ropes and they're just as good as the left-wing NGOs. So you end up with a kind of stalemate at present, but I don't see much prospect … They've got very sophisticated working with Catholic countries, with Muslim countries, working on issues like abortion and that sort of thing. They've formed their own coalitions and what not, but it's defensive in nature.[22]

Conclusion

The evidence strongly suggests that the Christian Right have hijacked the human rights and humanitarian assistance agenda. Conservative evangelicals were instrumental in focusing the attention of both the Clinton and Bush administrations on religious persecution in southern Sudan. The increased focus on religious persecution and a commitment to taking religious freedom as seriously as other aspects of freedom and democracy by US governments was largely achieved by pressure from the Christian Right. The International Religious Freedom Act and the mandate to record progress on religious freedom throughout the world are notable advances that would not have been achieved without them. The Christian Right were able to develop and work with disparate alliances to achieve their objectives. In promoting religious freedom, they were careful not to limit the scope to just Christian persecution but also campaigned against Baha'i and Jewish persecution. Inevitably, the main focus has been on Christian persecution, in particular by Muslim or Communist countries. Working together with allies and fellow members in Congress, and through orchestrated campaigns by supporters, they have been able to maintain pressure on the administration to link religious freedom with humanitarian and military assistance. The Christian Right, as we have seen, have favourite causes, and the plight of Christians in southern Sudan, North Korea, China, Saudi Arabia, Pakistan, Eritrea and Iran tends to dominate. This tends to skew the administration's focus and downplay more serious human rights issues (with the exception of Sudan and North Korea) in Burma, Iraq, Somalia, Zimbabwe, Turkmenistan, Equatorial Guinea, Chad, Ivory Coast, Haiti and Uzbekistan.

The distribution of humanitarian assistance, which used to be the prerogative of USAID, has now been extended to incorporate most government departments. Through the Faith-based and Community Initiatives directives FBOs now receive significant amounts of government funding to deliver services while proselytizing. Hundreds of millions of dollars have been awarded to organizations based on their religious affiliation rather than on their ability to deliver services successfully. The programme has privileged Christian organizations over other faiths and secular organizations, enabling them to acquire lucrative government-funded contracts that provide them with credibility and leverage in their attempts to convert nationals in the host countries in which their activities are conducted. The confusion between service provision and proselytizing is unclear and causes confusion in the minds of service deliverer and recipient. With no checks and balances in place, it is hardly surprising when Muslim countries, in particular, fail to see the difference between Christian organizations promoting Christianity and Christian foreign policy. This is all the more problematic when the leaders of favoured FBOs are publicly hostile towards Islam and the Prophet Muhammad.

At the same time as Christian Right organizations and politicians are castigating Muslim countries for persecuting Christians and FBOs are actively seeking to convert Muslims, their counterparts at the UN are determinedly entering into political alliances with Islamic countries in pursuit of a conservative social agenda. Conservative evangelicals have done their best to smother progress on gender equality, gay rights, reproductive health, children's rights and HIV/AIDS prevention by restricting sex education and the use of condoms, promoting a discredited policy of abstinence that only works in the minds of parents of white evangelical teenagers. In order to achieve these objectives they have entered into alliances with the most repressive regimes in the world, fully aware of the inconsistencies and unchallenged by memberships that are largely untroubled by foreign affairs until mobilized to engage by the myriad organizations on the Christian Right and their churches.

Over the past decade, the focus in the United States on human rights and humanitarian assistance has become sharper than ever before. The influence of the Christian Right movement on US policy on human rights and humanitarian assistance has been significant, albeit in a largely defensive and negative way, setting back progress in many areas, reducing the effectiveness of service delivery and opposition to human rights abuse, and linking US foreign policy assistance with Christian proselytizing. An incoming administration may set US humanitarian assistance and human rights policy on an even keel. Nevertheless, the Christian Right is better equipped, resourced and organized than ever before. The movement is determined to maintain its privileged status and influence, with strong support in Congress, with well-disciplined rapid response organization from committed members, and with both main political parties increasingly aware of the power of conservative evangelicals and the need to activate or ameliorate that support.

5

Dominion and the Environment

> So God created man in his own image, in the image of God created he him; male and female created he them. And God blessed them, and God said unto them, Be fruitful, and multiply, and replenish the earth, and subdue it: and have dominion over the fish of the sea, and over the fowl of the air, and over every living thing that moveth upon the earth. (Genesis 1:27–28)
>
> While the earth remaineth, seedtime and harvest, and cold and heat, and summer and winter, and day and night shall not cease. (Genesis 8:22)

Over the past few years, American evangelicals have become increasingly willing to step outside their traditional concerns on abortion, stem-cell research, homosexuality, sexual promiscuity, prostitution and pornography. Evangelicals have engaged with issues surrounding religious persecution, poverty, HIV/AIDS and now, potentially the most divisive issue of all, the environment and global warming in particular. The issue is treated here as a foreign policy issue because the stance of the Bush administration, supported by the majority of the Christian Right, puts it in confrontation with foreign governments and reflects conservative evangelicals' reluctance to allow international law and treaties they perceive to be against US interests to dictate American actions. The United Nations' Intergovernmental Panel on Climate Change (IPCC) and increasing numbers of evangelicals accept the evidence for and agree on the potential solutions to global warming, but the Bush administration and the Christian Right dispute the arguments.

This chapter contends that suggestions of a split within the Christian Right over environmental policy have been greatly exaggerated and that their broad opposition to environmentalism has enabled the Bush administration to resist pressure to sign up to international treaties on climate change. The Christian Right combine anti-environmentalism with an eschatology that predicts the imminent return of Christ and the creation of a new heaven and a new earth. This understanding of the end times and opposition to multilateral bodies such as the European Union and United Nations has reinforced the anti-environmentalist positions adopted by the Bush administration. Contrary to popular opinion, the Christian Right on the whole are not divided over the environment and, with a few dissensions, remain to all intents and purposes a reactionary force resisting evidence of human-made climate change.

The chapter considers IPCC reports on Climate Change and examines the administration's record on global warming. There is some evidence to suggest that in the final months of the Bush presidency the administration's position on global warming began to modify. The chapter examines the role of the Christian Right in supporting Bush's opposition to the Kyoto Protocol and effective measures to combat global warming. The Christian Right's interpretation of scripture and contestation of scientific evidence on global warming are challenged by fellow evangelicals within and outside the movement. The chapter examines this fractious dispute before analysing how the traditional Christian Right position has undergirded the Bush administration's approach to environmental policy.

Science, Climate Change and the Bush Administration

The *Fourth Assessment Report* of the UN Intergovernmental Panel on Climate Change (IPCC, 2007) represents the most definitive statement so far on the impact of climate change. The report considers both human and natural causes of global warming over a long period. It concludes, with a very high degree of confidence, that there has been a marked increase in carbon dioxide, methane and nitrous oxide in the earth's atmosphere since 1750 because of human activities such as burning fossil fuel and the change of land use. The evidence of increasing average air and sea temperatures, melting snow and ice, and rising sea level is described in the report as 'unequivocal'. The report suggests that most of the observed increase in average global temperatures over the past half-century is very likely due to the increase in greenhouse gases produced by human activity.

The IPCC report is sufficiently nuanced to provide some basis for argumentation by environmentalists and by others who dispute the evidence of global warming. Each successive report on climate change that is published, however, further emphasizes that there is now consensus among most scientists working in the area of climate change that global warming and bizarre weather patterns are increasing as a result of human activity, and in particular emissions from the burning of fossil fuels. Certainly this is the view of UN Secretary General Ban Ki-moon, who called a meeting of world leaders at the United Nations on 24 September 2007 to discuss how to replace the Kyoto Protocol, whose agrement on restrictions on greenhouse gas emissions is due to expire in 2012. Ban Ki-moon told the leaders of over 150 nations participating that the 'scientists have very clearly outlined the severity of the problem' and that 'the cost of inaction will far outweigh the cost of early action' (Hodge, 2007). President Bush decided not to attend the event, sending Condoleezza Rice in his place. He did attend a private dinner, however, with the secretary general and leaders of the major emitting countries and those most at risk from global warming (Hodge, 2007).

Ban Ki-moon's meeting coincided with the start of the 62nd General Assembly session, which had climate change as its focus. Bush organized an alternative meeting later in the week, which was attended by mid-level officials from fifteen other major emitting countries. There was considerable suspicion at the meeting that this was an attempt to usurp the UN global emissions reduction programme. Bush and Rice, after years of denial, acknowledged that the USA was a major contributor to global greenhouse emissions and climate change. The solution, however, was not more regulation, but for each country to make its own decisions about how best to reduce emissions. The US favoured technological innovation, and felt that other proposed solutions would harm economic growth in the developed and developing world by starving the latter of fuel. Bush proposed an international fund to help developing nations acquire clean energy technology (Broder, 2007a, 2007b; Hodge, 2007). The president ruled out any mandatory legislation to bring about greenhouse gas reductions, preferring a voluntary approach: 'We will set up a long-term goal for reducing global greenhouse-gas emissions ... Each nation must decide for itself the right mix of tools and technologies to achieve results that are measurable and environmentally effective' (Broder, 2007b).

While the new acknowledgement by the administration of US culpability in climate change was welcome, the lack of willingness to countenance international regulation of greenhouse gas emissions suggested that Bush was more concerned to maintain and protect US corporate interests than deal with the issue during his remaining sixteen months in office. Kevin Phillips (2006) details the relationship between corporate interests and the Christian Right within the Republican Party, a relationship that serves to encourage the oilman and conservative evangelical Bush's world-view. Phillips divides the Christian Right into two camps on the environment, Dispensationalists and Reconstructionists. The first group interpret current world events such as tsunamis, rising energy prices and wars as signs of the end times and therefore conclude that Christians should welcome the imminent return of Christ and not concern themselves with energy policy. Reconstructionists, on the other hand, believe that a theocracy is necessary in America to hasten the Lord's return and are therefore more willing to countenance Christian involvement in environmental matters. Both groups, Phillips points out, believe that the earth is less than 10,000 years old and disagree about anthropogenic explanations of global warming (Phillips, 2006: 66).

The shared interests of fiscal conservatives, corporate interests and conservative evangelicals meet in the Republican Party and, more secretively, in the Council for National Policy. Leaders in the oil, gas, coal and car industries make common cause with the 'economically undemanding religious right' (Phillips, 2006: 67) and business lobbies aware of the power of such groups within the GOP seek to gain their support (Phillips, 2006: 237). Christian Right stalwarts James Dobson, Richard Land and the late D. James Kennedy set up the Interfaith Council for Environmental Stewardship (ICES) in 2000 to provide an environmental lobby group supportive of business and developmental approaches to Christian stewardship. The Action Institute for the Study of Religion and Liberty adopts a similar approach and challenges environmentalist approaches favoured by the green lobby (Philips, 2006: 66, 238).

The main governmental bodies concerned with the environment are the Environmental Protection Agency (EPA) and the Departments of the Interior and Energy. During the Bush administration, Gale Norton served as secretary of the interior (2001–06). Norton had previously worked for James Watt (1979–81), a Pentecostal and secretary of the interior, who was forced to resign after upsetting ecologists with his lack of concern for the environment based on his eschatological position. She also worked for the Coors-financed Mountain States Legal Foundation and interior secretary Donald Hodel, who went on to lead the Christian Coalition. Norton's appointment reflected the close linkage of the Bush administration, the Christian Right and corporate interests. Gale encouraged the opening up of the Arctic National Wildlife Refuge for oil production and other measures favourable to the oil industry. The Department of the Interior has recruited and lost a number of employees from and to the oil industry. The closeness of Gale's office to industry became even more apparent with her appointment to a senior legal position with Shell after leaving office (Macalister, 2007).

The administration's pro-business environmental policies have also enjoyed strong support in Congress, with conservative evangelicals in prominent positions, including Tom DeLay, House Majority Leader (2003–06) and James Inhofe, chair of the Senate Environment and Public Works Committee (2003–07). Bush's denial of the seriousness of global warming and his confidence in business to deal with the problem through research and development have been reflected in the suppression of at least two reports urging action to combat global warming. In 2002, a Pentagon-commissioned report on climate change was rejected.[1] The following year an EPA report on the environment omitted any reference to anthropogenic global warming, despite its having been included in an earlier draft. The section was replaced by a reference to a study funded by the oil industry (Kaplan, 2005: 105). Core supporters had upheld the Bush administration record on global warming but other evangelicals, including conservatives, became increasingly exercised by the lack of attention to the environment.

Evangelicals Divided over Creation

In February 2006, a nationwide survey of born-again or evangelical Protestant Christians revealed increasing evangelical concern for the environment. The survey, funded by the Evangelical Environmental Network, revealed that 54 per cent believed a person's Christian faith should encourage them to focus on environmental issues. Half felt steps ought to be taken to reduce global warming even at a high economic cost for America, including 40 per cent of conservative evangelicals; 63 per cent believed that global warming issues need addressing immediately.[2] Later in the year, a Pew Forum survey confirmed the upsurge of environmental interest among evangelicals, including Bush's core support. Among white evangelicals attending church at least once a month, 45 per cent confirmed that environmental issues had been addressed from the pulpit. Seven out of ten evangelicals felt there was solid evidence that the earth was getting warmer and 37 per cent that it was due to human activity. More white evangelicals felt that stricter environmental controls were worth the cost than were concerned they would hurt the economy (47 : 38 per cent). White evangelicals had more favourable views of the environmentalist movement than conservative republicans did (49 : 43 per cent) and were less hostile (40 : 50 per cent) (Pew Forum, 2006e).

The two surveys revealed the depth of evangelical interest in environmental issues, heightened by an awareness of climate change through pictures of melting icebergs, thinning Arctic sea ice, the separation of the Larsen B ice shelf from the eastern side of the Antarctic Peninsula, and Hurricane Katrina. The environment had become an increasingly important issue for the evangelical left since the early 1990s and more so from 2000 onwards as the scientific evidence grew stronger. The pro-business Christian Right mainstream and Bush administration strongly opposed this emphasis. However, by 2002 even some leaders in the Christian Right were beginning to call for action to tackle global warming. This seeming split in the Christian Right ranks has been hailed in the media as the beginning of the end for the Christian Right and as representing a generational shift (Cornwell, 2006; Tooley, 2006; Sachs, 2006; Luo and Goodstein, 2007). The defection of leading members of the National Association of Evangelicals and of Joel Hunter, who had been invited to become president of the Christian Coalition, to the environmentalist camp caused considerable anger and consternation among the Christian Right, which swiftly descended into bitterness and recrimination.

The Evangelical Climate Initiative

Evangelical scientists' concerns on climate change were raised at the international climate negotiations in The Hague in November 2000. They were particularly concerned about the potential effects of climate change on the world's poor. In the summer of 2002 evangelical scientists organized a conference in Oxford warning of the dangers of climate change and calling for action as part of a Christian acceptance of responsibility to protect God's earth. Jim Ball, executive director of the Evangelical Environmental Network, persuaded vice president of the NAE Richard Cizik to attend the conference. Cizik became convinced of the necessity for fellow evangelicals to be involved in practical action to reduce global greenhouse emissions and to take responsibility as God's stewards for the environment (Cizik, 2007). After the conference, a 'What Would Jesus Drive?' educational campaign was launched, asking Christians to consider the impact of transport pollution and oil dependency on the environment and the poor. In 2004, evangelical leaders met at Sandy Cove, Maryland, and covenanted to take a lead on environmental or creation care issues, deepening their theological understanding of the issues and engaging church members and fellow Christian leaders on climate change, attempting to reach a consensus within twelve months.

Twenty-nine evangelical leaders, the majority of whom were not members of the Christian Right, signed the Sandy Cove Covenant. There were, however, a few signatories among well-known figures within the Christian Right, including the NAE's president Ted Haggard, vice president Richard Cizik, and the vice president of National Ministries Bob Wenz. There were also influential opinion formers from Christian media, including the editors of *Christianity Today* and *Charisma*, the most popular evangelical magazines. The signatures of prominent members of the NAE was controversial because of their status as an umbrella body representing the diverse constituency of left- and right-leaning evangelicals leading 30 million church members. The organization continued with its political engagement in issuing a report later in the year. *For the Health of the Nation: An Evangelical Call to Civic Responsibility* begins with a reminder of the power of the evangelical lobby, totalling a quarter of all US voters, and includes a call to protect God's creation:

> As we embrace our responsibility to care for God's earth, we reaffirm the important truth that we worship only the Creator and not the creation. God gave the care of his earth and its species to our first parents. That responsibility has passed into our hands. We affirm that God-given dominion is a sacred responsibility to steward the earth and not a license to abuse the creation of which we are a part. We are not the owners of creation, but its stewards, summoned by God to 'watch over and care for it' (Gen. 2:15). This implies the principle of sustainability: our uses of the Earth must be designed to conserve and renew the Earth rather than to deplete or destroy it. (NAE, 2004: 11)

The NAE policy document calls on evangelicals to demonstrate their love for Jesus not just by winning souls but also by caring for the environment. Evangelicals are encouraged to recycle and conserve resources, while government is urged to encourage the sustainable use of resources including fuel, to protect wildlife and to reduce pollution (NAE, 2004: 12). Out of the policy document and the concerns of evangelical scientists, the Evangelical Climate Initiative (ECI) developed. The ECI accepted the findings of the IPCC and its former chair, a British evangelical, John Houghton, and released a document on 8 February 2006 signed by eighty-six prominent evangelicals entitled *Climate Change: An Evangelical Call to Action.*

The document makes four main claims with a pledge from the signatories to spread their message and seek ways for government and individuals to implement the necessary actions. First, the document claims that 'human-induced climate change is real'. Second, it observes that 'the consequences of climate change will be significant, and will hit the poor hardest.' The third claim is that 'Christian moral convictions demand our response to the climate change problem.' Fourth, the document insists that 'the need to act now is urgent. Government, businesses, churches, and individuals all have a role to play in addressing climate change – starting now.'[3] The ECI recommends federal legislation to bring about carbon dioxide emissions reductions. The call to action was again signed by prominent evangelicals, including Rick Warren, senior pastor of Saddleback Church and author of the bestseller *The Purpose Driven Life*, but not this time by executive officers of the NAE, who had been warned off by the Christian Right. The most significant defection from the mainstream Christian Right position on the environment was Joel Hunter, who was set to take over the leadership of the Christian Coalition, an offer that was withdrawn because of his desire to expand the traditional Christian Right core issues to include poverty and the environment.

Hunter, pastor of the 12,000-strong Northland Church, Longwood, Florida, has taken a lead in causing the Christian Right to reflect on their position on the environment. He argues that whatever evangelicals' perspective on global warming, they all have a shared interest in and responsibility for caring for the environment:

> Every major religion has a moral mandate to take care of the Earth. For those who look to the Bible for instruction, it is the first responsibility given to man: 'The Lord God took the man and put him into the garden of Eden to cultivate it and keep [protect] it' (Gen: 2:15, NASB[4]). Our moral obligation, then, does not depend on the rate our planet is warming, or even whether the main cause is human activity. We are to refrain from harming God's creation – period. Few Christians or persons of other faiths (or no faith) would disagree with that statement. (Hunter, 2007)

Joel Hunter is not dismissive of his opponents among colleagues in the Christian Right and has sought to take on board their market-based approaches to tackling the problem. He cautions against climate-change scepticism, which he is fearful would delay the reforms considered necessary to avert environmental catastrophe. Hunter acknowledges that for many evangelicals active participation in environmental activism is tantamount to lack of faith in God's care for humanity. The message evangelicals in the Creation Care movement are sending to their peers is that caring for the environment is an act of faith and obedience. Hunter and others within the movement are eager for evangelicals to be in the vanguard of environmental reforms rather than trailing behind radical environmentalists who do not share their conservative social agenda (Hunter, 2007).

The other leading defector from mainstream Christian Right thinking on the environment is Richard Cizik. Throughout the past quarter of a century Cizik has been the most influential voice of the NAE in Washington, lobbying on matters of concern to evangelicals. A pro-Bush conservative, Cizik's Christian Right credentials are impeccable, and yet by 2004 he was calling for evangelicals to become active environmental campaigners in order to protect God's creation. He has used his privileged position within the NAE to call for action on global warming, withstanding attempts from Christian Right leaders, including James Dobson and Charles Colson, to remove his platform. Ted Haggard, president of the NAE until revelations of his relationship with a male prostitute were revealed, prevented Cizik and other NAE officials from endorsing the *Evangelical Call to Action* because it had not received the unanimous endorsement of the NAE Board following criticism from leading members of the Christian Right.

The letter sent to the NAE on global warming demonstrates the considerable power wielded by conservative evangelical patriarchs. Twenty-two leading conservative evangelicals, many of whom were not even members of the NAE, signed the letter, causing Haggard to feel compelled to comply with their demands. Signatories included Charles Colson (PFM), James Dobson (FOF), John Hagee (Cornerstone Church), D. James Kennedy (Coral Ridge), Richard Land (ERLC), Richard Roberts (Oral Roberts University), Louis Sheldon (TVC), Donald Wildmon (AFA) and Alan Wisdom (IRD). The letter points out that global warming is not a consensus issue and that there should be room within evangelical circles to disagree about the extent of the problem and prospective solutions. The letter ends 'with love and respect' but contains a clear instruction to the association:

> Further, we signatories who are members of the NAE believe that if the NAE wishes to take an official position on global warming or any other issue, it should do so through its formal process within the general council. Individual NAE members or staff should not give the impression that they are speaking on behalf of the entire membership, so as not to usurp the credibility and good reputation of the NAE.[5]

Criticism of Cizik has continued unabated from the Christian Right patriarchs, who accuse him of diverting attention onto global warming and away from core campaign issues such as abortion, same-sex marriage, sexual abstinence and morality. In March 2007, Dobson, Gary Bauer, Tony Perkins, Paul Weyrich and Don Wildmon sent another letter to the NAE calling for Cizik's resignation. Richard Land did not sign the letter and none of the signatories was a member of the NAE. The letter insists that if Richard Cizik 'cannot be trusted to articulate the views of American evangelicals' then he should be made to resign (Goodstein, 2007). Jerald Walz, vice president of operations at the IRD, has also opposed Cizik on the board of the NAE. IRD issued a statement criticizing Cizik for stepping outside his NAE remit and advocating policy positions that 'go well beyond any plain scriptural teaching. None of them has been authorized by the NAE board. None of them would have consensus support in the evangelical community' (Americans United, 2007; Christian Century, 2007). This time the NAE board under new president Leith Anderson backed Cizik, reaffirming policy documents on torture and *For the Health of the Nation*, and praising Cizik (Goodstein, 2007; Christian Century, 2007).

Cizik has attempted to bring a pro-business conservative evangelical constituency round to a position of supporting action on environmental issues, considering that such support is part of a continuum of Christian Right social issues. In the environmentalist film *The Great Warming*, Cizik was interviewed at length. In the interview, he criticizes the Republican leadership for holding back progress on climate change and advocates evangelicals using their position of influence in the party, which he puts at between 40 and 50 per cent of the Republican base, to effect change. He believes that there has been a lack of evangelical engagement on the issue because of a lack of leadership from the pulpit, a reluctance to embrace big government solutions to tackling global warming, and apocryphal beliefs teaching that this is a sign of the end times and therefore there is no need to take action. Cizik dismisses end-time thinking on the environment as heretical.

Cizik acknowledges that evangelicals do not wish to be a part of the environmentalist movement but rather feel that biblical teaching and their own religious experience and tradition naturally lead to an environmentalist position:

> So when evangelical Christians make the connection between the call to protect the innocent, the unborn, and the call to be stewards of the world that God has created, when they make the connection between the two, there will be no hesitation to speak out on environmental concerns.[6]

Richard Cizik has received a great deal of publicity for his creation-care message, including a feature in the Green Issue of *Vanity Fair* magazine in May 2006. He attracts publicity from the secular media and opprobrium from the Christian Right patriarchs because of the perception that he represents a decisive split in the ranks of the Christian Right that marks the end of their influence as a cohesive force in American politics.

The Cornwall Alliance for the Stewardship of Creation

The dispute between Cizik, Hunter and other creation-care evangelicals and the mainstream Christian Right is contested theologically and politically. Both sides claim to be adhering to biblical standards regarding care for the environment and concern for the poor. The Christian Right, through groupings such as the Cornwall Alliance for the Stewardship of Creation, formerly known as the Interfaith Stewardship Alliance (ISA), dispute the scientific findings of the IPCC, and consider that care for the poor includes encouraging and equipping them to develop economically by embracing the free market and gaining access to industry and technology. Climate change is not seen as being sufficiently important to distract conservative evangelicals from pursuing their social agenda. As we have seen, at times this fractious dispute has erupted into highly personalized and vitriolic abuse. The

National Center for Public Policy Research has actively sought to discredit the ECI and the Evangelical Environment Network. Amy Ridenour of the National Center summed up the suspicions of many on the Christian Right:

> What we are finding so far is what we expected to find: the group is a far-left environmental project funded by leftists with an interest in environmental issues and no track record of promoting or supporting Christianity, evangelical or otherwise. We are seeking, among other things, evidence that donors also fund explicitly anti-Christian activities. This would demonstrate that their interest here is definitely not the promotion of Christianity, but the hijacking of Christianity for political purposes. (Biddison, 2006)

The Christian Right approach to global warming embraces a three-part strategy: disputation of the scientific evidence on climate change, stressing the importance of development for mature and developing economies, and dismissing creation care as a distraction from their core mission or as a left-wing attempt to split the Christian Right and weaken the American economy. The first two parts of the strategy find their most forthright expression in a document produced by the Cornwall Alliance in July 2006, *A Call to Truth, Prudence, and Protection of the Poor: An Evangelical Response to Global Warming*. The document, signed by over 120 leading members of the Christian Right, scientists, pastors and theologians, offers an alternative to the ECI's *Evangelical Call to Action*, one which it claims will improve conditions for the poor more effectively.

The *Call to Truth* commends the *Call to Action* signatories for speaking out on 'a public issue of ethical concern (Cornwall Alliance, 2006: 1). The report then proceeds to challenge each of the ECI's four claims on climate change, which it describes as assumptions. The first assumption, that carbon dioxide 'emissions from fossil fuels are the main cause of warming', is critiqued on the strength of other studies indicating that natural causes may outweigh anthropogenic causation, that rising carbon dioxide emissions follow rather than lead global warming, and that the impact of land-use conversion is underemphasized (Cornwall Alliance, 2006: 2–3). The second claim, that 'global warming will be catastrophic, especially for the poor', is challenged on the basis of the scientific evidence. The authors question the idea that temperatures will rise as high as the IPCC claims and that even if they did it would not be as catastrophic as suggested. They provide contrary opinions about sea level rises, heat waves that are more frequent, droughts and extreme weather events, increases in tropical diseases, more intense hurricanes and decreased agricultural yield in poorer countries. The Cornwall Alliance also disputes notions of a scientific consensus surrounding anthropogenic global warming, which it describes as an illusion (Cornwall Alliance, 2006: 3–10). For the Alliance increased carbon dioxide emissions would be beneficial inasmuch as they reduce severe cold-related deaths and increase agricultural yield while reducing desertification (Cornwall Alliance, 2006: 4–8).

The other part of the ICI document's second claim considers that climate change will hit the poor hardest. The contrary report believes that 'mandatory reductions in fossil fuel use' would have significantly more impact than increased global temperatures. Reducing energy use, the authors claim, would slow economic development, reduce productivity and increase costs, adversely affecting the living standards of the poor. The Cornwall Alliance would accept tradable permits to deal with pollution but reject a regulatory approach that would place a cap on national or global emissions (Cornwall Alliance, 2006: 11–13). It emphasizes a market-orientated approach in line with traditional Republican thinking:

> Put simply, poor countries need income growth, trade liberalization, and secure supplies of reliable, low-cost electricity. Rather than focusing on theoretically possible changes in climate, which varies tremendously anyway with El Niño, La Niña, and other natural cycles, we should emphasize policies – such as affordable and abundant energy – that will help the poor prosper, thus making them less susceptible to the vagaries of weather and other threats in the first place. (Cornwall Alliance, 2006: 13)

The third and fourth claims of the ECI document suggest that the IPCC evidence demands an evangelical response to climate change and that the need to act is urgent. *The Call to Truth* agrees with the call to love of neighbour and stewardship but disagrees over the requisite course of action. They argue strongly that the global poor are better served by economic development and increased wealth than by reducing carbon dioxide emissions. The real threat to the world's poor is seen by the Alliance as a lack of clean water, indoor plumbing, sewerage, electricity for refrigeration and air conditioning, employment, medical care and adequate nutrition, and effective legal and economic systems (Cornwall Alliance, 2006: 14). In the battle between the creation-care environmentalists and Christian Right stewardship, the latter claim the moral high ground, arguing that denying the benefits of economic growth through access to fuel resources, including fossil fuel, nuclear energy and hydroelectricity, is 'unconscionable' (Cornwall Alliance, 2006: 14–15). The Alliance supports efforts to improve energy efficiency but advocates leaving it to the market:

> We agree that it is wise to pursue increasing energy efficiency through the development of new technologies. But a program that can only be done by government mandate is by definition not a program that the market deems cost effective. We believe the market is a better judge of cost effectiveness than bureaucrats and politicians. What are needed are *prudent* policies that reflect actual risks, costs, and benefits; an honest evaluation of sound scientific, economic, and technological data; and unbiased application of moral, ethical, and theological principles. (Cornwall Alliance, 2006: 15)

The Cornwall Alliance suggests that, rather than helping the poor, ECI policies will lead to increased hardship and even death for the world's poor. Global warming, it argues, will have mixed rather than catastrophic results. Using a simple cost–benefit analysis the Alliance claims that insignificant reductions in global temperatures through curbing greenhouse gas emissions are not worth the damage caused to the economic prospects and life chances of individuals in developing nations. The document commends the Copenhagen Consensus in which eight leading economists, including three Nobel prizewinners, prioritized major problems facing humanity and the solutions proposed to alleviate them based on their cost-effectiveness. Seventeen problems were considered, including three related to global warming, which were all placed bottom of the list of priorities (Cornwall, 2006: 18). Just as the ECI promised through its *Call to Action*, so the *Call to Truth* commits the signatories to communicate its message and 'oppose quixotic attempts to reduce global warming' (Cornwall Alliance, 2006: 19).

The Cornwall Alliance sums up its politico-theological position in the Cornwall Declaration, setting out seven aspirations, which reflect its ideological commitment to capitalism, the market economy and conservative Republican values:

> 1. We aspire to a world in which human beings care wisely and humbly for all creatures, first and foremost for their fellow human beings, recognizing their proper place in the created order.
> 2. We aspire to a world in which objective *moral principles – not personal prejudices* – guide moral action.
> 3. We aspire to a world in which right reason (including sound theology and the careful use of scientific methods) guides the stewardship of human and ecological relationships.
> 4. We aspire to a world in which *liberty as a condition of moral action is preferred over government-initiated management* of the environment as a means to common goals.
> 5. We aspire to a world in which the *relationships between stewardship and private property are fully appreciated*, allowing people's natural incentive to care for their own property to *reduce the need for collective ownership and control* of resources and enterprises, and in which collective action, when deemed necessary, takes place at the most local level possible.
> 6. We aspire to a world in which *widespread economic freedom* – which is integral to private, market economies – makes sound ecological stewardship available to ever greater numbers.
> 7. We aspire to a world in which advancements in agriculture, industry, and commerce not only minimize pollution and transform most waste products into efficiently used resources but also improve the material conditions of life for people everywhere. (emphasis added)[7]

The thinking behind the Cornwall Declaration informs the policy positions adopted by Christian Right patriarchs such as Dobson and Land. Richard Land informed me that the economic cost of adopting the Kyoto Protocol would affect people at the economic margins for very little gain in terms of temperature reductions. Therefore, 'someone needs to speak up for the human cost of some of these environmental measures that are being proposed.'[8] He felt that the dangers of overreaction on climate change could have the same impact as warnings about the damage caused to the environment and human health by the use of DDT. The restrictions on DDT usage, for Land, have resulted in the unnecessary deaths of 1 million children due to malaria, for want of DDT. He summarizes the environmental priorities of fellow members of the Christian Right:

> What my segment of evangelicalism is going to be arguing is, of course, we need to be stewards of Creation but we need to balance the environmental issues with the human cost on people who are least able to bear those costs. And that the ultimate value is not nature. The ultimate value are [*sic*] human beings, and that we are going to be arguing for – we're going to be the advocates for human beings who may be asked to bear a disproportionate cost.[9]

Land argues in favour of the developed world minimizing its carbon footprint in order to enable greater development with reliable energy sources for the developing world. Those energy sources, he argues, are too expensive because the developing world has to compete with the developed world. He advocates 'a massive commitment' to the use of nuclear energy in the developed world, which would then 'make petroleum energy and other carbon-based energies more affordable and much more accessible to the developing world'.[10] Such an outlook is anathema to Cizik, Hunter and the ECI but is supported by Land's fellow Southern Baptists, who passed a resolution at their conference in 2007, warning against overreaction to global warming and of the need to consider the economic consequences of any action (Gorski, 2007).

The economic arguments of Land and other leading conservative evangelicals rally supporters around a discourse about how best to help the global poor and the US economy at the same time. There are other discourses, which also affect Christian Right approaches to climate change. These centre on evangelicals' suspicion of science that places primacy on scientific evidence over theological belief and biblical literalism. This is revealed in the evolution-versus-creationism/intelligent design debates, and the disputation over the age of the earth, which most evangelicals consider to be between 6,000 and 10,000 years old. Further suspicions are aroused by scientific evidence about the sentience of fetuses, stem-cell research and sexual health. As a result, the default position for conservative evangelicals is suspicion of scientific evidence and an inclination to disbelieve without corroborating biblical evidence. Both sides in the dispute over climate change seek to establish the strengths of their position based on scripture first and then scientific validation for their preferred interpretation.

Apocalyptic Thinking

A further discourse on the environment maintains that because of the proximity of the return of Jesus there is no need to be concerned about such temporal matters. Hal Lindsey (2006), author of the best-selling *The Late Great Planet Earth* and *Satan is Alive and Well on Planet Earth*, appeals to a great many conservative evangelicals by relating global warming to the end times, despite Richard Cizik's characterization of such views as heretical.[11] Lindsey's apocryphal and prophetic writings focus on signs of the end times and the return of Jesus. Global warming, tsunamis and hurricanes are for Lindsey the 'birth pangs' before the Lord's return. Quoting from Matthew 24 and Luke 21 he identifies as key signs religious deception and turning to the occult, wars and rumours of wars, international upheaval, ethnic clashes, earthquakes, famines and plagues. There is a further birth pain, which he relates to global warming:

> And there will be signs in the sun, in the moon, and in the stars; and on earth distress of nations, with perplexity, the sea and the waves roaring; men's hearts failing them from fear and the expectation of those things which are coming on the earth, for the powers of heaven will be shaken. (Luke 21:25–56, New King James Version)

Lindsey uses the above passage to demonstrate that global warming is 'primarily caused by what is happening in the sun and moon' and not because of human activity. It is the 'distress and perplexity' of the nations that sums up the climate change debate. Rather than arguing in favour of one or other of the positions, Lindsey embraces, and calls on fellow evangelicals to do likewise, the environmental changes and problems that herald Christ's return. Lindsey fully accepts the worsening environmental conditions, but believes they should inspire evangelism rather than environmentalism, to save the souls that face destruction without conversion to Christianity (Lindsey, 2005).

Lindsey cautions fellow evangelicals about being deceived by arguments for creation care and environmentalism, considering them to be a plot by liberals 'both [to] advance their one-world, anti-nationalism agenda and to raise money for their own personal political agendas' (Lindsey, 2007a). Rather, evangelicals should be confident in the promises of God that there will never be another Noah-like flood and that seasonal cycles would continue (Genesis 8:22). Before things become too catastrophic, Christians can be confident that these are the end times (Matthew 24:33–34; Luke 21:25–58) (Lindsey, 2007a, 2007b). Such views inform evangelicals that there is no need to engage in environmental concerns, and indeed that such engagement indicates a lack of trust in God and gullibility to left-wing machinations that seek to bring about world government and the Antichrist.

Christian Right Influence on Bush Policy on the Environment

The Bush administration has consistently applied a pro-business approach to the environment, including opening up the Arctic nature reserve for oil production and a reluctance to accept scientific findings on anthropogenic climate change and global warming. The refusal to commit America to the Kyoto Protocol on greenhouse emissions has enabled US business to continue polluting the atmosphere without economic penalties or incentives to develop alternative technologies and reduce US dependency on fossil fuels. Domestic political opposition to this business-friendly approach has been muted by Republican majorities in the House of Representatives for six of the eight years of Bush's term, and Senate GOP majorities for slightly over half that term. Congressional representatives and senators have been reluctant to risk prices and job prospects by capping greenhouse gas emissions.

Although President Clinton signed up to Kyoto in 1998, he never sent it to Congress for ratification. Indeed, a year earlier the Senate passed the Byrd–Hagel resolution 95 : 0, which declared that unless it could be demonstrated that implementation would not harm the US economy, and developing countries were obliged to sign up, then the Senate would not ratify the treaty. Bush's unwillingness to commit to mandatory emissions reductions received widespread support from both parties until the Democrats regained the Senate in 2007. Even proposed programmes of research on abrupt climate change and the introduction of a market-driven tradable greenhouse gas allowances system were defeated in the Senate 55 : 43, with all Christian Right senators, including Allen, Brownback, Frist, Inhofe, Santorum and Smith voting against, on 30 October 2003.

The Christian Right and the Bush administration's interests have been ably served in the Senate by James Inhofe (R–Oklahoma), chair of the Senate Environment and Public Works Committee (2003–07). Inhofe has become one of the most informed senators on the issue of climate change, and up until the end of 2006 had made eight speeches from the floor of the Senate on the subject of global warming – more than any other politician. Inhofe's scepticism about anthropogenic global warming pre-dates the ISA and Cornwall Alliance and involves a lengthy and considered critique of Kyoto and the four IPCC reports.

As committee chair, Inhofe has argued that the claim that global warming is anthropogenic is untrue and based on flawed science, that carbon dioxide increases do not cause catastrophic disasters but are actually beneficial for the environment and economy. He further argues that Kyoto would place a huge financial burden on America and especially poorer citizens. Indeed, the motivations for Kyoto are a European plan intended to handicap the US economy through carbon taxation and regulations (Inhofe, 2003, 2005, 2006). He has used Senate speeches linking environmental groups with a partisan Democrat political agenda and criticized media coverage on global warming (Inhofe, 2004, 2006).

Inhofe's support for the Bush administration's strategy on the environment, coupled with the reluctance of congressional representatives and senators to pursue a policy with little electoral advantage in the face of the economic cost of implementing reductions in greenhouse gas emissions, enabled Bush to maintain his indifference to successive IPCC reports. The existence of contrary opinions, no matter how lacking in credibility, legitimized the administration's unwillingness to commit to mandatory emissions targets in international agreements. However, a combination of factors has belatedly led to a reconsideration of administration attitudes to global warming.

The evidence of global warming has become increasingly difficult to ignore, despite conflicting reports. Hurricane Katrina produced an environmental shock to the American polity only slightly less significant than the political and security shock of 9/11. The attention paid to environmental issues by the Republican governor of California Arnold Schwarzenegger has brought global warming to the attention of the GOP. The involvement of high-profile non-partisan evangelical leaders such as Rick Warren and Bill Hybels in creation care and the defection of Christian Right leaders Cizik and Hunter to the environmentalist camp has inevitably caused some reflection on global warming positioning for the administration and the Christian Right more broadly. The Democrat takeover of both Houses of Congress in the 2006 midterm elections, the build-up to the presidential elections in 2008, and the end of Bush's presidency all combine to enable the president to make nominal concessions on climate change.

The international recognition accorded to Al Gore and the IPCC, through the award of the 2007 Nobel Peace Prize and the Oscar won by the film *An Inconvenient Truth*, built pressure on the administration to accept what it already knew: that anthropogenic global warming required immediate action. The disastrous intervention in the Middle East, intended to provide greater access to Iraqi oil supplies, and the ongoing War on Terror, have obliged the president to consider alternative energy sources. The Christian Right, and Christian Zionists in particular, have been very supportive of efforts to develop biofuels and lessen the reliance on oil supplies from volatile Islamic countries. In acknowledging the anthropogenic nature of climate change and making vague promises to encourage market-based solutions to develop cleaner fuel technology and biofuels, Bush has delayed the taking of serious action on the issue until he has safely left office.

On 17 January 2007, members of the NAE and the Center for Health for the Global Environment launched an 'Urgent Call to Action: Scientists and Evangelicals Unite to Protect Creation', claiming consensus on a range of environmental issues. The ISA, before changing its name to the Cornwall Alliance in May 2007, reaffirmed its support for Bush's policies and denied any such consensus between evangelicals and scientists. In a letter to the president, E. Calvin Beisner, ISA national spokesman, challenged the claims of the 'Urgent Call' and urged him to seek truth rather than consensus. The 'truth' the Christian Right expect the president to find will take longer than the remainder of his time in office, but the statement sends out a signal of continuing support from the mainstream of his core constituency.

Conclusion

Members of the Christian Right have on the whole loyally supported Bush's environmental policy and reluctance to engage with the issues of global warming. The preferred stance on environmental issues for the key leaders of the Christian Right has been to support US business interests, domestically and internationally, in the belief that economic growth without too much federal or international regulation will lead to higher living standards for America and the developing world. Conservative evangelicals favour market-based solutions rather than government regulation to deal with sensitive issues such as global warming. This position accords with that adopted by the Bush administration. Hence the Christian Right have found themselves in the position of defending administration policy rather than pressing for their own agenda. The policy of non-action on environmental issues has been ably defended by the ISA, the Cornwall Alliance, Senator James Inhofe and the votes of Republicans, including conservative evangelicals in both houses of Congress.

The notion that there has been a significant cleavage within the Christian Right over environmental policy has been greatly exaggerated. This has been the product of wishful thinking on the part of environmentalists, liberals and the Christian Left. While it would be wrong to minimize the importance of the defections of Joel Hunter and Richard Cizik to the environmentalist lobby, the overwhelming majority of conservative evangelical leaders have not altered their position. The combination of Hal Lindsey's approach and that of the Cornwall Alliance represents the mainstream Christian Right view; it is difficult to envisage Cizik and Hunter convincing this section of evangelicalism to engage in environmentalism, even under the label of creation care.

PART III

6

Blessing Israel

> And I will bless them that bless thee, and curse him that curseth thee: and in thee shall all families of the earth be blessed. (Genesis 12:3)[1]

Throughout the last two millennia, Christians have enjoyed an ambiguous relationship with Judaism and Israel. The early disciples were Jewish, as indeed was Jesus himself; however, the decision of Saul (later Paul) and Barnabas to take the gospel to the gentiles resulted in controversy that has remained unabated ever since (Acts 15:1–31). What should be the relationship between Jew and Gentile? Are the promises of God, described in the Bible, still relevant for Israel and the Jews or have the Church and Christians replaced biblical Israel (Romans 9:1–11:36)? Over the centuries, the Church tended to accept the latter interpretation of replacement theology, beginning with Justin Martyr's *Dialogue with Trypho* in the middle of the second century. The teachings of Augustine and John Chrysostom in the fourth century contributed to the depiction of the Jews as Christ-killers and their subsequent persecution at various times in pogroms throughout the Christian world. King Edward I expelled all Jews from England by edict in 1290, and they weren't permitted to return until the rule of Oliver Cromwell. The Spanish Inquisition routinely tortured and executed Jews over two centuries. Reformation leader Martin Luther encouraged persecution of the Jews on the grounds that they would not convert to Christ. The Papacy looked the other way as 6 million Jews were slaughtered in the Holocaust. Since the founding of the State of Israel, and more especially since the Six Day War of 1967, there has been a shift in emphasis among the majority of the American Christian Right to considering the State of Israel and the Jewish people as being God's people and an essential component of the end times.

In this chapter, we consider how this new emphasis has sought to influence US foreign policy in the Middle East. Beginning with the background to US support for Israel, the chapter goes on to consider how Christian Right eschatology informs their attitude towards Israel. We examine how the most prominent grouping, the Christian Zionists, have built close working relationships and developed links with other sympathetic parties. The chapter continues by analysing the movement's modus operandi and its impact on US foreign policy. It concludes that, although Christian Zionist support is not a necessary condition for US support for Israel, it helps create the conditions that preclude a peaceful resolution of conflict and even incites such conflict in a way that is detrimental to the interests of both the United States and Israel.

US support for Israel has been a fairly consistent aspect of American foreign policy since the State of Israel was declared on 14 May 1948. Over the subsequent decades that support has grown closer and become more resolute. There have been some tensions as US security and economic interests in the Arab world have come into conflict with this support. Secretary of State George C. Marshall advised President Truman that US interests lay in the Persian Gulf, securing oil supplies and reducing Soviet influence in the region. President Eisenhower adopted friendly relations with Israel but recognized that such support risked inflaming Arab resentment, radicalization and Soviet influence. He demanded the withdrawal of Israeli, French and British troops during the Suez Crisis in 1956. Eisenhower erected a Chinese wall between US–Israeli and US–Arab relations that has remained to this day (Allin and Simon, 2003: 125). Overall, Republican administrations have traditionally been more willing than Democratic ones to challenge or control Israel's behaviour. During the various attempts to broker peace settlements in the region the State Department has worked on the basis of Israel trading 'land for peace', appealing to Arab governments and the Palestinians to accept that only the USA has sufficient influence with Israel to bring about a settlement. Whether US administrations are able, or even willing, to help broker a realistic settlement is more dependent on domestic sources of foreign policy than State Department diplomacy, as we shall see.

The United States has diverted around one-fifth of its foreign aid assistance to Israel, averaging around $3 billion per annum, amounting to over £100 billion since the state was founded. In 2008, this contribution was to reduce to $2.4 billion in military aid while Israel will remain the largest beneficiary of US foreign assistance (IMFA, 2006). In July 2007, however, the State Department announced a new military aid package of $30 billion over ten years, a 25 per cent increase in real terms.[2] Unlike other aid recipients, Israel receives this money as a lump sum at the beginning of the financial year and is not required to account for how it is spent. In addition, the United States supports Israel militarily from its defence budget, writes off various loans, provides special grants, makes available the latest military hardware, and shares intelligence. Since 1985 Israel has been the beneficiary of a bilateral Free Trade Area Agreement with the USA and from 1987 has been designated as a 'major non-NATO ally'. The United States has steadfastly supported Israel through successive administrations, brokering ceasefires and peace settlements with Egypt and Jordan, and vetoing resolutions critical of Israel in the UN Security Council. The US–Israel relationship is unique and has become a permanent feature of US foreign policy even when this has not always been in America's best interest:

> The continuing and deepening amity between Israel and the United States has been defined by various American administrations in terms ranging from the preservation of Israel as a 'basic tenet' of American foreign policy, with emphasis on a 'special relationship' between the two nations, to a declaration of an 'American commitment' to Israel. (IMFA, 2006)

In March 2006, two prominent realist International Relations scholars, John Mearsheimer and Stephen Walt, produced one of the most damning assessments of the US–Israel relationship and its detrimental impact on US foreign policy. In 'The Israel Lobby', published in the *London Review of Books* (Mearsheimer and Walt, 2006a), and their subsequent book, *The Israel Lobby and U.S. Foreign Policy* (2007), the authors argue that US foreign policy in the Middle East is determined by a pro-Israeli lobby comprising Jews, Christian evangelicals and neoconservatives. This 'Israel Lobby', they claim, dominates Congress and the executive, think-tanks and the media. It also monitors academic discourse and uses its resources, influence and threats to promote a pro-Israel bias in US foreign policy, even when this is against America's national interest (Mearsheimer and Walt, 2006a, 2006b, 2007). The authors, although part of the US foreign policy establishment for many years, have been vilified by the Lobby and face the usual charge of anti-Semitism experienced by any academic who questions Israel's conduct in the Middle East. They have raised an important debate about the nature and role of US support for Israel, a debate to which this chapter contributes. Mearsheimer and Walt, although acknowledging the influence of Christian evangelicals and neoconservatives, concentrate in their writings on the 'Jewish lobby' and in particular the role of the American Israel Public Affairs Committee (AIPAC). This chapter is more concerned with the Christian Right's advancement of a pro-Israel agenda.

The Christian Right's pro-Israel agenda was considered by them to have received a significant boost with the election of George W.

Bush in 2000. They, for both domestic and foreign policy reasons, welcomed the result, and yet most Jewish voters, traditionally the most enthusiastic supporters of Israel, continued their traditional support for the Democratic candidate. As David Frum, one of George Bush's former speechwriters, pointed out:

> It would be almost impossible to invent a candidate less likely to appeal to Jewish voters than George W. Bush. His personality seemed to fuse together in one body the three personality types most calculated to frighten and annoy Jews: the redneck, the Bible-thumper, and the upper class frat boy. His social conservatism worried Jews, his apparent anti-intellectualism offended them, and above all, they mistrusted his 'born on third base' background. (Frum, 2003: 246–7)

Yet, as Frum goes on to say, Bush emerged 'as one of the staunchest friends of Israel ever to occupy the Oval Office' (Frum, 2003: 248). In the remainder of the chapter, we consider the extent to which this is attributable to the influence of the Christian Right.

Christian Right Eschatology

The Christian Right are not a homogenous grouping but rather contain many nuances and differing emphases, in particular in relation to Israel. However, over the past few decades a consensus in relation to Israel has emerged within the movement around Christian Zionism. Christian Zionism has a long history, although it only achieved ascendancy in evangelical circles in the United States in the latter half of the twentieth century. Christian Zionism traces its origins back to the early nineteenth century and the teachings of John Nelson Darby (1800–81) and the Plymouth Brethren. Darby spent a considerable amount of time in the United States between 1862 and 1877 preaching a fundamentalist interpretation of the Bible, which was to influence the Niagara Conference of 1875, a gathering that brought together American fundamentalists and produced a creed in 1878 calling for the restoration of Jews to a homeland in Palestine. Darby's teaching was also to influence two of the most prominent revivalist preachers in American history, Dwight L. Moody in the late nineteenth century and Billy Sunday in the first two decades of the twentieth. They, along with Cyrus Scofield's Reference Bible, the main Bible for Christian fundamentalists in America throughout the twentieth century, became the main vehicle for disseminating Darby's interpretation of the Bible and contributed to the ascendancy of Christian Zionism within the movement.

Darby's teaching as disseminated by Moody, Sunday and Scofield complemented the teachings of William Hechler (1845–1931) and William Blackstone (1841–1931), author of *Jesus is Coming* (1878). Former Israeli prime minister Benjamin Netanyahu describes Blackstone as a leading Christian Zionist and acknowledges that the movement pre-dates the modern Zionist movement by fifty years (Netanyahu, 1994: 16). Hechler befriended the Jewish Zionist pioneer Theodor Herzl, author of *Der Judenstaat* (1896), and the efforts of Zionists from two of the three Abrahamic faiths provided the impetus for the Balfour Declaration in 1917, Jewish resettlement in Palestine and the formation of the State of Israel in 1948.

The theological underpinning of Christian Zionism is known as 'premillennial dispensationalism'; it takes a literal interpretation of the Bible to contend that God has a covenant with the Jewish people that is eternal, exclusive, and cannot be abrogated, according to Genesis 12:1–7, 15:4–7, 17:1–8; Leviticus 26:44–5; Deuteronomy 7:7–8 (Wagner, 2003b). The history of humanity, according to John Nelson Darby, can be divided into seven time periods, or dispensations, beginning with the Garden of Eden and ending with the Second Coming of Christ, his thousand-year reign with the Church (the millennium), followed by the judgement of the unbelievers. In such thinking, God has given the land of Canaan as an everlasting possession to the Jewish people (ICEJ, 2006a). The modern State of Israel is seen as the fulfilment of biblical prophecy, and therefore Israel's right to the biblical Promised Land is to be supported and defended. Indeed the promises of blessing and cursing in Genesis 12:3 are dependent, for Christian Zionists, upon support for Israel. The destiny of the Church is intimately bound to the destiny of Israel in two distinct and parallel covenants. The first covenant is with the physical descendants of Abraham, through Isaac not Ishmael, namely the Jews. The second covenant is with the spiritual descendants of Abraham, the Church.

Christians eagerly await the return of their messiah, Jesus, but before this can occur, certain biblical prophecies must be fulfilled, according to Christian Zionists. These prophecies, which are largely apocalyptic, are found in the books of Daniel, Zechariah, Ezekiel, Revelation, and the final two chapters of Paul's first letter to the Thessalonians. In brief, Christian Zionists interpret such passages to indicate that before the messiah returns, Jews from around the world will return to the State of Israel. The true Church, comprising only born-again Christians, living and dead, will be raptured, physically taken up to heaven to be with Christ, in an instant (1 Thessalonians 4:13–17). Those remaining on earth will experience seven years of tribulation, or overwhelming suffering, during which an Antichrist will emerge and the world will move inexorably towards a final battle that could mark the destruction of civilization, the battle of Armageddon. This will take place, according to Christian Zionists, at Mount Megiddo in Israel. Just in time, Jesus will return with all the church, those who were raptured, and win a decisive victory before establishing a reign with his church that will last one thousand years (Matthew 24:30; 2 Thessalonians 1:7; 1 Peter 1:13; Revelation 1:7). Christian Zionists, agreeing with John Hagee, interpret Revelation 19–21 to mean that, after the thousand years,

> living unbelievers and the wicked dead now raised to life will be judged at the [literal] great white throne judgement. They will then be cast into the lake of fire, while the saved [born-again Christians] will live forever with Christ in a new heaven and earth. (Hagee, 2006)

Such dispensationalist thinking dominated those churches and believers influenced by Darby, but for mainstream Christianity the late nineteenth and much of the twentieth century were dominated by liberal theology and modernism as churches sought to accommodate scientific teaching, in particular evolution, and German higher criticism. Belief in the literal truth of the Bible and its inerrancy was scorned as churches, seeking to remain relevant, adapted to modernity. Many literalists turned their back on mainstream Christianity and political involvement to pursue a separate existence, developing churches, Bible colleges, schools, evangelistic missions at home and abroad, and religious publishing companies. It was only in the 1980s that they re-emerged as a major religious and political force (Brog, 2006a: 52) within the Christian Right. Subsequently, they became the most vocal and politically active group among Christian evangelicals, and the best coordinated within the Republican Party.

The political contribution of the Christian Right is not simply motivated by the desire to promote their version of morality but is deeply influenced by eschatology that places humanity towards the end of Darby's sixth dispensation, just before Christ's imminent return. This proffers a pessimistic analysis that the condition of the world will get progressively worse until God rescues the Church, leaving the world to its fate before Christ's triumphal return. John Hagee, the pre-eminent contemporary Christian Zionist, provides ten 'prophetic' signs of the end times that believers are to anticipate. These include the 'knowledge explosion' (Daniel 12:4), plague in the Middle East (Zechariah 14:12–15), the rebirth of Israel (Isaiah 66:8–10), and the return of the Jews to Israel (Jeremiah 23:7–8). The end of 'gentile control' of Jerusalem (Luke 21:24), international instant communication (Revelation 11:3, 7–10), and days of deception (Matthew 24:4) are further signs. There will also be 'famines, and pestilences', and earthquakes (Matthew 24:7), and 'as in the days of Noah' debauchery and apostasy (Matthew 24:36–39). Hagee argues that with the State of Israel's 'rebirth' in 1948 and the reunification of Jerusalem under Israeli control from 1967, the return of Christ is imminent (Hagee, 2007: 127).

Hagee's *Jerusalem Countdown*, is but one of a burgeoning series of 'prophetic' end-time publications enjoying phenomenal sales. Hal

Lindsay's *The Late Great Planet Earth* (1970), which started the trend, has sold over 47 million copies, and was made into a film narrated by Orson Wells. Tim LaHaye and Jerry Jenkins have sold over 70 million copies of their twelve-book series *Left Behind*. The series details the events that the authors imagine, based on their literalist interpretation of the Bible, will take place after all born-again Christians and children are raptured, leaving behind all non-Christians and Jews. The books have been adapted for children and made into films and computer games, becoming a publishing phenomenon. What such authors have in common is the premillennial anticipation and embracing of wars, rumours of wars, bloodshed, violence and natural disasters. Rather than abhorring and seeking to avoid war, Christian Zionists eagerly anticipate such conflict as a sign of the approaching rapture and return of Christ. The Bible has more resonance for them than today's newspapers; all events are interpreted in the light of a premillennial dispensationalist reading of key texts.

In the Christian Zionist mindset, the events of history centre on the biblical Land of Israel. For them the Palestinian Authority territories are Judea and Samaria, Iraq is Babylon and Iran is Persia, Syria is Assyria, the European Union (EU) is the Roman Empire, and Russia becomes Gog and Magog (Ezekiel 37, 38), which will join together with the Arabs to attack Israel. The great army that will come against Israel according to Revelation 9:16 is identified variously as one or more from the UN, EU, China or Russia (Northcott, 2004: 61). The Jews must occupy the Promised Land, including the West Bank, and rebuild the Third Temple, either next to or on the site of the al-Aqsa Mosque and the Dome of the Rock, Islam's second holiest site, depending on which Christian Zionist is writing or speaking. After the rapture, the Antichrist (variously from Europe or the UN) will appear and form one world government before the battle of Armageddon and the return of Christ.

Little wonder that Christian Zionists have little confidence in the Middle East peace process Quartet, which beside the United States includes the EU, UN and Russia, each of which could produce the

Antichrist, be the harbinger of one world government, and go to war against Israel, according to Christian Zionist eschatology. Events such as 11 September 2001, Hurricane Katrina, and even Ariel Sharon's stroke are viewed through an eschatological prism, indicating either God's displeasure or the proximity of the end of the age. According to such a mindset there is nothing that can be done to alter the course of events ordained by God but, in supporting Israel, nations will receive God's blessing and approval (Genesis 12:3). If nations oppose Israel then they will be cursed by God and judged upon Jesus' return, based, according to Christian Zionists, on how they have treated Israel and the Jewish people (Hagee, 2007: 118). Hagee, LaHaye and Lindsey are not isolated voices but express views held by up to 25 million evangelicals in the United States (Wagner, 2003b).

Christian Zionism and the Israel Lobby

Mearsheimer and Walt (2006b, 2007) identify the Israel Lobby as having three component parts: Jewish Americans/AIPAC, Christian evangelicals and the neoconservatives. Of the three groupings, it is now the Christian evangelicals, or more specifically Christian Zionists, who are now in the ascendancy. The authors identify Gary Bauer, Jerry Falwell, Ralph Reed, Pat Robertson, and former majority leaders in the House of Representatives Dick Armey and Tom Delay as leaders within the Israel Lobby. With the exception of Jerry Falwell, who died in May 2007, these prominent Christian Right leaders are certainly at the forefront of promoting a pro-Israel agenda in US foreign policy. It is important to emphasize that not all members of the Christian Right are also Christian Zionists. A minority contend that the Church has replaced Israel in covenantal relationship with God; others emphasize the need for Jews to convert to Christianity; and still others see the United States as a chosen nation and relations with Israel as based on US foreign policy and strategic interests rather than biblical promises. However, it appears that almost every prominent right-wing evangelical leader is now anxious to identify with the

Zionist cause, including James Dobson, Tony Perkins, Tim and Bev LaHaye, and John Hagee.

This was not always the case. The origins of this dramatic change in the influence of Christian Zionism among the churches and American politics go back to the late 1970s, and the formation of the Moral Majority. Falwell's four organizing principles were the issues of abortion, traditional marriage, a strong US defence, and support for Israel (Brog, 2006b). The CNP has also worked for the past quarter of a century steadfastly to promote a 'moral majority' agenda, including support for Israel.

The Moral Majority's successor, the Christian Coalition, founded by Pat Robertson and led initially by Ralph Reed, has continued to maintain support for Israel as a major priority for the organization and US foreign policy. Since its foundation, there has been an exponential growth in the formation of pro-Israeli support groups and lobbies. These include Richard Hellman's Christians' Israel Public Action Campaign (CIPAC), designed as a Christian equivalent of AIPAC and the arranger of solidarity missions to Israel; Christian Friends of Israel; the Jerusalem Prayer Team; and Bridges for Peace, which was established in 1976 to support Jewish immigration to Israel. Churches including Cornerstone Church in San Antonio, Texas, Faith Bible Chapel in Arvada, Colorado, and Maranatha Chapel in San Diego have particularly emphasized the importance of blessing the Jewish people and supporting Israel, organizing annual celebrations to in the country's honour. Other organizations have emerged with Jews and Christian Zionists working alongside one another to advance the interests of Israel. These include Jews for Jesus and the International Fellowship of Christians and Jews (IFCJ), founded in 1983 by Rabbi Yechiel Eckstein. IFCJ, with its campaigning website 'Stand for Israel', seeks to strengthen American support for Israel. Its *On the Wings of an Eagle* programme assists Jewish emigration from the Former Soviet Union, Argentina and Ethiopia (Brog, 2006a: 162–3).

These disparate groupings duplicate and overlap each other's ministries and ensure that issues concerning Israel are never far from the religious–political agenda. The Christian Zionist movement came of age in February 2006 when Pastor John Hagee from Cornerstone Church brought together 400 leading Christian Right church pastors to form a Christian-style AIPAC, on a far bigger scale than anything achieved by CIPAC. Hagee, angered by widespread recrimination following Israel's destruction of Iraq's nuclear reactor site in 1981, had tried to start a similar umbrella grouping twenty-five years earlier but the venture failed to get off the ground. The 400 pastors, in 2006, committed themselves and their churches to involvement in Christians United for Israel. CUFI's stated aims are to unite Christian supporters of Israel so that they speak 'with one voice for a common cause', to establish 'rapid response' systems to lobby Capitol Hill, and to organize 'Night to Honor Israel' events 'so that the Jewish people can see and feel Christians expressing the love of God to them without a hidden agenda' (Horowitz, 2006). The hidden, or not so hidden, agenda for conservative evangelicals is the conversion of Jews to Christianity and compliance with their understanding of biblical principles. During the first eighteen months, CUFI experienced tremendous interest from evangelical groups across the United States, and 'Nights to Honor Israel' have been held at cities throughout the country, including an annual Israel summit in July, in Washington DC. The first summit attracted 3,500 people for teaching and a national Night to Honor Israel celebration, during the Feast of Tabernacles in October 2006, addressed by former CIA director Jim Woolsey.

CUFI is rapidly becoming a major player in US foreign policy, enjoying good access to the Republican Party at local and national level, Congress, the Bush administration and the 2008 GOP presidential contenders. The executive board comprises executive director David Brog, who is a former chief of staff to Senator Arlen Specter and cousin of former Israeli prime minister Ehud Barak. Brog is Jewish, with excellent contacts on Capitol Hill, and is ideally placed to represent Christian Zionists to Israel and the domestic Jewish community. Founder and national chairman John Hagee, senior pastor of the 18,000-member Cornerstone Church, San Antonio, serves on the board, together with George Morrison, senior pastor of Faith Bible Chapel, Arvada; Gary Bauer, president of American Values; Michael Little (CBN); and, until his death in May 2007, Jerry Falwell. The organization appoints regional, state and city directors and has successfully drawn in other leading members of the Christian Zionist movement. These include leading members of the 'Word of Faith' movement such as Billy Joe Dougherty and Kenneth Hagin (Oklahoma), Happy Caldwell (Arkansas) and leading proponent of the prosperity gospel Kenneth Copeland (Texas), each appointed state director in their home state.

Christian Zionists have sought to forge links with other supporters of Israel including neoconservatives and the Jewish Lobby. Neoconservative support for Israel is extensive and includes columnists such as George Will, late *Wall Street Journal* editor Robert Bartlett, and Charles Krauthammer. Former UN ambassadors Jeanne Kirkpatrick and John Bolton (although he told me he is not a neoconservative, his views are as close as to make such differences a matter of semantics) are also strong advocates for Israel.[3] Members, or former members, of the Bush administration, including Elliott Abrams, Douglas Feith, 'Scooter' Libby, Richard Perle, David Wurmser, and architect of the Iraq War and disgraced president of the World Bank Paul Wolfowitz are also advocates of Israel (Mearsheimer and Walt, 2006a: 15, 20).

Although not sharing the same ideological agenda, neoconservatives and Christian Zionists have found common cause in support of Israel. For neoconservatives, this has more to do with Israel's importance to the projection of American power in the Middle East and supporting a liberal democratic ally in the region. Neoconservatives and Christian Zionists have united around support for Likud and its leaders, especially Menachem Begin, Benjamin Netanyahu and Ariel Sharon, before the establishment of Kadima. Neoconservatives have sought a return to an aggressive, proactive first-term Reaganite foreign policy, where a strong US military is able to advance US interests around the world, by force if necessary. In *Project for the New American Century*, prominent neoconservatives advocated the imperative of American leadership in the world. Increased defence spending was considered necessary in order to

> strengthen our ties to democratic allies and to challenge regimes hostile to our interests and values ... to promote the cause of political and economic freedom abroad [and] ... to accept responsibility for America's unique role in preserving and extending an international order friendly to our security, our prosperity, and our principles. (PNAC, 1997)

Israel is considered one of those allies and an indispensable part of an international order conducive to American interests. The statement of principles was signed by twenty-five prominent neoconservatives, including many who would play a prominent part in implementing US foreign policy in the Middle East, such as Dick Cheney, Donald Rumsfeld, Paul Wolfowitz, Elliott Abrams, Paula Dobriansky and Zalmay Khalilzad. Also on the list was the name of former GOP presidential candidate Gary Bauer, who helped develop links with the Christian Right. The neoconservative declaration of faith was preceded by publication of a strategy document prepared for Benjamin Netanyahu, the Likud candidate in the 1996 Israeli elections. The document, *A Clean Break: A New Strategy for Securing the Realm*, was prepared by the Institute for Advanced Strategic and Political Studies (IASPS), whose members included leading neoconservatives Richard Perle, James Colbert, Charles Fairbanks Jr, Douglas Feith, Robert Loewenberg, David and Meyrav Wurmser. The report advocated abandoning the Oslo Peace Accords, undermining Arafat's role among the Palestinians, striking Syrian military targets in Syria and Lebanon, removing Saddam Hussein from power in Iraq, and abandoning Israel's 'socialist foundations' (IASPS, 1996). Donald Wagner argues that such a strategy helped achieve victory for Netanyahu and set the modus operandi for successive Likud administrations (Wagner, 2003c).

Christian Zionists have little problem supporting neoconservatives' call for an aggressive foreign policy based on 'military strength and moral clarity' providing Israel's interests are advanced (PNAC, 1997).

Such a stance is rather more problematic when it comes to building relationships with a Jewish Lobby where the 'moral clarity' of neoconservatives and the Christian Right are anathema. Traditionally the Jewish community in America is liberal on the touchstone issues for the Christian Right, including homosexuality, abortion, separation of church and state, and overwhelmingly votes for the Democratic Party. Many remain suspicious of the Christian Right's agenda in supporting Israel and seeking to cooperate with Jewish organizations. After centuries of persecution, mistrust, claims of replacement theology, the Holocaust, and evangelistic campaigns to convert them to Christianity, many American Jews remain to be convinced of Christian Zionism's philo-Semitism. There is concern that anti-Semitism has been a feature of Christian Zionist thought and that Jews are seen as pawns to be manipulated in fulfilment of dubious biblical promises that will hasten the Second Coming of Christ (Zunes, 2004). Any affinity, or concern, for the Jewish people can be perceived as purely instrumental in order to achieve the return of a Christian messiah and either the conversion or punishment of those Jews who have not recognized him.

John Hagee is accused of blaming the Jews for anti-Semitism, suggesting that the Holocaust was part of a divine plan to force Jews to move to Israel, and that many will be killed in the apocalyptic war that results in the return of Jesus. Born-again Christians have been raptured before this eagerly awaited event (Wilson, 2007). In his bestselling book *Jerusalem Countdown* Hagee does indeed write that

> Their own rebellion had birthed the seed of anti-Semitism that would arise and bring destruction to them for centuries to come … it rises from the judgement of God upon his rebellious chosen people.
>
> … No one could see the horror of the Holocaust coming, but the force and fear of Hitler's Nazis drive the Jewish people back to the only home God intended for the Jews to have – Israel. (Hagee, 2007: 9, 133)

Anti-Defamation League national director Abraham Foxman, although welcoming the support of Christian Zionists, recognizes that they have very different agendas. Foxman suspects Hagee, the late Jerry Falwell and Robertson of having ulterior motives in supporting Israel to do with proselytizing to Jews, supporting the return of Jews to the Jewish homeland to hasten the Second Coming, leading to the war of Gog and Magog, and even seeking support from Jews for their social agenda (Zahavy, 2006a). Gershom Gorenberg, author of *End of Days*, sums up his interpretation of Christian Zionism:

> The Jews die or convert. As a Jew, I can't feel very comfortable with the affections of somebody who looks forward to that scenario … They don't love real Jewish people. They love us as characters in their story, in their play, and that's not who we are, and we never auditioned for that part, and the play is not one that ends up good for us. If you listen to the drama they're describing, essentially it's a five-act play in which the Jews disappear in the fourth act. (CBS, 2003)

For liberal Jews the Christian Right support for Israel is problematic because of its social agenda domestically and in Israel. Christian Zionists are seen by them as being an obstacle to the peace process in their forming of alliances with right-wing Israeli politicians and supporting the settlements programme politically and financially. In rejecting the Land for Peace strategy, encouraging the development of illegal settlements in the West Bank and Gaza (until 2004), and limiting successive US administrations' willingness to exercise leverage over Israel to achieve peace, US Christian support for Israel is seen as part of the problem rather than the solution. For others, including Axe Foxman and David Harris, executive director of the America Jewish Committee, Israel needs all the support it can get, and although they remain aware of Christian Zionist proselytizing tendencies and eschatological motivation that support is welcome. For Harris, the American Jewish community cannot afford the luxury of choosing its friends, for 'The end of time may come tomorrow, but Israel hangs in the balance today' (Broadway, 2004).

Christian Zionists are aware of this suspicion and great efforts have been made to reassure the Jewish community, and AIPAC in particular, of the genuineness of their philo-Semitism. Gary Bauer, co-founder of Stand for Israel, has led efforts to reach out to AIPAC. In 2002, Stand for Israel held a conference and lobbying session the day after AIPAC's annual conference, inviting many of the same speakers and pledging support for Ariel Sharon's polices (Wagner, 2003c). The key speaker, Gary Bauer was invited the following year to address the AIPAC conference. A similar invitation was extended to John Hagee in 2006. CUFI appointed a Jewish executive director specifically to build bridges and persuade sceptics that the organization was sincere and willing to tone down its evangelistic impulse to convert Jews. David Brog has addressed numerous meetings and given many interviews to the Jewish media on behalf of his organization denying anti-Semitism and conversion objectives. For Brog, Christian Zionists are righteous gentiles in the same tradition as Corrie ten Boom and other Christians who helped Jews during the Holocaust because of their recognition that they were God's chosen people (Brog 2006a, 2006b, 2006c; Glazov, 2006; Zahavy, 2006b).

Over time many Jewish doubts about the sincerity of the Christian Zionist movement have been assuaged, largely based on the latter's willingness to vocalize and campaign in support of Israel, contribute financially to Israel, cooperate in alliances between Christians and Jews, and also due to the attitude of the Begin, Netanyahu and Sharon governments. The relationship between Likud and American Christian Zionists began in 1977 following the election of Menachem Begin as Israeli prime minister. Begin started to reach out to the Christian Right in America at the same time as they were beginning to merge as a force in US politics. Begin invited Jerry Falwell to Israel on an official visit in 1978. A year later, Falwell received a Lear jet as a gift from the Israeli government, in recognition of his friendship towards them around the time that the Moral Majority came into being (Theocracy Watch, 2005; Broadway, 2004). Over the following three decades, conservative Israeli leaders have continued to reach out to the Christian Right. Former Israeli Prime Minister Benjamin Netanyahu is a regular visitor and speaker at Christian

Zionist conferences and to leaders in the United States. Netanyahu addressed the 2007 CUFI Washington summit by video link and spoke at the Value Voters summit in October 2007. Ariel Sharon also frequently met with Christian Right leaders both in the USA and during their regular visits to Israel.

The Israeli tourism industry sponsored hundreds of evangelical pastors on free trips to Israel to gain their political support and encourage them to return with Christian tour parties. Timothy Weber recounts that the Israeli government sent Yona Malachy of the Department of Religious Affairs to study Christian fundamentalism in America. Malachy worked closely with Christian Zionist groups, which greatly enjoyed the attention in the 1980s, and reciprocated by taking increasingly pro-Israeli stands as they began seeking to influence the American political process (Weber, 2004). Pat Robertson, who, like Jerry Falwell and John Hagee, has made scores of trips to Israel, was honoured in February 2004 by Israeli tourism minister Benny Elon for 'saving Israel's tourism from bankruptcy' after encouraging hundreds of thousands of evangelicals to visit Israel each year, despite US government warnings about the terrorist threat following 9/11 (Broadway, 2004).

Christian Zionist churches and parachurch organizations, including the National Leadership Conference for Israel, hold regular conferences, large-scale rallies, and national advertisement campaigns in support of Israel. Significant financial assistance has been given to encourage Jewish settlement in the Occupied Territories. The Jerusalem Prayer Team and Christian Friends of Israeli Communities, which twins evangelical churches with West Bank settlements, support about one-third of all settlements financially through individual donations. Other groups, including IFCJ and Bridges for Peace, support emigration from the former Soviet Union and other parts of the world, and pay for education programmes, flights and resettlement costs. Yechiel Eckstein estimated in 2004 that evangelical contributions to Israel could exceed $25 million per annum (Weber 2004; Broadway, 2004; Mayer, 2004). John Hagee's Cornerstone Church has donated millions of dollars, and CBN hundreds of thousands of dollars, to support Jewish immigration to Israel as Christian Zionists have demonstrated a practical commitment to Israel (Brog, 2006a: 165). We next consider how they seek to utilize this support to achieve their objectives.

Modus Operandi

The Christian Right have become well aware of their importance in Washington as one of the main political players. They represent a core constituency of between 40 and 75 million (McMahon, 2006) and account for around 40 per cent of George Bush's vote in the 2004 elections. Some 74 per cent of white evangelicals voted Republican in 2004, and 72 per cent in the mid-term elections two years later, despite Iraq, and the Haggard and Abramoff scandals. Through the churches and television ministries, they are an organized group, which can be and is regularly mobilized. Unlike many other groups, right-wing Christians can be depended on to vote. They have been prepared to throw their considerable financial weight behind favourite causes, of which support for Israel is becoming an increasingly important one. The Christian Right spread their message from the pulpits and across the airwaves each week. CBN claims a domestic audience of 80 million and TBN some 92 million viewers. James Dobson's *Focus on the Family* claims to have 1 million people on its mailing list and a potential radio audience of 220 million. Ralph Reed, co-founder of Stand for Israel, summed up this new confidence, stating that 'Christians have the potential to be the most effective constituency influencing foreign policy since the end of the Cold War … They are shifting the center of gravity in the pro-Israel community to become a more conservative and Republican phenomenon' (Firestone, 2002).

Christian Zionists have tended to base their modus operandi on AIPAC, as one of the most successful special-interest groups in America. This includes lobbying on Capitol Hill, in the White House and even in state congresses. The objective is to ensure that Israel is the single most important consideration at all levels of government. Politicians are nurtured, supported, reviled and opposed in direct relation to their support for Israel. A conditioning process is developed, whereby a politician is unable to approach issues that relate to Israel without first considering how a considerable number of her or his most vociferous constituents are going to react. No peace proposals can be debated on their own merits without considering whether support for any initiative could lose votes. The Christian Right's thorough infiltration of the Republican Party means that the party's electoral fortunes depend on Christian Right finance and foot soldiers to win elections. The pro-Israel lobby operate a pincer movement, with AIPAC able to harness Democrat votes in support of Israel and the Christian Right doing the same with Republican ones. Supporters of Israel, on both sides of the political divide, will be judged by the movement not just on moral compass issues but on the degree of commitment to Israel. Politicians found guilty of taking a neutral stance or pro-Palestinian position on US policy in the Middle East are likely to find themselves targeted and vilified, while their electoral opponents benefit from extra funding, media coverage and campaign workers courtesy of the Christian Right.

Politicians' support for Israel is monitored and recorded through scorecard voting, established by Christian Right organizations including the Christian Coalition, FRC and Eagle Forum. Voting records are disseminated to churches and constituents to inform voters whether or not their representative is 'on message'. For those politicians supportive of Israel, they have the benefit of a steady stream of campaign workers, interns and volunteers from Christian Right colleges and universities, including Patrick Henry College, Liberty University, Bob Roberts and Regent University. Christian Right groups have encouraged members to become staff members on Capitol Hill to help increase their influence. The strength of the Christian Zionist constituency is demonstrated by the holding of conferences, summits and rallies in support of Israel in Washington DC and major cities across the USA.

CUFI and Stand for Israel have led the way in preparing rapid-response networks among their supporters to react immediately to any issues arising that might adversely affect their agenda for Israel. At the click of a mouse supporters can be mobilized to email, telephone, fax and write to politicians expressing their approval or disapproval of proposals or actions relating to Israel. At various times throughout the year constituents can be called upon to lobby their congressional representative or senator in person. The annual CUFI Washington–Israel summit culminates in a mass lobby of Congress when thousands of constituents gently remind their representatives that their continued support and 'God's blessing' are dependent upon their attitude towards Israel and the Jewish people.

Christian Right access and influence also extend to the White House. George W. Bush had been his father's point man to evangelicals in the 1992 election and this constituency became his base constituency when he assumed office in 2001. Karl Rove had developed relations with the Christian Right to secure Bush's re-election and, along with Tim Goeglein and Elliott Abrams, formed a triumvirate of insiders liaising with the Christian Right over social/values legislation, faith-based initiatives and Israel. Leading members of the Christian Right were granted privileged access to the president and his advisers, being consulted in person or by conference call on steps in the habitually stalling peace process. The Christian Right, who under previous Democrat and Republican administrations, with the exception of the Reagan administration, had been political pariahs, were now welcome in the corridors of power, where they used their position to argue strongly for unequivocal support for Israel.

The Christian Zionist lobby seeks to control the debate and agenda on Israel. This control extends to the media, where the majority of radio stations are unashamedly conservative and the religious stations overwhelmingly right-wing evangelical and allow no room for dissenting opinions on Israel. Newspapers that run stories and op-ed pieces criticizing Israel are inundated with telephone calls and emails of complaint and threats within just a few hours. Christian Zionists complement similar campaigns by AIPAC and use advocacy and disinformation to 'correct' articles or reports they disagree with. The Christian Right media willingly provide access to leading members of the Republican Party and conduct supportive interviews, which serve propaganda rather than journalistic purposes. Christian Zionists also have the ability to spend vast sums of money on advertising campaigns as they seek to influence public and elite opinion in support of Israel.

The movement is interested in perpetual support for Israel and carefully monitors academic discourse concerning the country. Students are encouraged to inform on lecturers and teachers who offer objective or dissenting views on Israel. Campus debate has become increasingly fractious on issues relating to Israel because of the vilification of opponents of Christian Zionism. At a recent conference held in the United Kingdom, attended by the author, a leading US academic refused to answer a question on Israel, afterwards explaining that he was hopeful of attaining a position in an incoming Democratic administration and that if he made any criticism of Israel his nomination would be opposed in the Senate. The home-schooling movement and evangelical universities enable dissenting views on Israel to be filtered and graduates trained for public service therefore take distorted thinking on the Middle East conflict and Israel into the next generation of policy planners.

The Impact of the Christian Right on Israel Policy

The Christian Right understandably rejoiced when George W. Bush assumed the presidency: they believed that they had their man in the White House. However, the reality of office and the responsibility to represent all the people rather than just white evangelicals inevitably created tensions between Bush and the Christian Right, and over time generated a sense of disappointment. This has been most vocally expressed with regard to Israel and the administration's attempts to resurrect a peace process. There are theological tensions, as

Bush's nationalism clashes with Christian Zionism. Michael Northcott considers Bush a premillennial dispensationalist because of his close association with Christian Zionist preachers Franklin Graham and James Robison. This association, Northcott claims, will allow Israel to reoccupy Palestine and rebuild the Temple (Northcott, 2004: 67–8). Unfortunately for Christian Zionists, Bush shows little sign of being committed to their cause and has endeavoured to pursue a Land for Peace strategy with a generalized commitment to a two-state solution with a viable Palestinian state. Many on the Christian Right have variously interpreted the Israel/Palestine Road Map as a betrayal and going against God's will.

Pat Robertson summed up the feelings of many co-religionists when addressing viewers of his *700 Club*:

> You know the prophet Joel speaks about those 'who divide my land'; that there is a curse on them. I think I would walk very, very softly if I were George Bush in this regard ... The crunch will come when he tries to divide Jerusalem ... I think he's going to incur the wrath of the Lord if he does that.

Robertson also suggested that Ariel Sharon's stroke and coma might have been the result of God's displeasure at the withdrawal from Gaza. Gary Bauer and the late Ed McAteer (Religious Roundtable) have spoken in favour of Eretz Israel and support the transfer of Palestinians out of the West Bank (Durham, 2004: 153). Ethnic cleansing may be on the agenda of Christian Zionists but certainly not of the administration. Here, there is a sharp distinction between Bush's Christian nationalism – his first priority as a Christian is the advancement of US objectives, as he understands them – and Christian Zionist prioritization of Israel and the fulfilment of end-time prophecy. Other differences emerge in attitudes towards Islam. Bush and Condoleezza Rice have emphasized that 'Islam is a peaceful religion' and distinguish between 'good' and 'bad' Muslims, whereas Christian Zionists baulk at making such a distinction and use the term 'Islamofascism' as part of an agenda which owes much to Huntington's clash-of-civilizations thesis. On a visit to England in November 2003, President Bush stated his belief that Christians and Muslims worship the same God, a view that was dismissed by Richard Land, who recalls telling a reporter from the *New York Times*: 'I appreciate that the President's making faith a part of his administration and a part of his policies but he is after all the commander-in-chief, not the theologian-in-chief and in this instance he is wrong.'[4]

Christian Zionist hostility to Islam is endemic and reflected in sermons and speeches by leading members of the movement. Franklin Graham described Islam as 'a very evil and wicked religion',[5] and Pat Robertson complained that 'when people talk about Islam as a religion of peace – it just isn't. This is baloney.'[6] Jerry Falwell described Muhammad as 'a terrorist',[7] while Jerry Vines, past president of the Southern Baptist Churches, considers the Prophet as 'a demon possessed paedophile' (Salpeter, 2002). Inside the administration first-term attorney general John Ashcroft explained his view of the difference between Islam and Christianity: 'Islam is a religion in which God requires you to send your son to die for him. Christianity is a faith in which God sends his Son to die for you' (Eggen, 2002). Such perceived differences have had an impact on attitudes towards the Middle East and account for the pressure Christian Zionists have sought to administer in order to achieve their objectives.

Under the Oslo Accords, Israel was to withdraw from areas of the West Bank, which were to be administered by the Palestinian Authority. However, in April 2002 the Israeli military launched an offensive in the West Bank. Bush immediately ordered Israel to withdraw, whereupon he experienced the full might of the Christian Zionist lobby for the first time. Jerry Falwell organized supporters to flood the White House with over 100,000 emails complaining about Bush's order and insisting on Israel's right to take whatever action it felt appropriate. Tom DeLay, Dick Armey and Trent Lott set out from Capitol Hill to admonish Bush in person, and, against State Department advice, Congress overwhelmingly adopted a resolution supporting Israel's actions and blaming Palestinians exclusively for the violence by a vote of 352 : 21 in the House and 94 : 2 in the Senate. The administration did an immediate U-turn and made no further objections to Israeli actions.

In the build-up to the Iraq War, Bush was desperate to receive support from at least some Arab states and launched a new Middle East peace initiative setting out his objective for separate Israeli and Palestinian states. The Road Map was a time-delineated process for achieving a peace settlement premissed on the unilateral abandonment of land occupied by Israel since 1967 in pursuit of a Palestinian state, and the trade-off was land for peace. Former ambassador Dennis Ross, President Clinton's Middle East peace negotiator, told me that he felt there was a trade-off, designed to appeal to the Christian Right, between the Road Map, promising to create a Palestinian state, which they would not like, and excluding Yasser Arafat as an interlocutor, which they did like:

> There were rumours that some of the Christian Right had a chance to look at the speech before it came out. And, in a sense, if you look at that speech, it embraced a Palestinian state but it also invasively said you can't deal with Arafat, you need a new Palestinian leadership. So you could argue that that part of the speech was Tom DeLay's imprint ... At least according to the rumour, he was allowed to go over the speech. I don't know if it's true. DeLay would have liked the 'no' to Arafat, might not have liked the idea of the Palestinian statelet but it's inconceivable that taking the tough positions on Arafat would be embraced because it said we wouldn't be dealing with the Palestinians at all. Basically, reform for the Palestinians before there could be such a state.[8]

The White House, nonetheless, received 50,000 postcards from core supporters protesting against the Road Map; thereafter George Bush remained silent on the subject, allowing all the deadlines to be passed without resolution. A similar scenario ensued after Bush criticized the Sharon government for its programme of targeted assassinations against Palestinian leaders in 2003. Again, thousands of emails, letters and telegrams flooded the White House as the rapid-response capacity of Christian Zionist organizations went into action. Within twenty-four hours, the administration had changed its approach and refused to comment on the assassinations of the wheelchair-bound Sheikh Yassin and Rantisi in 2004. Since 2003, the administration has made neither implicit nor explicit criticisms of Israeli actions.

The administration learnt the lessons of these encounters and increasingly sought to take Christian Zionists into their confidence and reassure them of the administration's support for Israel. When Ariel Sharon decided to overturn the Road Map and unilaterally withdraw from Gaza, while increasing and strengthening settlements in the West Bank, the White House took Christian Zionists into their confidence. A special meeting was called with their leaders, Elliott Abrams and Tim Goeglein, to reassure them that Gaza was not part of biblical Israel and that the administration supported Sharon's actions in that Israel would enjoy the mutual objective of becoming more secure (Perlstein, 2004). Although many Christian Zionists objected, it was left to Pat Robertson and a few others to raise public objections, but no coordinated campaign challenged the administration's position.

Support for Sharon and hostility towards Palestinian leader Yasser Arafat were shared by the Christian Right and the Bush administration. This dual position strengthened the hand of Sharon and weakened that of the Palestinians in stalled negotiations. The USA pressured the Palestinian Authority into removing Arafat as interlocutor and replacing him in peace negotiations with the more amenable Mahmoud Abbas (Abu Mazen). Arafat was held as a virtual prisoner in his compound by the Israeli military, from the time of the Israeli occupation of Jenin until his death in 2004, without any US criticism. Yasser Arafat's refusal to accept the previous administration's peace plan led to the rejection of his role as an interlocutor with Israel. Instead, Abbas was feted by the USA and Israel as their chosen representative for the Palestinian people, first as prime minister and then following Arafat's death as leader of Fatah and president of the Palestinian Authority. Abbas was seen as being far more amenable to US interests and more likely than opposition groups to agree to peace on inferior terms than that offered to Arafat by Barak and Clinton in 2000.

As part of a wider neoconservative democratization strategy the Bush administration encouraged democratic elections in the Palestinian Authority in order to strengthen the position of Abbas. Before the elections AIPAC and Christian Zionists encouraged congressional calls for Hamas not to be allowed to participate in the elections. On 15 December 2005, a Sense of Congress resolution insisted that 'no US assistance should be provided to the Palestinian Authority if any representative political party holding a majority of parliamentary seats within the Palestinian Authority maintains a position calling for the destruction of Israel'. The resolution passed with 418 votes for and only 1 vote against. Hamas, however, won the elections, taking 44 per cent of the popular vote.

Whereas Arafat sought to negotiate from a position of strength, Abbas was willing to negotiate on Israeli terms, promising to reign in opposition to Israel, control violence, and agree to abide by the Road Map. Palestinian resistance to Israel was seen as particularly crucial in Sharon's decision to withdraw unilaterally from Gaza in 2004. The credit for that retreat was given to Hamas rather than Fatah and helped to bring about their victory in the parliamentary elections. The electorate rejected the failed peace strategy of the Road Map, which had brought little respite to Palestinian suffering or progress towards a two-state solution and contributed to the corruption of Fatah. The refusal of America, Israel and their allies to recognize the Hamas victory in the most democratic elections to take place in an Arab country, and their imposition of economic and political sanctions and refusal to hand over tax revenues collected by Israel on behalf of the Palestinian Authority, further polarized opinion in the Occupied Territories and increased support for Hamas.

The United States adopted a policy intended to strengthen Israeli security and marginalize radical Islamic tendencies among the Palestinians. There would be no contact with or financial assistance given to Hamas until they recognized the State of Israel, renounced violence and accepted previous agreements. US financial and military support would go to Abbas and Fatah as they attempted to suppress Hamas in Gaza and build a unity government that could curtail Palestinian violence and specifically attacks on Israel. Elliott Abrams, and Vice President Cheney's national security advisers David Wurmser and John Hannah sought to organize a hard coup against Hamas by supplying arms and training to Fatah activists and providing $86.4 million for Abbas's security detail under Mohammed Dahlan. Rice, Elliott and US envoy to the Middle East peace process David Welch actively promoted a strategy which sought to encourage the military defeat of Hamas and their removal from power by urging new elections or the formation of a government without Hamas representation (Perry, 2007: 1–2; Perry and Woodward, 2007; de Soto, 2007).

The Bush administration was determined to bring down the Hamas government from the outset. Outgoing UN special envoy to the Middle East Peace Process, Alvaro de Soto, in an end-of-mission report leaked to the *Guardian* newspaper, was scathing about America's contribution to the deepening crisis in the Occupied Territories. De Soto reveals a policy geared to defend Israeli interests by bullying other members of the Quartet into disproportionately bringing pressure to bear on Palestinians to abide by the Road Map while allowing Israel to change facts on the ground, without reproach. Quartet envoy and former president of the World Bank James Wolfensohn was frustrated in his attempts to move the peace process forward by the State Department. His attempts to broker agreement on access and movement in the Palestinian Territories were 'intercepted – some would say, hijacked – at the last minute by US envoys and ultimately Rice herself' (de Soto, 2007: 7).

Following the 2006 parliamentary elections, de Soto recalls that Welch and Abrams threatened that if the UN did not review all projects and programmes with the Palestinian Authority 'it could have repercussions when UN budget deliberations took place on Capitol Hill' (de Soto, 2007: 18). Despite the reservations of the other three members of the Quartet, Israel was encouraged to withhold the Palestinian tax revenue necessary to provide services and pay wages for government employees, including teachers, doctors and police. According to de Soto, US representatives told other envoys that they did not want Israel to transfer the revenue owed (de Soto, 2007: 20, 33).

Following its election victory, Hamas sought to form a government of national unity, along the lines of the one formed for a short period after the Mecca agreement in March 2007. The USA made it known to Fatah and independents that they wanted Hamas to be obliged to try and govern on their own, while pressuring Abbas to call fresh elections and take Hamas on militarily and politically (de Soto, 2007: 21, 23). The combination of economic and political sanctions on Hamas and supplying weaponry to Fatah resulted in the descent into civil war in Gaza, as an inevitable and not unwelcome – from a Bush administration perspective – consequence of their policy. Welch twice mentioned at envoys' meetings in Washington DC, before the Mecca summit to resolve the conflict in Gaza, that he liked 'this violence' because it meant that 'other Palestinians are resisting Hamas' – a cavalier disregard of the human catastrophe that had erupted in Gaza (de Soto, 2007: 21).

All the while the Bush administration failed to put any pressure on Israel to take steps towards peace, to release political prisoners, or to ease its oppressive policies restricting the movement and civil liberties of Palestinians. With a lack of progress on peace negotiations, humanitarian suffering as a result of the economic restrictions placed on Hamas and later unity government, the situation in the Palestinian Authority inevitably polarized between warring factions. Hamas eventually seized de facto control of Gaza in June 2007, and Abbas responded by replacing the unity government led by Haniyeh with one approved by the United States and Israel. The immediate reaction of the Israeli and American governments was to welcome this undemocratic measure and release funding to support Abbas and Fatah in an attempt to ostracize Hamas from the electorate. At the time of writing, it appears that such an administration, undergirded by US and Israeli support, is unlikely to enjoy popular legitimacy and achieve any peace settlement that includes a contiguous Palestinian state on the West Bank and Gaza with East Jerusalem as its capital.

As the Palestinian Authority has spiralled into crisis, the Christian Right's and Israel's claim that there is no partner for peace has become a self-fulfilling prophecy. The objectives of Christian Zionists are being achieved with the American government 'blessing Israel' by not pressuring it to concede land, abandon settlements, dismantle the separation wall, or deal equitably with Palestinians in East Jerusalem. The Christian Right continue to encourage and support efforts by Congress to persuade the president to move the US embassy from Tel Aviv to Jerusalem, as the indivisible capital of Israel. Throughout the Clinton and Bush presidencies Congress has passed such resolutions only to have them overturned on a six-monthly basis by presidential veto, until such time as a peace settlement has been reached. In the meantime, Israel continues to be a major recipient of US aid despite being one of the most prosperous countries in the region; at same time, the Palestinian Authority is unable to pay its employees' wages.

In the summer of 2006, following the seizure of three Israeli soldiers by Hezbollah in a cross-border raid, Israel launched a devastating pre-planned attack on Southern Lebanon and Beirut. The fighting lasted from 12 July until a UN-brokered ceasefire came into place five weeks later, after at least 1,100 Lebanese and 43 Israeli civilians had been killed, and 900,000 fled their homes (BBC News, 2006). While much of the world called for an end to the slaughter, the Bush administration resisted any attempts to resolve the conflict, to enable Israel sufficient time to destroy Hezbollah and, in so doing, Syrian and Iranian influence in Lebanon. The Israeli assault coincided with a CUFI summit in support of Israel in Washington DC, the participants of which lobbied Congress and the White House. David Brog claims that

> [T]he arrival in Washington at that juncture of thousands of Christians who came for one issue and one issue only, to support Israel, sent a very important message to the Administration and the Congress, and I think helped persuade people that they should allow Israel some more time. (Blumenthal, 2006)

The House of Representatives passed Resolution 921 on 20 July 2006 'condemning the recent attacks against the State of Israel, holding terrorists and their state sponsors accountable for such attacks, supporting Israel's right to defend itself, and for other purposes'. The resolution passed with 410 votes for and just 8 against. Israel's inability to defeat Hezbollah and the experience of hundreds of rockets landing in northern Israel undermined the Kadima government of Ehud Olmert. Christian Zionists believe that such a setback is temporary and is but a prelude to future confrontation and the re-election of their friend Benjamin Netanyahu as Israeli premier.

The war against Hezbollah was seen by many in the Bush administration as a proxy war against Iran, Hezbollah's main ally and benefactor. Iran is seen by Israel and the Christian Right as being the single greatest threat to Israel's existence. Statements by President Mahmoud Ahmadinejad calling for Israel to 'be wiped off the face of the map', the hosting of a Holocaust-denial conference, and the development of a nuclear programme all deepen Israeli insecurity and the call for action in support of Israel from the Israel Lobby in America. Iranian sponsorship of Hezbollah, Hamas, Islamic Jihad, the al-Aqsa Martyrs Brigades, and the Popular Front for the Liberation of Palestine–General Command, and support for Shiite militias in Iraq, make the country the number-one foreign enemy of the Christian Right. The US experience in Iraq and Afghanistan means that the Bush administration has, at the time of writing, been unwilling to take military action to weaken Iranian influence in the region. The Christian Right, along with neoconservatives, have been particularly bellicose in suggesting military action against Iran to protect Israel and US interests in the region.

President Bush met with a number of Christian Right leaders, including James Dobson, early in May 2007 to maintain support for his 'War on Terror' strategy. Dobson left the meeting seeking to convince his supporters that the USA faced the real possibility of an Iranian nuclear, chemical or biological attack that could destroy one or even ten cities. Dobson argued that somebody should be saying:

'We are being threatened and we are going to meet this with force – whatever's necessary' (Blumenthal, 2007b). Like Dobson, John Hagee accuses Ahmadinejad of being a new Hitler and urges early and decisive military action against Iranian nuclear facilities, even though he predicts this will lead to Iranian 'suitcase' and 'dirty' nuclear bombs in major cities (Hagee, 2007: 5, 52). According to Hagee, America or Israel must launch a pre-emptive strike against Iran because for 'Israel to wait is to risk committing national suicide' (Hagee, 2007: 53). For Hagee, confrontation with Iran is but another sign of the end times and to be welcomed as such, another opportunity to please God by protecting Israel.

> There is a clear and present danger to America and Israel for a nuclear Iran. There will soon be a nuclear blast in the Middle East that will transform the road to Armageddon into a racetrack. America and Israel will either take down Iran, or Iran will become nuclear and take down America and Israel. (Hagee, 2007: 4–5)

CUFI has sought to influence the administration through expressing concern to individual members of the administration, presidential candidates and Congress. Members lobbied congressmen and senators in support of the Iran Counter-Proliferation Act of 2007 to tighten sanctions on Iran and prevent US nuclear cooperation with Russia, which has assisted Iran's nuclear programme. The organization also lobbied vigorously and successfully at state level to prohibit state investment in Iran. Florida legislators unanimously passed the Protecting Florida's Investments Act[9] as did their Californian counterparts in approving the California Public Divest from Iran Act.[10] At the CUFI Washington Summit 2007, Hagee described President Ahmadinejad as the 'head of the beast' of radical Islam. For Hagee it is '1938 all over again and Ahmadinejad is Hitler'. He warned that Iran was 'working night and day' and will not respond to diplomacy, but rather is 'stalling for time' before attacking Israel and America. With his voice rising to a crescendo, Hagee declared, 'He [Ahmadinejad] will do it!' For Hagee, the only option for America and Israel is to consider a pre-emptive strike against Iran.[11]

Although Christian Zionists enjoy support in the White House, that influence does not extend to the highest levels within the State Department. It is the State Department, however, rather than the White House or Pentagon, that is conducting US policy on Iran at the time of writing. Former ambassador John Bolton, when interviewed, dismissed Christian Right influence on Iran:

> Right now, their influence on the State Department is practically nil. So, they still have an influence on the president, but I believe, for example, that we need to have military force an option if Iran isn't going to stop. I can't see any reason why they are going to stop, so I think military force, certainly regime change, as a practical matter, is definitely something that has to be a priority. But whether they will influence Bush to the point where he changes the policy the State Department is pursuing is, I think – obviously, we can't know the answer – but I don't see any signs of it happening.[12]

The Christian Right have experienced some setbacks of their own, with the fallout from the Foley, Abramoff and Haggard scandals costing them dearly in terms of lost seats and influence in the 2006 mid-term elections. Leading Christian Zionist supporters, including Tom DeLay, Dick Armey, Bill Frist and Rick Santorum, are no longer in Congress, and Ralph Reed was humiliated in his attempt to become lieutenant governor of Georgia. Prominent religious leaders including Ed McAteer, Jerry Falwell and James Kennedy have died. The end of George Bush's presidency will bring to a close an era when the Christian Right have one of their own in the White House. However, an incoming Republican president would still be beholden to the Christian Right should this be the outcome in 2008.

All the leading GOP contenders courted the Christian Right. John McCain, despite accusing Jerry Falwell and Pat Robertson of being 'agents of intolerance' in 2000, built bridges with them, including delivering the commencement address in 2006 at Falwell's Liberty University and mobilizing religious supporters behind an 'Americans of Faith for McCain' campaign (Holley, 2007; Cooperman, 2007). McCain had breakfast with John Hagee on 29 January 2007 to seek his support for his candidacy and later turned up at the Middle East briefing sessions of CUFI's 2007 Washington Summit. Hagee reported to CUFI members and supporters that McCain's comments on Israel 'are on target! He gets it!'[13] McCain was endorsed by Hagee and Rod Parsley, one of the new generation of televangelist Christian Right leaders and a CUFI regional director.

Following the loss of both Houses of Congress to the Democrats, Bush and Rice sought to shore up support for their policy in Iraq and the Middle East more generally by seeking to reactivate the Middle East peace process. The State Department views the Palestinian–Israeli conflict as a major obstacle to persuading Arab states to support its policies in Iraq. Secretary of State Rice was particularly anxious to resurrect the stalled process but her efforts have been thwarted by a combination of the Jewish and Christian Zionist lobbies. Both groups, along with Israeli officials, see Elliott Abrams, deputy national security adviser, rather than Condoleezza Rice as the main point of contact with the administration on the Middle East. Abrams informed Jewish communal and Republican leaders that Rice's frequent trips to the region were simply to keep European and moderate Arab countries 'on the team'. He is also reported to have told both groups that Bush would act as 'an emergency brake' to prevent Israel being forced into a deal and that any progress would be very limited (Guttman, 2007). Former UN envoy Alvaro de Soto decries 'the tendency that exists among US policy-makers and even amongst the sturdiest of politicians to cower before any hint of Israeli displeasure, and to pander shamelessly before Israeli-linked audiences' (de Soto, 2007: 48).

Throughout his presidency George Bush has been very supportive of Israel both financially and in not applying pressure to bring about a peace settlement that would lead to a withdrawal from all the territory occupied since the Six Day War, including East Jerusalem. In the first six years of the Bush presidency, declared American assistance to Israel amounted to over $17 billion (see Table 7.1). As previously mentioned, a ten-year agreement signed in 2007 provides Israel with a further $30 billion in military assistance. Over the

TABLE 7.1 US grant assistance to Israel, FY 2001–06 ($ million)

Year	Military	Economic	Jewish refugee resettlement	American schools & hospitals	Other grants	Total
2001	1975.6	838.2	60.0	2.3		2876.1
2002	2040.0	720.0	60.0		28.0	2848.0
2003	3086.4	596.1	59.6			3742.1
2004	2147.3	477.2	49.7	3.2	9.9	2687.3
2005	2202.2	407.1	50.0			2659.3
2006	2280.0	237.6	50.0			2567.6
Total	13731.5	3276.2	329.3	5.5	37.9	17380.4

Source: adapted from Clyde R. Mark, 'Israel U.S. Foreign Assistance', Congressional Research Service, 12 July 2004; and US State Department, USAID, Congressional Budget Justification for FY2007 Foreign Operations, March 2007.

course of every administration since 1967, the Israeli government has sought to change facts on the ground by extending and developing settlements in the occupied Palestinian Territories. These have experienced exponential growth since the Road Map was unveiled, without condemnation from the Bush administration, creating a situation in which a contiguous Palestinian state becomes impossible.

Security cooperation, including Israeli advice on counterinsurgency operations in Iraq, has grown stronger as the War on Terror has progressed. The Bush administration and Republican and Democratic Congresses have proved trusted friends of Israel. The 107th to 110th Congresses have passed numerous resolutions expressing support for a two-state solution, while unequivocally condemning Palestinian violence and largely ignoring Israeli violence. Resolutions have expressed solidarity with Israel in the fight against terrorism and insisted that the Palestinian Authority hands over all arrested 'terrorists' to Israel, and that the administration suspend all relations with Yasser Arafat.[14] A House resolution at the time of the West Bank incursion by Israel troops stated that it

> stands in solidarity with Israel as it takes necessary steps to provide security to its people by dismantling the terrorist infrastructure in the Palestinian areas; remains committed to Israel's right to self-defense and supports additional assistance to help Israel defend itself.[15]

The House of Representatives overwhelmingly condemned the 9 July 2004 decision of the International Court of Justice to declare Israel's security barrier, or separation wall, built on occupied territory, illegal and stating that it should be dismantled.[16] Both Houses of Congress have been united in backing Bush's policy towards Israel and the Palestinian Authority, authorizing the requisite funds, seeking to defend and protect Israel's interests by legitimating changing circumstances. They have studiously avoided any condemnation of Israeli actions, including attacks on civilian areas, targeted assassinations, and arrests of democratically elected members of the Palestinian parliament. The seizure of Palestinian territory behind the separation wall, the withholding of taxes needed to run the Palestinian Authority, and the failure to meet obligations under the Road Map, including the construction of an airport and seaport in Gaza, and freedom of movement between Gaza and the West Bank, have all been ignored.

A bipartisan consensus exists that supports a two-state solution on Israeli terms and backs Abbas and Fatah (post-Arafat) as the party most willing to acquiesce. Resolutions in support of Israel receive near unanimous support in both Houses, with fewer than twenty-five congressional representatives and senators prepared to vote against this trend. Christian Zionists push at an open door in being able to enlist congressional support for their position. A prominent Christian Zionist, Senator Brownback, demonstrated this confidence in introducing a joint resolution in April 2007 'providing for the recognition of Jerusalem as the undivided capital of Israel before the United States recognizes a Palestinian state, and for other purposes'.[17]

Unequivocal US support for Israel is also clearly demonstrated in the UN Security Council. The Bush administration has continued the practice of previous administrations of vetoing any reprimand of Israeli actions, no matter how justified. By July 2007, Bush's UN representative had vetoed nine UN Security Council resolutions submitted either singly or jointly by eighteen different countries, including Jamaica, Colombia, South Africa and Singapore. There appears to be a reflex action from successive administrations to reject any criticism of Israel. Such criticism is perceived to come from Islamic countries largely for domestic consumption and can be safely ignored. However, even a cursory examination of the wording of such resolutions reveals an even-handed approach to violence, conflict and peace in the situation. The main difficulty for most of the nine vetoed resolutions lies in their request that both parties, Israelis and Palestinians, refrain from violence and abide by international law, including the Geneva Convention.

The Bush administration has determined to shield Israel from any blame for its actions or acknowledgement that these are a contributory factor to increased tensions in the region. Despite this partisanship, which would seem to preclude America from negotiating a lasting peace treaty, both the PLO and Israelis see its role as almost indispensable in reaching agreement. The Israelis know that they have America on their side of the negotiating table and Palestinians are aware that Israel will only move if the Americans make it worth their while. Alvaro de Soto in his report sums up the Israeli and US approach:

> When push comes to shove Israel can accept an intrusive US third-party role because they know that the US is a close ally which can be counted on not to betray it or even pull any surprises – the US usually floats proposals with the Israelis before presenting them to the Palestinians. Israelis also take advantage of their unique ability to influence the formulation of US policy. (de Soto, 2007: 26)

The question remains as to whether the Israel Lobby, and especially Christian Zionists, are influencing Bush's policy on Israel or whether these policies would be pursued anyway. Is Bush motivated by US strategic and national interests or eschatology? Richard Land has no doubts:

> I must tell you that I have known the president since 1988. I have at least three or four conversations with the president every year and weekly conversations with people in the administration. I have never heard the president, nor any of the president's advisers, ever mention the idea that God has a special covenant with Israel. And I have never seen any books on the shelves of White House offices that I've visited that would – no Tim LaHaye books, no books about Israel and the Second Coming. I believe that the Bush foreign policy is based on the foreign policy of the United States ever since Harry Truman was one of the first to recognize the existence of the Jewish state in 1948. That America stands behind Israel's right to exist within secure borders and at peace with her neighbours, and not be driven into the sea. And that, as the only stable democracy in the Middle East, Israel is the most reliable ally of the United States.[18]

George Bush is the first US president specifically to call for a two-state solution to the Israel–Palestinian problem and in doing so has incurred the anger of many Christian Zionists. For many, including Land, part of blessing Israel is accepting its right to make its own negotiations even if that means giving up land for peace. For Hagee, and others, there are no negotiables, including the status of Jerusalem. At the Washington Summit, Hagee declared to the applause of the 4,500 Christian Zionists present, 'there will be one Jerusalem that shall not be divided – for anyone – not now – not ever.' Bush has sought to pursue his own policy in advancing US as well as Israeli interests, while trying to keep a wide range of Christian Zionists content.

Attempts by Bush to kick-start the peace process and the Road Map at the end of 2007 with a conference in Annapolis, Maryland, and subsequent visit to the region in January 2008 aroused anger among the Christian Right. Many members flooded the White House with emails, this time organized by Richard Scarborough of Vision America, which end with a plea to the president: 'As a Bible-believing Christian, I do not support the division of Jerusalem. And I ask you to stop supporting it also. Do not give Jerusalem to radical Islam.'[19] Within weeks of the initiative being reignited, Israel produced plans to continue building settlements in East Jerusalem, refusing to consider that this constituted occupied territory; meanwhile rockets continued to be fired into Israel from Gaza.[20] The prospects for peace are slim but nonetheless Bush is reported to be hopeful of a peace settlement based on a two-state solution.

Conclusion

A key aspect of Bush administration foreign policy has been the tensions that have existed between realist and idealist principles. Inspired initially by the neoconservatives, the administration sought after 9/11 to use its military superiority to project US power, using Iraq as a catalyst, to transform the Middle East into democratic states with open markets. As the backlash of Iraqi insurgency, Taliban revival in Afghanistan, increased international terrorism and the growth in support for fundamentalist Islam in the region undermined such a policy, the administration soon surrendered to the realpolitik of protecting US interests and support for Israel as a strategic ally. In so far as these objectives complemented Christian Zionist objectives, Bush enjoyed the support of the Israel Lobby. George Bush has followed a long tradition of US presidents in supporting Israel and seeking to negotiate a two-state solution to resolve the Israeli–Palestinian conflict that has dragged on for six decades. He has followed a traditional approach of land for peace with the added dimension that the dispute has become embroiled in the larger context of the War on Terror and the Iraq War.

Israel has been accepted as a partner in the War on Terror by virtue of its confrontation with radical Islamic movements in the Palestinian Territories and Lebanon. The prospect of a Palestinian state, via the Road Map, was offered as a token for British and pro-Western Arab support in attacking Iraq and overthrowing Saddam Hussein. Any possibility of a contiguous Palestinian state based on pre-1967 borders is initially premissed on recognition of the State of Israel, abiding by existing agreements and ending violence, before another series of supplemental conditions are imposed. Bush's and

Rice's actions can be seen as promoting US security interests by supporting an ally in a vital region, maintaining a lucrative source of business for US arms manufacturers, and appeasing pro-Western Arab governments with populations broadly supportive of the Palestinians. Bush's actions are unlikely to have been any different whether the Christian Right pressured him or not.

Bush's policy towards Israel and the Palestinian territories is determined first and foremost by US national security interests. He has demonstrated a willingness for Israel to give up land for peace, as demonstrated in his enthusiastic response to Sharon's unilateral decision to withdraw from Gaza. He would like to see a democratic and peaceable Palestinian state on the West Bank and Gaza, despite Christian Zionist support for Israel's retention of all occupied territory and the expulsion of Palestinians from the West Bank, as advocated by, among many others, the late Ed McAteer (CBS, 2003). The Christian Right do not have their way on the recognition of Jerusalem as the undivided capital of a Jewish state in perpetuity, or on moving the US embassy to Jerusalem from Tel Aviv. They were unable to halt the pull-out from Gaza, or prolong Israel's 2006 conflict with Hezbollah. At the time of writing, they have been unsuccessful in persuading Bush to launch an attack on Iranian nuclear sites, as urged by John Hagee and James Dobson. So, in what sense can this book make the claim that the Christian Right, and Christian Zionists in particular, have an influence on policy towards Israel?

I believe that Christian Zionists are significant players in administration policy towards Israel because of their central place within the Republican Party. They are well organized and coordinated, with leaders who enjoy unparalleled access to the administration and Congress. Through Abrams, Goeglein and, until his resignation, Rove they are regularly consulted and kept informed on US foreign policy in the Middle East. Through their sermons, lobbying, media campaigns, publications and broadcasting Christian Zionists provide support for an aggressive US militarism and unequivocal support for Israel. At times, such a strategy runs counter to US foreign policy interests and discourages friendly criticism of Israel that might check actions that contribute to the lack of stability in the region. Such a one-sided approach precludes the possibility of America acting as an honest broker in any potential Middle East peace settlement, and ties it to a corrupt PLO as the only acceptable interlocutor, regardless of the democratic mandate of Hamas. Christian Zionist support is not a necessary condition for US support for Israel but it does help create the conditions that preclude a peaceful resolution of conflict and even incites such conflict in a way that is detrimental to the interests of both the United States and Israel.

Christian Zionists recognize their differences with Bush, and their support for him is conditional upon his support for Israel. In adopting an uncompromising stance for Israel and against Islam, they provide succour to those within the administration who seek military solutions to the region's problems while threatening Bush's and Rice's attempts to appeal to pro-Western Arab governments to support the US position. The eschatological position of the Christian Right, encouraged by the apocalyptic writings of LaHaye, Jenkins and Hagee, means that they are unconcerned about the prospect of war – particularly against Iran, Syria, Hezbollah and Hamas-controlled Gaza – and indeed see this as a positive sign of the end times to be encouraged. This impulse to war can be successfully resisted by the State Department and White House but can become irresistible as well-organized voters bombard politicians with demands for action.

The attempt of the Christian Right to influence foreign policy in the region is most clearly demonstrated in America itself. The prominence given to Israel as a political issue is attributable to a combination of factors, including support for a fellow democracy, the influence of neoconservatives and the Jewish lobby, but also significantly the efforts that conservative evangelical preachers, politicians and writers make in order to keep it at the top of the agenda. In any debate on Israel, contrary opinions are vehemently attacked with accusations of anti-Semitism, and critics of Israeli policy are marginalized, isolated and targeted for removal from academic posts and newsrooms by the Israel Lobby, including Christian Zionists. Think-tanks, policy forums and reportage are dominated by the Lobby, effectively closing down the opportunity to devise alternative strategies to bring about an equitable settlement of the Palestine–Israel dispute. In blessing Israel, the Christian Right have encouraged and strengthened a US policy that has cursed the Palestinians to further hardship and suffering, internecine conflict, and little prospect of achieving a viable Palestinian state.

7

The War on Terror

> Some Westerners, including President Bill Clinton, have argued that the West does not have problems with Islam but only with violent Islamist extremists. Fourteen hundred years of history demonstrate otherwise. The relations between Islam and Christianity, both Orthodox and Western, have often been stormy. (Huntington, 1997: 209)

> The face of terror is not the true faith of Islam. That's not what Islam is all about. Islam is peace. These terrorists don't represent peace. They represent evil and war. (George W. Bush)[1]

In February 1998 Osama bin Laden called for a jihad against the Jews and 'the crusaders', the outworking of which was to result in the devastating attacks on the Twin Towers in New York and the Pentagon on the morning of 11 September 2001. Over 3,000 people died in these attacks on symbolic targets of US military and economic power, which changed, in a few hours, the foreign policy imperatives of the new president and his successors for a generation. President Bush had assumed office earlier in the year having campaigned on the basis of not embarking on reckless foreign adventures, unlike his Democrat predecessor. The appointment of Condoleezza Rice as National Security Adviser in the White House led to the assumption that a realist foreign policy would come to dominate US geopolitical thinking after Clinton's Wilsonian departure in the post-Cold War era. Al-Qaeda's attack on the American homeland changed that pragmatic approach and led to a new era in US foreign policy defined by the global 'War on Terror'.

As the dust clouds were settling from the collapse of the Twin Towers, many Americans were asking the question, 'why do they hate us?' Rather than considering the possibilities that US foreign policy may have contributed to such animosity, the president foreclosed discussion by declaring that America, and indeed the West, in general, was hated because 'they', whoever 'they' were, envied America's freedom, liberty, democracy and prosperity. The question that also arose for many, in an America steeped in notions of American exceptionalism and John Winthrop's *City on a Hill*, was where God was in all this. Did 'they' also envy or hate 'our' faith? Were the events of 11 September to be interpreted as terrorism, carried out in pursuit of political objectives, or as a religious war pitching Islam against Christianity?

In this chapter, we examine how the Christian Right, as the main supporter of and leading advocate for Bush's War on Terror, has attempted to turn the war into a crusade. We begin with an examination of how conservative evangelicals and the Bush administration have variously interpreted the War on Terror using Samuel Huntington's *Clash of Civilizations* thesis as a starting point. We look at how the differing interpretations have influenced policy during the long war. The projection of US military power into the Middle East led many Christian Right organizations to consider the War on Terror to be an ideal opportunity to evangelize at home and abroad, arousing Muslim accusations that it was a Christian crusade against Islam. The chapter goes on to look at how conservative evangelical influence in the Middle East, within the administration and the military, has grown over the past few years as a result of policies designed to promote religious freedom. There is considerable nuance in the approach of the Christian Right towards Muslims at home, which tends to be pacific, and abroad, which is hostile. The chapter continues with an exploration of the extent to which Islamophobia is having a detrimental effect on US foreign policy. Finally, the chapter considers whether the long War on Terror is shorthand for a war against Islam.

The Clash of Civilizations

In the aftermath of 11 September, speaking on Pat Robertson's *700 Club*, Jerry Falwell lay the blame for the terrorist attack not on the terrorists but on liberals, whom he accused of bringing God's wrath on America:

> I really believe that the pagans and the abortionists and the feminists and the gays and the lesbians who are actively trying to make that an alternative lifestyle, the ACLU, People for the American Way, all of them who have tried to secularize America, I point the finger in their face and say, 'You helped this happen'.[2]

Falwell's views represented an automatic response laying the blame for the attacks on the Christian Right's domestic enemies. Such views were widely discounted even within the Christian Right, apart from syndicated columnist Ann Coulter, who agreed with Falwell but felt that Senator Edward Kennedy and America United's Rev. Barry Lynn should have been included in the list.[3] The early assumption that the attack was the work of al-Qaeda, a Wahhabi terrorist organization, led many commentators and members of the Christian Right to reconsider Samuel Huntington's 1993 thesis on the clash of civilizations, which seemed cogent in explaining the attack. *The Clash of Civilizations and the Remaking of World Order*, Huntington's fuller exposition of the thesis, went back to the top of the bestseller lists. Huntington's thesis is simply that following the Cold War the fundamental source of conflict will be cultural rather than ideological or economic. The world divides, according to Huntington, into seven or eight major civilizations (Western, Confucian, Japanese, Islamic, Hindu, Slavic-Orthodox, Latin American, and possibly African). The conflicts of the future, he claims, will lie on the fault lines between the different civilizations (Huntington, 1993).

Huntington claims that the main confrontation will be between the West and Islam because of the demographics of Muslim population, with large numbers of unemployed and disaffected young people. The Islamic resurgence has increased confidence in Muslim values at the same time as Western universalism and power projection into the Muslim world are fuelling resentment. The collapse of Communism has removed a common enemy, leaving the two as sole protagonists in a world where interaction is as inevitable as it will become intolerable for both sides. There is also the added complication for Huntington that Islam and Christianity will also clash because they are both missionary faiths intent on converting each other to what they hold to be the one true faith (Huntington, 1997: 211). Huntington makes it clear that the conflict he predicts is not with radical Islam or Wahhabism but with Islam itself:

> The underlying problem for the West is not Islamic fundamentalism. It is Islam, a different civilization whose people are convinced of the superiority of their culture and are obsessed with the inferiority of their power. The problem for Islam is not the CIA or the U.S. Department of Defense. It is the West, a different civilization whose people are convinced of the universality of their culture and believe that their superior, if declining, power imposes on them the obligation to extend that culture throughout the world. (Huntington, 1997: 217–18)

Many criticisms can be and have been made of the 'clash of civilizations' thesis, not least that Huntington demonstrates at best a superficial knowledge of Islam, many of his facts are empirically wrong, and his thesis shows every sign of becoming a self-fulfilling prophecy (Fox and Sandler, 2006; Ruthven, 2004). Here, however, my intention is not to challenge the theory but rather to demonstrate that, although Huntington is not a conservative evangelical, his opinion resonates with many on the Christian Right and corroborates their world-view.

Shortly after 11 September, Steven Snyder of International Christian Concern wrote an open letter stating that America 'is witnessing what Christians in other parts of the world have been enduring for some time. We are at war with an unseen enemy that has demonstrated its resolve to launch a "jihad" (holy war) on Americans, Christians, and Jews' (Green, 2001). Charles Colson had no doubts about the efficacy of Huntington's thesis, declaring that 'great clashes of world view – that is how people understand the ultimate reality – continue to divide the world, and will do so until the end of history when the Lord returns'. For Colson, and indeed most evangelicals, Islam and Christianity are diametrically opposed to one another. Christian doctrine, he argues, must be defended while rigorously seeking to convert Muslims and resist Muslim attempts to do likewise (Colson, 2002). Similar statements are made regularly from conservative evangelical pulpits, radio stations and television broadcasters to the Christian Right faithful, blurring demarcation lines between Islam and its fundamentalist derivative.

Although Bush initially described the US response to the terror attacks as a crusade, such terminology was swiftly corrected. The administration was determined to avoid a 'clash of civilizations' response to the 11 September attacks. In part, this was due to pragmatic considerations that a sizeable proportion of US citizens are Muslim, that key trading partners and military allies are Muslim nations, and that most of the world's oil reserves are located in Muslim lands. For the most part, however, it reflects the views of Bush himself that Islam is not a monolithic entity and that the radical Islam of al-Qaeda and others represents a different type of Islam to that practised by moderate Muslims throughout America and the rest of the world. In Bush's Manichaean world-view of good and evil, freedom and oppression, democracy and totalitarianism, there is also room for good and bad Muslims. Bush is a committed Christian but is also comfortable with mainstream believers from other faiths, respecting their beliefs more than the lack of faith of atheistic and agnostic Americans. Before making his official statement to Congress on 20 September, Bush convened a meeting with twenty-seven religious leaders including evangelicals, Catholics, Mormons, Muslims, Buddhists, Sikhs and Hindus (Maddox, 2003: 399). He followed this up between 17 September 2001 and 5 December 2002 with no fewer than twenty-one speeches in which he praised Islam. He has consistently described Islam as a religion of hope, charity, mercy, comfort and peace.

> I have assured His Majesty [King Abdullah of Jordan] that our war is against evil, not against Islam. There are thousands of Muslims who proudly call themselves Americans, and they know what I know – that the Muslim faith is based upon peace and love and compassion. The exact opposite of the teachings of the al-Qaeda organization, which is based upon evil and hate and destruction.[4]

While such comments infuriate most of Bush's supporters on the Christian Right, there is an assumption that he has to say that in order to unite the nation behind the War on Terror and reduce the risk of harm to troops engaged on the front line. The president and, in particular, his most effective speechwriter Michael Gerson were able to unite much of the country, and certainly conservative evangelicals, behind the president's response to the attacks by using language that resonated with his religious base and reflected the mood of the country. Each speech referring to the War on Terror was punctuated with dichotomous rhetoric that contrasted goodness and evil, darkness and light, a sense of higher calling and mission against a moral outrage, of high responsibility and courage in the face of adversity. Speeches used biblical and hymnal references substituting God for America and vice versa. When Bush described Iraq, Iran and North Korea as 'an axis of evil' in the 2002 State of the Union address he was able in an instant to summon images that resonated with the American people – memories of Ronald Reagan's resolution and ultimate victory over Communism, the exceptionalism and high calling of America, and the triumph of Jesus over evil in dying on the cross but rising again to life. In an exceptional time, the Christian Right hailed Bush as God's man in the White House. General Jerry

Boykin expressed the view of many members of the Christian Right, then and now, at a church service in October 2003:

> Then this man stepped forward and he looked America in the eye and he said 'We will not forget, we will not falter and we will not fail.' Now ask yourself this: why is this man in the White House? The majority of Americans did not vote for him. Why is he there? And I'll tell you this morning he's in the White House because God put him there for such a time as this. God put him there to lead not only this nation but to lead the world, in such a time as this. (Kaplan, 2005: 21)[5]

In posing the conflict with al-Qaeda and other radical Islamists as a battle between the forces of good and evil, civilization and barbarism, rather than Christianity and Islam, Bush signalled a change in foreign policy emphasis from pragmatic realism to an idealism that would not simply defend American values but seek to advance those values throughout the world. The president's moral discourse resonated with the neoconservative wing of the Republican Party and strengthened the interdependency of the Christian Right and neoconservatives. Neoconservatives occupied key positions within the administration, with Paul Wolfowitz deputy secretary of defense, Douglas Feith under-secretary of defense for policy, and Richard Perle a member of the Defense Policy Board. Lewis 'Scooter' Libby, the vice president's chief of staff, and Elliott Abrams, in charge of the National Security Council for Near East, Southwest Asian, and North African Affairs, were convinced neoconservatives (Kline, 2004: 456). The future ambassador to Afghanistan, Iraq and later the UN, Zalmay Khalilzad, and undersecretary for democracy and global affairs Paula Dobriansky would be significant actors in the Bush Middle East strategy. Fellow travellers included the vice president Dick Cheney, the defense secretary Donald Rumsfeld, and – Fukuyama would argue – the President himself (Fukuyama, 2006: 46). By the end of 2006, most of the neoconservatives, apart from Elliott Abrams, who has developed a strong relationship with the Christian Right over Middle East policy and was promoted to deputy national security adviser, had been forced out of the administration because of the Iraq debacle and the failure of democracy-promotion efforts in the region.

In the aftermath of the 11 September attack, the neoconservatives were the only ones prepared and with a ready-made plan to project American power abroad. The plan required a cataclysmic event – another Pearl Harbor – to advance their foreign-policy objective of expanding American values of free markets, moral conservatism and democracy around the world on the back of significantly increased military expenditure. The neoconservative vision was clearly set out in a statement of principles by the Project for the New American Century, signed by Abrams, Cheney, Libby, Rumsfeld, Wolfowitz, Khalilzad and Dobriansky; and by the president's brother Jeb. The signatories also included Francis Fukuyama, who has since recanted, leading members of the Christian Right Gary Bauer and William Bennett, and Frank Gaffney, a regular commentator on security affairs at Christian Right gatherings (PNAC, 1997).

The quick response to al-Qaeda's attack was the realist one of attacking the state where the terrorists were based, overthrowing the Taliban, killing or capturing Mullah Omar and Osama bin Laden, and destroying the terrorist infrastructure. Reflecting Bush's sense of divine mission, Operation Enduring Freedom was initially called Operation Infinite Justice, until it was pointed out to the president that perhaps only God could distribute infinite justice. Such a plan was relatively uncontroversial and was approved of by the Christian Right leaders; liberals and pacifists questioned the legality of punishing a country for the crimes of individuals or organizations based there.

Bush rejected offers from the Taliban to hand over bin Laden to an Islamic court in another country or to consult with the Organization of the Islamic Conference. Instead, he seized the opportunity to restore American prestige and extend America's global reach by establishing US military bases in the former Soviet Union's Central Asian Republics, with the agreement of the host countries and Russia. In so doing, Bush effectively agreed to overlook human rights abuses in Chechnya and the Central Asian Republics in return for Russian and the republics' support in the War on Terror. The US military entered an ongoing civil war in Afghanistan on the side of the Northern Alliance, themselves notorious violators of human rights, and achieved a rapid victory at the cost of the lives of around a thousand, mainly civilian, Afghanis. Later elections secured victory for a pro-Western government, but five years after the war Mullah Omar and Osama bin Laden had been neither killed nor captured, al-Qaeda had recovered their strength, and the Taliban had resumed control of large sections of the country.

Following the easy initial victory in Afghanistan, neoconservatives and the Christian Right saw an opportunity to link the War on Terror to unfinished business in Iraq. President Bush was certainly amenable to such encouragement. Although his father's advisers cautioned against invading Iraq because of the danger of the country disintegrating and increasing the influence of Iran, Turkey and Syria, it was felt that the risks were far outweighed by the prospect of projecting American power in the region. A successful invasion could result in the establishment of permanent bases, control over oil resources, the removal of a human-rights-abusing dictator who had defied US hegemony, and the establishment of a free-market democracy. Added to the mix was the defiance and lack of cooperation shown by Saddam Hussein to the UN in their fruitless search for the weapons of mass destruction that American and British intelligence insisted must be there. For the neoconservatives, Iraq represented a wonderful opportunity to send a message to Iran, Syria, North Korea, and other states they did not approve of, that pre-emption was the new modus operandi and that they had better reform or they would be next. For the Christian Right, Saddam Hussein's missile attacks on Israel during the first Gulf War and his support for Palestinian resistance groups and suicide bombers made Iraq an obvious next target. George Bush himself had a personal score to settle: a failed assassination attempt by Iraqis on his father. For Cheney and the corporate backers of the Republican Party, Iraq represented a wonderful opportunity to open up the oil industry to

US companies, boost the arms industry and award lucrative reconstruction contracts to supporters.

The one problem was the lack of legitimate reasons to go to war with Iraq. The regime was being contained, US/UK control of a no-fly zone over Iraq and selective strikes against air defences and military targets over the previous ten years had rendered Iraqi defences ineffective, and UN inspectors were being given access, albeit reluctantly, to Iraqi weapons and chemical facilities. In the effort to justify invading Iraq and overthrowing the regime, the Bush administration, supported by the Blair government, sought any scrap of information that would confirm their hypothesis that Iraq had weapons of mass destruction and was prepared to use them against other countries, including Israel. If they did not use such weapons themselves then there was the possibility that they would pass them on to terrorists who would attack America or its allies. Using information from Iraqi defectors, anxious to impress their new benefactors, and from intelligence services, eager to deliver what their employers were looking for, misinformation was accumulated and manipulated in briefings, documents and UN briefings in an attempt to bypass international law, which rules out regime change. In the process, the Bush administration, with the loyal assistance of the British government, was able to mislead its electorate and foreign governments into believing that Iraq had weapons of mass destruction.

In reality, the decision to attack Iraq had been made in the weeks following 11 September, and by 21 November 2001 Bush had instructed Donald Rumsfeld to start planning for the invasion (Woodward, 2003, 2004; Clarke, 2004). The driving force propelling America to war with Iraq was Vice President Cheney and a cabal of neoconservatives within the administration. Bush's decision to go to war was from the earliest stages encouraged, supported and justified by a combination of neoconservatives outside government and the Christian Right. An open letter on 3 April from the Project for the New American Century (PNAC), signed by, among others, Bauer, Bennett and Gaffney, made the case for linking support for Israel to the War on Terror; and, regarding the line in the sand drawn by the president, Iran, Iraq, Syria and Yasser Arafat were in the 'against us' camp:

> Furthermore, Mr. President, we urge you to accelerate plans for removing Saddam Hussein from power in Iraq. As you have said, every day that Saddam Hussein remains in power brings closer the day when terrorists will be not just airplanes with which to attack us, but chemical, biological, or nuclear weapons, as well. It is now common knowledge that Saddam, along with Iran, is a funder and supporter of terrorism against Israel. Iraq has harbored terrorists such as Abu Nidal in the past, and it maintains links to the Al Qaeda network. If we do not move against Saddam Hussein and his regime, the damage our Israeli friends and we have suffered until now may someday appear but a prelude to much greater horrors. (PNAC, 2002)

The claims about Iraqi links with al-Qaeda were a complete fabrication but have been used by Bush continuously to obfuscate and shore up domestic support for the ill-conceived Iraq War. Before the letter, Israeli Prime Minister Sharon attempted to persuade the Bush administration to incorporate the Israeli–Arab conflict into the War on Terror, but the president carefully avoided doing so. Following assurances from Karl Rove that 'our folks' saw the Israeli–Palestinian conflict as part of the War on Terror, Bush began a process of isolating the Palestinian leader and pressing ahead with plans to remove Saddam Hussein (Frum, 2003: 258–9).

As the commitment to regime change in Iraq became more public, key figures within the Christian Right were eager to provide theological justification for such action. Richard Land organized a letter stating that a pre-emptive military strike on Iraq would be legitimate under Just War Theory. The letter was co-signed by Chuck Colson, PFM; Bill Bright, founder and chair of Campus Crusade for Christ; D. James Kennedy, president of Coral Ridge Ministries Media; and Carl Herbster, president of the American Association of Christian Schools (Anderson, 2002). This advice was contradicted by almost every other religious leader in the United States and, more importantly, for the 25 per cent of the US population who are Catholic, by Pope John

Paul II, who declared that 'war is never just another means that one can choose to employ for settling differences between nations' (John Paul II, 2003). The Pope insisted that war could only ever be the very last option, under very strict conditions, and could not ignore the impact on the civilian population before and after military operations. Bush refused to see a delegation of leading ministers from mainstream denominations, including his own United Methodists, opposing the war (Wallis, 2005: 133). Land, Robertson, Falwell and other leading members of the Christian Right played an important role in reducing the impact of the Pope's and traditional churches' opposition to the war, enabling Bush to claim to be on the right side of a Manichaean struggle between the forces of good and evil. A Christian nationalist theme developed in the 2003 State of the Union address and subsequent speeches invoking the 'power, wonder-working power, in the goodness and idealism and faith of the American people' – a description usually given of Jesus.

Land's letter and subsequent statements were based on his notion of Just War, derived from Christian ethics and in particular *jus ad bellum* to legitimate going to war. Under 'Just War' a sovereign authority must wage war for it to be just, and there must be just cause. Further, the intentions must be pure, with the outcome being better than the result of having not acted. There must be a reasonable prospect of a successful outcome and every effort should have been made to avoid conflict (Evans and Newnham, 1998: 288). Land was clear in his view then and has remained unrepentant:

> Under certain conditions, war is justified as a least-bad alternative. The first condition is that there is a just cause. Our cause in Iraq is just; it may be one of the nobler things we have done in recent history. We went to liberate a country that was in the grip of a terrible dictator who had perpetrated horrible atrocities and crimes against humanity, against his own people, and against his neighbors. We removed him, and we're giving the Iraqis the ability to defend themselves and to build a stable democracy. We have a responsibility and an obligation based on the blessings that have been showered upon us to help others when we can. (Land, 2007: 206)

Christian Right backing for the Iraq War and linkage with the War on Terror were loud and consistent enough for Bush's core constituency in the conservative evangelical churches to embrace conflict enthusiastically. In March 2003 on CNN's *Larry King Live*, John MacArthur of the Grace Community Church, Sun Valley, California, was one of four clergymen discussing 'What would Jesus do about war with Iraq?' MacArthur's position was the default position for the Christian Right. War with Iraq was justified and would be approved of by Jesus. Taking Bible passages out of context, MacArthur claims Jesus' approval for war in Luke 14:31 and Luke 22:36. Although he specifically states that the war is not a Christian war, he emphasizes that Bush is a Christian president and that Saddam Hussein prayed to the wrong God, that Muslim beliefs are wrong and that they will be condemned to an eternal hell with eternal punishment. For MacArthur the issue was not whether to go to war with Iraq or not but rather that the war against Iraq started with its involvement in the events of 11 September.[6] (As we know, there was no such involvement.)

Throughout the build-up to war with Iraq and in the following years it has been the Christian Right's leadership and conservative evangelicals sitting in church or in front of Christian television that have been the most vociferous and enthusiastic supporters of the war; a support strengthened by calls to see the conflict in spiritual terms of a battle between good and evil. As in life, where believers are exhorted to wage a constant and vigilant battle against the forces of evil, so the War on Terror (and Iraq) would be long and difficult. Whenever support for the war has been strained, the president and his speechwriters have been able to rely on language that would resonate with supporters and stiffen resolve. A president who did not seek advice from his father, Bush Senior, but rather appealed to a 'higher father', was a president conservative evangelicals could call their own (Woodward, 2004: 421). A president who could tell the Palestinian prime minister Mahmoud Abbas that 'God told me to strike at al-Qaeda and I struck them, and then he instructed me to strike at Saddam, which I did, and now I am determined to solve the problem in the Middle East', is speaking in terms the Christian Right relate to and appreciate.[7]

Conflicts in Afghanistan and Iraq are ongoing, at the time of writing, with little prospects of resolution. Al-Qaeda has proved remarkably resilient and has regrouped to provide an increasing threat to United States' interests throughout the world, including opening up a front in Iraq that previously did not exist. Bush's War on Terror has been expanded to include the Sunni and Shiite resistance in Iraq; Israel's confrontation with the Palestinians, in particular Hamas and Islamic Jihad; Hezbollah in Lebanon; and the Iranian government of President Ahmadinejad. These confrontations and the involvement of the Christian Right in influencing policy were the subject of the previous chapter and so will not be considered again here; however, it is important to note that they have consistently applied the twin principles of support for US power projection and unreserved support for Israel. For Christian Zionists such as Robertson and Hagee the issue is seen in apocryphal terms as a possible sign of the end times; it is held to be vital for America's health and prosperity that it firmly supports God's chosen people, the Jews. At the time of writing, a determined campaign is being waged by conservative evangelicals and the increasingly less influential neoconservatives to destroy Iran's developing nuclear energy plants, and in so doing open another front in the War on Terror.

Religious Freedom and Proselytizing in the Combat Zone

The Bush administration's strategy in the global War on Terror has been both military and political. Bush and his National Security and State Department teams have emphasized the need to promote democracy in the Middle East in order to bring about a peaceful world order. In order to secure the support of pro-American Muslim countries and as a reward for Prime Minister Blair's support, President

Bush announced commitment to a two-state solution and involvement in an Israeli–Palestinian peace process and a strategy to democratize the Middle East, starting with Iraq, which would serve as a catalyst for peace, democracy and prosperity in the region. In a speech to the National Endowment for Democracy, on its twentieth anniversary, Bush asserted that Islam was consistent with democratic rule, affirmed his commitment to helping bring about such political change, and formulated the American secret for success:

> Successful societies guarantee religious liberty – the right to serve and honor God without fear of persecution. Successful societies privatize their economies, and secure the rights of property. They prohibit and punish official corruption, and invest in the health and education of their people. They recognize the rights of women. And instead of directing hatred and resentment against others, successful societies appeal to the hopes of their own people.
>
> … The establishment of a free Iraq at the heart of the Middle East will be a watershed event in the global democratic revolution.[8]

Regular visitor to the White House and leading advocate for war Richard Land considers that Bush's policies resonate with conservative evangelicals. For Land, and the Southern Baptists he represents, the only answer to 'Islamic jihadism' is modernity and representative governments. Evangelicals appreciate that democracy and religious freedom provide the best opportunity to spread the Christian message, including the right to change faiths.[9] The conservative evangelical experience in Sudan and the fight to achieve the International Religious Freedom Act gave the Christian Right considerable influence in ensuring that religious freedom was included within the post-Saddam Iraqi constitution. Religious freedom is evangelical shorthand for being able to evangelize within ostensibly Muslim countries. The military conflict encouraged a rush of missionary activity and training to share their faith with Muslims in the Arab world.

Richard Land presents the respectable face of conservative evangelicalism, stressing nuance, duty and responsibility, religious freedom, and an imperative to evangelize for the benefit of non-believers. Many others in the Christian Right make little attempt to moderate their approach to reach a wider audience. Glenn Miller, interviewed on the *700 Club*, said that the war in Iraq had nothing to do with oil but rather was concerned about Jehovah God breaking the 'power of deception' exercised by the 'false God Allah' over 1.2 billion Muslims.[10] The military battle was also being fought in the spiritual realm and represented an opportunity to share 'the good news of salvation'.

A plethora of organizations either sprang up or were revitalized by war in the Middle East. These include the Crescent Project, Arab World Missions, the Center for Ministry to Muslims, the Arab Communications Center, the Columbia Institute of Muslim Studies, and the Zwemer Institute of Muslim Studies, each offering training in reaching 'Muslims for Christ'. Other groups such as Red Sea Missions, Arab World Ministries, Frontiers, Harvest for Christ, Samaritan's Purse, and the Association of Baptists for World Evangelism provided Americans determined to harvest souls in the 10/40 window the opportunities to do so. Would-be missionaries are encouraged by many of these organizations to enter Muslim countries as students, as health and welfare workers, or as IT consultants in order to circumvent laws regarding proselytizing. Esther Kaplan records that the Southern Baptist Convention had one thousand missionaries in the 10/40 window and were distributing food boxes with text from John 1:17 in Arabic stating that 'the law indeed was given through Moses; grace and truth come through Jesus Christ'. According to her research Samaritan's Purse allocated $194 million to send missionaries to Iraq; in addition, In Touch Ministries, Atlanta, circulated a pamphlet entitled *A Christian's Duty* to thousands of US troops in Iraq (Kaplan, 2005: 14–16).

In 2004, the *Los Angeles Times* reported that there were thirty evangelistic missions operating in Iraq.[11] After three years of conflict in Iraq, despite the resources that have been provided to faith-based organizations, their attempts to convert Muslims to Christianity have proved futile, and inded half the indigenous Iraqi Christian population have fled the country. Christian proselytizers are unable to operate because of the Iraqi resistance, who have targeted Iraqi Christians and their churches.[12] The identification of Christianity with the occupation by coalition forces has been strengthened by presidential language that only just stops short of describing US actions as a crusade. In George Bush's notorious 'Mission Accomplished' speech, aboard the USS *Lincoln* on 1 May 2003, he told troops that they 'carry a message of hope – a message that is ancient and ever new. In the words of the prophet Isaiah, "To the captives, come out, and to those in darkness, be free."'

Iraqis and Afghans can be forgiven for considering the occupying US troops as a Christian army. Muslim members of the armed services are rare. Traditionally, volunteer recruitment to the US military comes disproportionately from the Southern and western states, where there are a higher proportion of evangelicals. In these areas of America, support for the war by conservative evangelical pastors and congregations encourages recruitment and retention in the War on Terror.

The appointment of General Jerry Boykin as deputy undersecretary for defense for intelligence, in charge of the hunt for Mullah Omar, bin Laden and Saddam Hussein, is reflective of the extent to which conservative evangelicals are involved at the highest levels in the US military. In a series of in-uniform speeches and sermons at churches in 2002 and 2003 the general recounted his earlier service in Somalia in 1993. He described a dark mark on a photograph he took of Mogadishu from an army helicopter as being a demonic presence, which God had revealed to him as the real enemy in Somalia. He recalled one of General Aidid's lieutenants saying on CNN that the Americans could not get him because Allah would protect him. Boykin pointed out that he knew 'that my God was bigger than his. I knew that my God was real and his was an idol.' He also told a congregation in Oregon that faith in God caused Special Operations forces in Iraq to be successful and warned the congregation that 'Satan wants to destroy this nation, he wants to destroy us as a nation, and he wants to destroy us as a Christian army.' In answering the question, 'why do they hate us?' Boykin told churchgoers in Sandy, Oregon, in June 2003 that it was because they are a Christian nation. 'We are hated because we are a nation of believers. Our spiritual enemy will only be defeated if we come against them in the name of Jesus' (Arkin, 2003; Rennie, 2003). Boykin came under intense criticism from politicians and the media for his statements. Although Bush refused to criticize the general's comments, Boykin was shortly afterwards transferred from his sensitive post.

Jerry Boykin reflects the growing assertiveness of conservative evangelicals in the military. Buoyed by the Bush presidency, born-again Christians are actively evangelizing within the Pentagon and occupying senior positions. A video produced in 2006 by the Christian Embassy, a conservative evangelical organization dedicated to converting and sustaining diplomats, government leaders and military officers, demonstrates the extent of Christian Right influence in the Pentagon. The video, which has since been removed from the Christian Embassy website, shows interviews conducted inside the Pentagon with senior officials and high-ranking officers in uniform. The Embassy organizes Bible studies attended by some forty generals, discipleship groups, prayer breakfasts and outreach events. The Flag Officer Fellowship provides an opportunity for fellow Christians to meet and be seen by fellow officers. The video has interviews with four generals and two colonels based in the Pentagon. Major-General Jack Catton shares his faith with fellow officers and believes this is making 'a huge impact because you have many men and women who are seeking God's council and wisdom, as we advise the chairman and the secretary of defense, Hallelujah!'[13]

Barry Lynn from Americans United has exposed further blurring in the separation of church and state in the military. An exposé of the Air Force Academy revealed egregious trivialization of minority faiths, including Mormons and Jews, and disrespect for non-believers. Lynn considers that trying to convert co-workers is a hierarchical prerogative rather than something the average enlisted person is doing.

There is a clear conflict of interest between conservative evangelicals proselytizing and the effective running of a diverse, multiethnic and multi-faith organization:

> When you're in a command structure and you have a guy who's obviously promoting patriotism and religion in the same breath and you expect to advance, or you want more flying time, you're going to be inclined to try to get along with that person. That's going to mean going to church and be visible there when he and his wife are there; you're going to do that.[14]

The influence of the Christian Right also extends to the battlefields of Iraq and Afghanistan. Over the past few years conservative evangelicals have taken over 50 per cent of the military chaplaincy posts, an integral part of the US military, and a ripe recruiting ground as bullets and missiles fly. One Southern Baptist chaplain at Najaf even offered soldiers the chance to swim in the swimming pool, if they were willing to convert and be baptized. Soldiers receive DVDs of their home church services; they attend church services, prayer meetings and Bible classes (Hedges, 2007; Layklin, 2003; Beaumont, 2007). This is neither surprising nor necessarily wrong, but it does reflect a US military made up disproportionately of conservative evangelicals who see themselves as being a Christian army. The combination of intense patriotism, American exceptionalism and born-again Christianity, involving the teaching that other faiths are inferior, false or satanic, is hardly conducive to cultural sensitivity and respect for other religions and traditions.

The US military receive support in their war efforts from mercenary forces in order to supplement troop levels, without the need for accountability to Congress or the American people. These private contractors are in receipt of hundreds of millions of dollars in government contracts to protect diplomats, installations and oil fields. The most notable of the mercenary forces active in the Middle East is Blackwater USA, run by former Navy SEAL Erik Prince, a leading member and benefactor of the Christian Right and funder of the Republican

Party. Blackwater have around 2,300 mercenaries employed around the world, equipped with state-of-the-art equipment, at the cost of half a million dollars in government contracts annually. Blackwater are currently deployed in Iraq and Afghanistan training troops and protecting US diplomats (who have included Bremer, Negroponte and Khalilzad), US diplomatic facilities and regional occupation offices. They have established a Special Forces camp a few miles from the Iranian border, have trained special forces in Azerbaijan, have provided security in New Orleans in the aftermath of Hurricane Katrina, and are anxious to secure contracts to be deployed in Darfur. In 2006, President Bush relaxed sanctions in Southern Sudan, and Blackwater are hoping to win contracts to train Southern Sudanese forces. Erik Prince is on the board of Christian Freedom International, a conservative evangelical organization heavily committed in Sudan and a leader in seeking to address persecution of Christians in Southern Sudan (Sizemore, 2006; Scahill, 2007).

The Prince family are also major benefactors of the Christian Right; Erik's father Edgar provided the start-up capital for Gary Bauer to start FRC and provided large financial contributions to James Dobson's Focus on the Family, Promise Keepers and the AFA. Prince's sister Betsy is married to Dick DeVos, son of Richard DeVos of Amway, another huge benefactor of Christian Right organizations and Republican candidates. Prince, Betsy DeVos and Richard DeVos are all members of the highly secretive Council for National Policy, along with Dobson and Bauer and numerous other neoconservatives and Christian Right leaders (Scahill, 2007). Blackwater is largely unaccountable, resisting attempts by Congress to track down its contracts and place it under military disciplinary codes of conduct. The Iraqi government condemned the organization for its heavy-handed approach towards security after the killing of seventeen civilians in September 2007 (Glanz and Rubin, 2007). In spite of Iraqi government demands for Blackwater to be withdrawn from the country, the company remains integral to US security plans in Iraq – an indication of lack of democratic control exercised by the US-backed Iraqi government. The privatized military contract service, run by conservative evangelicals, represents further indication of the expanding influence of the movement in the War on Terror.

Islamophobia and the Christian Right

There is a division among conservative evangelicals over Islam. As we have seen in earlier chapters, at the United Nations the Christian Right are willing to collaborate with Muslim countries and organizations on issues surrounding the family, abortion, sex trafficking, prostitution and HIV/AIDS. Some are even willing to discuss support for Israel and religious freedom in Arab countries, as witnessed at a meeting organized by Pentecostal evangelist Benny Hinn and attended by leading next-generation conservative evangelicals and ambassadors from nine Arab states.[15] Such cooperation largely goes unnoticed by regular members of interest groups and churches. Instead, Christian Right leaders, with a few exceptions, demonstrate open hostility towards Islam with varying degrees of nuance. In the more considered announcements made by leaders of the movement, a distinction is drawn between moderate and radical Muslims. Christian Right leaders regard Islam as a false religion and its followers as deceived and heading for damnation. They are still willing, however, to cooperate over issues of mutual interest but without conceding respect for the others' faith.

Shortly after making his infamous comments about Islam being 'wicked, violent and not of the same god', Franklin Graham, a regular speaker at Republican conventions, stated that he did not consider Islam to be 'a wonderful, peaceful religion'. He reminded NBC viewers that 'it wasn't Methodists flying into those buildings … It was an attack on this country by people of the Islamic faith' (Mansfield, 2004: 140). Jerry Falwell described Muhammad as a 'terrorist … a violent man, a man of war'.[16] Not wishing to be outdone, Pat Robertson has kept viewers to CBN's *700 Club* regularly informed about what he sees as the evil and dangers of Islam. The *700 Club* broadcasts throughout America and to many countries in Europe, the Middle East and Latin America. Robertson is regarded as the voice of Christian America for much of the world; consequently his views, although not always reflective of the Christian Right more broadly, have considerable influence.

On 24 April 2006, Robertson cautioned his viewers that just as America had not listened to what Hitler had to say in *Mein Kampf* and had therefore been unprepared, so it was not listening to what Muslims are saying: 'We are not listening to what not only the radical Muslims but Islam in general, we're not listening to what it says.' Robertson draws no distinction between radical and moderate Islam, and in so doing has brought Islamophobia into the Christian Right mainstream. Warning his viewers that those Muslims who wished to leave their religion faced death, he went on to ask, 'whoever heard of such a bloody, bloody, brutal type of religion? But that's what it is. It is not a religion of peace' (28 April 2006). On 19 September 2006, after a report on al-Qaeda's response to Pope Benedict XVI's controversial remarks about Islam, Robertson told his viewers that 'the leaders of al-Qaeda are calling for a holy war between Islam and Christianity. It's going to come, ladies and gentlemen.'

On 21 October 2001, interviewing Robert Spencer about his new book, *The Truth about Muhammad: Founder of the World's Most Intolerant Religion*, Robertson told the audience that 'the president ... has actually done the nation a great disservice by saying – quote – that "Islam is a religion of peace" – it's actually a political system isn't it?' He goes on to describe the Quran as 'teaching warfare, so at the core of this faith is militant warfare'. Robertson's recurring theme is that America needs to wake up to an Islamic threat that is all about violent jihad, which has not been appreciated even by moderate Muslims.

In the contest for the Republican presidential nomination in 2008 Mike Huckabee was also outspoken about the threat of radical Islam:

> A more successful U.S. foreign policy needs to better explain Islamic jihadism to the American people. Given how Americans have thrived on diversity – religious, ethnic, racial – it takes an enormous leap of imagination to understand what Islamic terrorists are about, that they really do want to kill every last one of us and destroy civilization as we know it. If they are willing to kill their own children by letting them detonate suicide bombs, then they will also be willing to kill our children for their misguided cause. The Bush administration has never adequately explained the theology and ideology behind Islamic terrorism or convinced us of its ruthless fanaticism. The first rule of war is 'know your enemy', and most Americans do not know theirs. (Huckabee, 2008)

Such concerns are now extending to organizations primarily concerned with social conservative issues, including FRC and FOF. Tony Perkins, president of FRC, described the War on Terror as 'a fundamental clash of world views', and James Dobson devoted five episodes of his daily radio programme to Islamic radicalism in March 2007 (Gilgoff, 2007). The war against radical Islam is a major concern for all organizations in the Christian Right and is described in apocryphal terms. The most vociferous exponents see the global War on Terror as World War III: radical Islam has replaced the fascists of World War II and the godless atheism of communism during the Cold War. This interpretation helps explain the Christian Right's enduring commitment to the war in Iraq as one battlefront in a war against what they consider the satanic forces of radical Islam, or 'Islamofascism'. In this battle, America and Israel join forces and the Middle East is the theatre of operations until jihadists strike America again.

The Christian Zionist movement, now under the leadership of John Hagee and CUFI, is increasingly vocal and influential in recasting the War on Terror as a war against 'Islamofascism', a term occasionally used by the president. In this war, America's support for Israel must be unwavering, Israel's enemies are America's enemies, Jerusalem must never be divided, and Iran must not be allowed to acquire nuclear weapons. Hagee developed this theme during speeches at AIPAC's 2006 annual conference and CUFI's 2007 Washington Summit: it is

1938 all over again; Ahmadinejad is Hitler and the world is waiting to see if he will be appeased or defeated; America is fighting a religious war against Islamofascism – a war America must win. Iran is considered to be a crucial component in the war against radical Islam and the stakes are high:

> If America loses this war with radical Islam – if we allow Iran to get and use nuclear weapons – the law of Sharia, the Islamic law, will rule America and the Western World. Christian churches and synagogues will be burned to the ground. Every Christian who refuses to denounce Jesus Christ to accept Allah will be decapitated. (Hagee, 2007: 35)

Hagee's comments reflect widespread belief in a struggle between Judeo-Christianity and Islam that cannot easily be resolved. At the Middle East briefing session, during the 2007 CUFI conference, the loudest cheers from 3,000 Christian Right activists went to Brigitte Gabriel, founder of the American Congress for Truth. Gabriel described the Arab world as having 'no soul', and warned that al-Qaeda, Islamic Jihad and Hamas had cells in over forty US states. She claimed that terrorists were marrying Arab women with American passports and 'breeding future terrorists'. When questioned about moderate Muslims, she replied, 'Where are the moderate Muslim voices? They are irrelevant because the moderates by their silence have become part of the radical agenda.'[17] Little wonder, then, that white evangelical Protestants have a less favourable opinion of Islam than other groups in American society and believe that Islam is more likely to encourage violence among its believers. Surveys conducted by the Pew Research Center showed that 46 per cent of those white evangelical Protestants questioned had an unfavourable opinion of Islam (36 per cent for all Americans) and 50 per cent considered it is more likely to encourage violence among its followers (36 per cent for all Americans).[18]

Although it is increasingly difficult to hear the Christian Right distinguishing between radical and moderate Muslims, some nuance still exists. Richard Land points out that Pat Robertson is becoming 'increasingly irrelevant' to evangelicals and that Hagee does not speak for a majority of evangelicals. He recognizes that there is a struggle but it is not against Islam but rather with 'radical Islamic jihadism':

> I am perfectly happy to have Islam as one of the faiths that's practised in the United States. I think the struggle that's going on in Islam is the most important struggle, ideologically, that's going on in the world today. The vast majority of the victims of radical Muslims are Muslims. The one common denominator of the extremists is that they are all from Muslim countries or they're all Muslim. There is a death cult that has taken hold in Islam and I think it comes from despair and this nihilism that has been bred by these countries that provide no real hope or opportunity to their populations. Radical Islam can't stand up against modernity; a medieval faith that has never had to contend with and interact with modernity – And the West had better understand that if someone's at war with you, you need to be at war with them. Radical Islamists want a caliphate across [the] Mediterranean [to] destroy Israel and destroy the USA. We're now in the Fourth World War and it's the struggle with radical Islamic jihadism. It's not a struggle between Islam and Christianity; it's a struggle between civilization and barbarism.[19]

The Bush administration has maintained the distinction between 'good' and 'bad' Muslims ever since 11 September and this view resonates with many but not all conservative evangelicals.

Conclusion

When the Bush administration, encouraged by neoconservatives, conservative evangelicals and corporate interests, sent US troops into Iraq in March 2003, the theatre of operations in the War on Terror moved decisively to that country. Al-Qaeda, which had previously not been present in the country, seized the opportunity to confront US troops in resisting the occupation and gaining valuable experience in urban warfare. Although most estimates place the extent of al-Qaeda involvement in the Iraq insurgency at no more than 3 per cent, the Bush administration has conducted a reasonably successful campaign convincing its core supporters that Iraq was involved in the attacks on America and that therefore Iraqis are the main opponents there today. The Bush administration considers Iraqi Sunni and Shia insurgents as being part of the War on Terror rather than a resistance seeking to end a foreign occupation.

The main, indeed the only, emphasis in the War on Terror is on Islamic groups and Islamic countries. In the list of 42 terrorist organizations outlawed by the Bush administration, 24 are Islamic organizations; a further 5 are Kurdish or Palestinian secular organizations; the remaining 13 include Continuity Irish Republican Army, Real IRA, Shining Path, the Tamil Tigers, Revolutionary Armed Forces of Colombia (FARC) and United Self Defence Forces of Colombia. Apart from involvement in Colombia as part of a concurrent war on drugs, the United States, throughout the War on Terror, has paid no heed to other terrorist groups.[20] The War on Terror specifically targets Muslim terrorist and radical groups and Islamic states accused of supporting terrorism in other countries.

The Christian Right, in alliance with neoconservatives, have been significant actors in the War on Terror. The support and encouragement of both groupings have been decisive in the administration interpreting the 11 September attacks as an ideological conflict in which the forces of radical Islam seek to destroy the West. Rather than seeking to deal with the attacks on America as terrorist incidents in which the perpetrators must be brought to justice, the conflict has been expanded to involve the occupation of two ostensively Muslim countries, and the possibility of confrontation with a third. The Christian Right–neoconservative alliance has been effective in persuading the president that the conflict is between Judeo-Christianity and radical Islam, a conflict that links Israel's and America's destinies.

The Christian Right have supported the president's decision to invade Afghanistan and Iraq and have been resolute in supporting the policy despite numerous setbacks. In the decision to attack Iraq evangelical Christian leaders played an important role in contradicting the Pope's advice that a pre-emptive strike did not meet the imperatives for Just War. Through extensive media coverage, they have convinced their supporters and members that there is a link between 11 September and Iraq, and that the war in Iraq is between the United States and al-Qaeda. In their support for Israel, they have used their influence with the White House and Congress to support Israeli actions in the Palestinian Occupied Territories and Lebanon, and urged military action against Iran's nuclear energy programme.

The War on Terror is led by a self-proclaimed born-again Christian, and is being fought by military personnel, disproportionately from evangelical backgrounds, who receive succour from military chaplains, half of whom are conservative evangelicals. The Christian Embassy has influenced the Pentagon, with conservative evangelicals represented at the highest levels of the military. The war has provided opportunities for Christian organizations to evangelize and win lucrative federal contracts to distribute assistance throughout the Muslim world, as part of a campaign to 'drain the swamp' and 'win hearts and minds'. Neoconservative attempts to privatize security have seen large contracts awarded to a mercenary organization run by prominent members of the Christian Right and benefactors of the Republican Party. The president's overtly Christian language and imagery in his speeches and unrehearsed asides, the 'mistakes' of describing the conflict as a 'crusade' of 'infinite justice', all convey the erroneous impression that the War on Terror is a Christian war against Islam.

The Christian Right have largely been unsuccessful in shifting the president from his position that 'Islam is a religion of peace' and of the desirability of working with Muslim countries in the War on Terror. The distinction between radical and moderate Muslims has been largely maintained despite attempts by Robertson, Graham and Hagee to blur the distinction. The president and administration have been able to call on Christian Right support without conceding to their demands on Israel or disastrous military action against Iran. The

War on Terror, which should more accurately be called a war against radical Islam, has exacerbated problems of international terrorism and increased anti-Americanism,[21] but could have fared worse if the Christian Right had been able to exert even greater influence over policy.

CONCLUSION

From Here to Eternity

Since the events of 9/11, the Christian Right have had greater opportunity to influence US foreign policy than ever before. They have enjoyed greater access to the White House than under any previous administration, with weekly conference calls to leading members and regular consultation on domestic and foreign policy on a whole range of issues from the Middle East, the war in Iraq, to global warming, religious freedom and HIV/AIDS policy. As a movement, they are no longer outsiders but have supporters within the administration and conservative evangelical fellow travellers, including the president himself. As Janice Crouse explains, 'It is a different situation for those of us who are Christian conservatives now. We are respected, our emails and our phone calls are answered and we do have access in ways that we did not have in the first Bush administration'.[1]

This book has been an attempt to move beyond the merely anecdotal and hysterical to consider the Christian Right on their own terms and demonstrate how they have sought to influence US foreign policy. The extent to which they have been successful depends on which foreign policy areas are considered. It is difficult to show conclusively the exact extent of influence by demonstrating how any specific aspect of foreign policy would have been different were it not for the involvement of the Christian Right. When considering policy towards Israel, for example, it is not possible to show a positive causation between hundreds of thousands of emails flooding the White House and a reduction in criticism of Israeli actions. This change in emphasis may have occurred anyway and the emails be simply coincidental; however, the likelihood is that such actions are significant and do not go unnoticed. Similar arguments could be advanced in attempting to find a causal link between the military–industrial complex, employment and the desire of congressional representatives to be re-elected, and yet few commentators would suggest that the influence is unimportant.

The picture that emerges is one of very serious foreign policy engagement, which flexes its muscles through an efficient lobbying machine honed over three decades. The mobilization of tens of thousands of activists and supporters to email, lobby, write and telephone politicians in Congress and the administration on specific foreign policy concerns constantly raises the profile of issues of concern to the movement. When these requests are backed up with orchestrated media campaigns, scorecard voting, financial support, and commitments to campaign for an incumbent's re-election campaign, they are inevitably taken seriously. The Christian Right, partly as a result of the work of Paul Weyrich and Gary Bauer, have formed tactical alliances with neoconservatives on a range of mutual interests, including support for Israel, religious freedom and the projection of US military strength to export America's Judeo-Christian values. The exact residual strength and capacity of the Christian Right, however, remain difficult to gauge although it has advanced so noticeably over the past eight years under a conservative Republican administration that was voted for overwhelmingly by conservative evangelicals in 2000 and 2004. To a great extent Christian Right aspirations and values have been promoted internationally by the Bush administration without the need for pressure or confrontation.

The evidence amassed in this book suggests that the Christian Right have been most effective as supporters rather than shapers of US foreign policy. The movement has been largely pushing at an open door in seeking to advance religious freedom, encourage democratization, deliver humanitarian assistance, support Israel, and restrict attempts by the international community to introduce equal rights legislation, an International Criminal Court, and carbon dioxide emissions reduction. In all these areas, the Bush administration has been delivering an agenda that generally, though sometimes not as successfully as they would like, meets with Christian Right aspirations. Conservative evangelicals in the foreign policy arena have been riding the Bush bandwagon rather than steering it, and confrontation has come when they seek a change in direction or want to steer more aggressively, as has occurred when, for example, opposing George Bush's Middle East Road Map and his attitude to Islam.

Christian Right support for US foreign policy objectives under a Republican administration is complemented by an evangelistic strategy that has served as an extension of American soft power. Through televangelism, radio broadcasts, evangelistic crusades and missions, conservative evangelicals and, in particular, the health and wealth teaching of Pentecostal, charismatic and renewalist televangelists such as Paul Crouch, Pat Robertson and T.D. Jakes, have introduced the American lifestyle, social conservatism and support for Israel to audiences across the developing world. Such teaching complements indigenous renewalist churches helping to fuel exponential growth in the movement across sub-Saharan Africa, Latin America and Asia. As we have seen, members of renewalist churches are more supportive of Israel and US foreign policy than fellow citizens and are more receptive to American values of self-help and capitalism. This provides a useful additional resource in promoting those values around the world in democracy and humanitarian assistance programmes.

Having the backing of a largely supportive politically active group of conservative evangelicals and right-wing Catholics has meant that the administration has been able to go further than it might have otherwise dared in pursuing its objectives. The decision to go to war against Iraq would have been even more keenly contested domestically had Richard Land and fellow Christian Right leaders not provided a Just War legitimation of the conflict despite contrary advice from the Pope and mainstream denominational leaders in America. The enthusiasm and support for US involvement in Iraq following Bush's declaration of 'mission accomplished' by the Christian Right helped in the exercise of maintaining troop numbers and in resisting the pressure to withdraw when it became obvious the victory had not been achieved. In terms of humanitarian assistance, the State Department and USAID would have been less willing to offend established and proven assistance providers such as Planned Parenthood, by enabling faith-based providers to deliver services. The Christian Right have further provided support for Bush's unilateralism by way of their steadfast role in international forums, particularly the UN, in resisting pressure to introduce or abide by international agreements, or reach consensus on issues such as Kyoto and the reduction of carbon emissions, CEDAW and equal rights, and the International Criminal Court.

The movement has been equally supportive on the issue of democracy promotion, which is always a controversial area and can be perceived by voters as spending taxpayers' money on a policy with negligible short-term gain. Conservative evangelicals have been grateful for the new opportunities the strategy has provided in opening up states and resources that traditionally have been closed to them. In the associated civil society area of religious freedom, they have actually set the pace, persuading the Clinton administration to introduce the International Religious Freedom Act, and enshrining religious freedom as an important measure in US diplomacy. They were instrumental, in alliance with neoconservatives and civil rights organizations, in pushing the Bush administration to get involved in southern Sudan and negotiate a peace settlement. It is the Christian Right who persuaded the Bush administration to engage with Africa as a whole, a continent that had been largely neglected by previous administrations. The Bush initiative on HIV/AIDS had been urged by secular humanitarian organizations for years, but it was the Christian Right, through Jesse Helms and others, who persuaded the president to provide $15 billion funding.

Ironically it is the realm of foreign affairs, where they are best organized and equipped, that the Christian Right have enjoyed least success. Academics and public alike have tended to perceive Israel as the issue where the Christian Right are most active and most effective. Christian Zionists have certainly been highly active in support of Israel throughout Bush's two terms in office. Eschatology has been the major driving force behind Christian Right thinking on Israel, but their views are not shared by the president as he has pursued, with wavering enthusiasm, a two-state solution to the Israeli–Palestinian problem. President Bush and his administration have shown no sign of having bought into the idea of end-times thinking, battles of Armageddon, or the return of Christ. Policy on Israel has been consistent, based on pragmatism, support for a fellow democracy and ally in the War on Terror, and opposition to radical Islam, not on biblical prophecy. The movement experienced some successes in terms of abandoning the late Yasser Arafat as a peace interlocutor, ending criticism of Israeli military operations in the West Bank and targeted assassination programme, and prolonging the Israeli attacks on Southern Lebanon and Hezbollah. In making its objections know the movement actually lent support and provided the administration with leverage to pursue a strategy that would otherwise have been harder to sell to domestic politicians and voters more anxious to see a peaceful resolution of the conflict.

The Religious Right have been regularly consulted by the administration but have been unable to persuade the president to move the US embassy in Israel from Tel Aviv to Jerusalem. They were unable to prevent US support for a unilateral Israeli withdrawal from Gaza.

They were also unsuccessful in ending Bush's continued commitment to a two-state solution, which inevitably means an Israeli withdrawal from parts of 'the promised land' occupied during the Six Day War. The Christian Right have been unsuccessful in persuading the president to change his views about the nature of Islam as a religion of peace and Muslims as people of faith who worship the one God. They have also, at the time of writing, failed to persuade Bush to attack Iran over its nuclear power programme and the perceived threat to Israel and US strategic interests. Should such an attack occur before the end of Bush's term the Christian Right will rally support and offer legitimation for it, in much the same way as they did before and after the Iraq conflict.

The Christian Right have enjoyed success during the Bush years. However, their influence is damaging to US interests in the short, medium and long term: by placing America against egalitarian progress in international forums; preventing measures designed to improve women's health, protect children and provide equality to homosexuals; by allying themselves with reactionary and human-rights-abusing governments around the world to support policies that restrict women's right to control their reproductive health; by placing the health of people, mainly in the developing world, at risk by restricting access to abortion and sex education; by banning stem-cell research designed to find cures for life-threatening illnesses; and by withholding condoms, the most effective weapon in the war against HIV/AIDS.

Christian Right denial of the anthropogenic causation of global warming continues to put the world at risk of environmental disaster by reducing pressure on the US government to cooperate with the international community and accept mandatory reductions in greenhouse gas emissions. Conservative evangelicals have led support for going to war and maintaining the occupation in Iraq. The Islamophobia expressed by leaders of the Christian Right reveals a deep-seated antipathy towards the Muslim world and seeks to identify Islam, rather than radical Islam, as America's enemy. The Christian

Right's proselytizing in the Muslim world, evangelization within the US military, and criticism of Muhammad and of Islam as a religion of peace, and unequivocal support for Israel despite its appalling treatment of Palestinians in the Occupied Territories – all create the impression within the Muslim world that America is leading a crusade against them. The delivery of humanitarian assistance by conservative evangelical organizations determined to convert patients, the hungry and the destitute to Christianity as their first priority will be seen as religious imperialism, to be added to the economic and cultural imperialism that causes so much consternation in the global South.

The Christian Right are currently training up a new generation of leaders who are intent on changing US society and foreign policy according to a narrow set of religious beliefs. As a movement, during the Bush years, they have reinforced the more reactionary and bellicose instincts of the president, reinforcing his Manichaean worldview that portrays America as good and those Muslims who take a contrary view as evil. The Christian Right are identified with the worst excesses of the Bush administration, as either instigators or supporters of policy, and share responsibility for reducing America's international standing and for fuelling hostility towards the country that is likely to continue for many years to come.

The Christian Right in the Future

Christian Right gains in the area of foreign policy have largely come about under the Republican presidencies of Ronald Reagan and George W. Bush. What does the future hold for the Christian Right after the 2008 elections? A Democrat administration might provide a temporary respite. But the Christian Right are preparing to be around as a major player in American politics and international affairs in perpetuity. Access to the White House is desirable for them, but not essential. After all, the International Religious Freedom Act was introduced despite opposition from Madeleine Albright, Clinton's secretary of state, because of support in Congress. The Christian Right will continue to organize and campaign around socially conservative issues at home and abroad. Under a Democrat administration it is unlikely that members of Christian Right organizations will take part in US delegations to the United Nations to discuss climate change or sexual health issues, but if the Republican Party is able to retake either the House or Senate, or indeed both, through the mobilization of Christian Right footsoldiers, then they will still exert considerable influence, especially on issues pertaining to Israel and religious freedom.

In the 2008 presidential primaries religion became an important issue as Democrats talked openly of their Christian faith in a way not witnessed since Jimmy Carter. This renewed openness to religion may lead to opportunities for the Christian Right to increase its support as more Democrat politicians are prepared to endorse socially conservative positions on abortion and stem-cell research. Although there have been no major Christian Right defections on climate change and the environment, this may change over time as the scientific evidence becomes incontrovertible and a Democrat administration endorses international agreements to reduce carbon emissions. A second Clinton administration, however, would be viewed with consternation by the movement because of her pro-choice and feminist views, thereby maintaining political polarization and redoubling efforts by the Christian Right to help Republicans retake Congress and win the 2012 election with a candidate they can unite behind.

Opponents of the Christian Right have looked with optimism to the emergence of new younger leadership within the movement to minimize its political significance. They can point to defections within the movement on global warming by Joel Hunter and Richard Cizik and the emergence of mega-church pastors such as Rick Warren, Bill Hybels and Joel Osteen, who are more concerned with evangelism and lifestyle than with partisan political activism, as a portent. The present leadership of the Christian Right are approaching their twilight years, and over the course of the first decade of the twenty-first century the pioneers of the movement have mostly died or retired.

Reports of the death of the Christian Right as a domestic and foreign policy actor, however, are greatly exaggerated. Dead leaders of the movement, such as Jerry Falwell and Lester Sumrall, have passed on the mantle to their sons, as has Pat Robertson, albeit this side of eternity. New leaders are emerging – such as John Hagee, Rod Parsley and Rick Scarborough, and maybe, after his showing in the Republican primaries, Mike Huckabee – who are every bit as hardline as their predecessors. The Christian Right have enjoyed their increased influence and the opportunity to help shape a conservative foreign policy agenda. As such they have no intention of leaving the world's stage any time soon.

Notes

Introduction

1. American Ethnic Geography, 'Map Gallery of Religion in the United States', www.valpo.edu/geomet/geo/courses/geo200/religion.html; accessed 23 January 2008.

Chapter 1

1. Richard Land, interview with the author, 19 July 2007, Washington DC.
2. Council for National Policy website, www.policycounsel.org; accessed 2 September 2007.
3. 'The Council for National Policy Past/Present Officers and Prominent Member Profiles', www.watch.pair.com/database.html; accessed 19 January 2008.
4. Ambassador Dennis Ross, Richard Land and Janice Crouse, interviews with the author 18–20 July 2007, Washington DC.
5. Eileen O'Connor, 'Bush's Faith-based Initiative', CNN.com, 29 December 2001, www.cnn.com/chat/transcripts/2001/01/29/oconnor.debrief/; accessed 20 January 2008.
6. Handout in welcome pack, Christians United for Israel, Washington DC/Israel Summit, 15–18 July 2007.
7. Information on the Center for Christian Statesmanship can be found at www.statesman.org, and on Evangelism Explosion from www.eeinternational.org.
8. www.christianembassy.com/content.asp?contentid=371; accessed 1 September 2007.

9. Christian Embassy, www.christianembassy.com/content.asp?contentid=359; accessed 20 January 2008.
10. Further information on the work of the Christian Embassy in Washington DC can be found at www.christianembassy.com.
11. Democracy Now website, 'God & the Presidency: An In-Depth Examination of Faith in the Bush White House', www.democracynow.org/article.pl?sid=04/10/20/1423216; accessed I May 2007.
12. Janice Crouse, interview with the author, 17 July 2007; and Richard Land, interview with the author, 19 July 2007, Washington DC.
13. Janice Crouse and Bill Sanders, interviews with the author, 17 July 2007, Washington DC.
14. *Time* magazine, www.time.com/time/covers/1101050207/photoessay/14.html; accessed 1 September 2007.
15. *Time* magazine, www.time.com/time/covers/1101050207/photoessay/19.html; accessed 1 September 2007.
16. *Time* magazine, www.time.com/time/covers/1101050207/photoessay/2.html; accessed 1 September 2007.
17. 'The Institute on Religion and Democracy Purpose Statement', www.ird-renew.org/site/pp.aspx?c=fvKVLfMVIsG&b=356299; accessed 6 September 2007.
18. World Congress of Families IV, Warsaw 2007: The Howard Center, http://worldcongress.org/WCF4/wcf4.co.htm; accessed 6 September 2007.
19. Statement Council for National Policy meeting on 7 February 1998, reported in *Washington Times*, 17 February 1998.
20. CUFI Membership Update for 29 January 2007.
21. Net Ministries: Christian Colleges and Universities, http://netministries.org/college.htm; accessed 1 September 2007.
22. Home School Legal Defense Association, 'About HSLDA', www.hslda.org/default.asp?; accessed 7 September 2007.
23. Ibid.
24. Generation Joshua, www.generationjoshua.org/dnn/Default.aspx?tabid=99.
25. Patrick Henry College, 'Statement of Mission and Vision', http://phc.edu/about/mission.asp; accessed 1 September 2007.
26. Ibid.
27. Patrick Henry College, 'Student Covenant and Honor Code', http://phc.edu/about/StudentCovenantHonorCode.asp; accessed 1 September 2007.
28. Patrick Henry College, 'Biblical Worldview Applications', http://phc.edu/about/BiblicalWorldviewApplication.asp; accessed 1 September 2007.
29. For further information on Regent University go to www.regent.edu/.

Chapter 2

1. Barry Lynn, interview with the author, 18 July 2007, Washington DC.
2. Further information about this radio ministry is available at www.lesea.com/broadcasting/index.cfm; accessed 24 January 2008.

3. Details of Focus on the Family International radio broadcasts can be found on www.oneplace.com/ministries/Focus_on_the_Family_International/; accessed 24 January 2008.
4. Franklin Graham's festivals or crusade details can be found at www.grahamfestival.org/index.asp; accessed 23 November 2007.
5. Joyce Meyer Ministries, www.joycemeyer.org.
6. For an interesting and detailed insight into the personal wealth of televangelists refer to the website of In Plain Site, which details the lifestyles of leading preachers in the renewalist movement, www.inplainsite.org/html/teleevangelist_lifestyles.html; accessed 9 September 2007.
7. For further information on Trinity Broadcasting Network see website www.tbn.org/.
8. *Broadcasting and Cable* magazine, 19 April 2004.
9. Daystar Television Network, www.daystar.com/links/about_us/about_daystar.htm; accessed 24 January 2008.
10. 'About CBN', www.cbn.com/about; accessed 9 September.
11. For further information on METV, see www.metv.org/; accessed 24 January 2008.
12. For more information go to www.fetv.tv/; accessed 24 January 2008.
13. www.operationblessing.org/about/history.asp; accessed 14 September 2007.
14. Joyce Meyer Ministries, www.joycemeyer.org/OurMinistries/WorldMissions; accessed 14 September 2007.
15. BBC News, 'US to get Africa command centre', 6 February 2007, http://news.bbc.co.uk/2/hi/americas/6336063.stm; accessed 14 September 2007.
16. Kenneth Copeland Ministries regular preach in Africa and attend ministers' conferences. See http://events.kcm.org.events.php; accessed 20 January 2008.
17. T.D. Jakes established *Terra Cotta International* as a ministry to help development projects and church growth in developing countries including Kenya. Jakes works with African ministries in a project known as Faith for Africa, http://thepottershouse.org/_downloads/FaithForAfrica.swk; accessed 20 January 2008.

Chapter 3

1. George W. Bush speech in Czernin Palace, Prague, Czech Republic, 5 June 2007.
2. Richard Land, interview with the author, 19 July 2007, Washington DC.
3. Wordsmyth, 'Reactions to Dubya's 2nd Inaugural', www.wordsmyth.btinternet.co.uk/CommentariatReactions.htm; accessed 29 September 2007.
4. Richard Land, interview with the author, 19 July 2007, Washington DC.
5. George Bush speech to National Religious Broadcasters, Nashville, 10 February 2006.
6. 'Bush Calls for Culture Change', *Christianity Today*, May (web only) 2004, www.christianitytoday.com/ct/2004/mayweb-only/5–24–51.0.html; accessed 6 September 2007.

7. Richard Land, interview with the author, 19 July 2007, Washington DC.
8. Ibid.
9. Rob Moll, 'Should Evangelicals Support Bush's Foreign Policy If He Can't Guarantee Religious Freedom?', *Christianity Today*, April 2006, http://ctlibrary.com/38710; accessed 10 September 2007.
10. Ibid.
11. Bill Saunders interview with the author, 16 July 2007, Washington DC.

Chapter 4

1. In 2007 the Center moved with Nina Shea to the Hudson Institute, Washington DC.
2. See http://persecution.org/Countries/sudan.html; accessed 16 April 2007.
3. 'Interview with Kristin Wright of Stand Today', *Christian Monitor*, 30 April 2005, www.christianmonitor.org/documents.php?type=Interviews&lang=English&item_ID=9&action=display&; accessed 22 January 2008.
4. Senior USAID official, interview with the author, Washington DC.
5. In fairness to Ambassador Natsios he did inform me of his antipathy towards the Religious Right, insisting that he was not a Christian conservative but rather a 'theologically conservative eastern orthodox Christian and I am philosophically on the right'. Email correspondence with the author, 9 July 2007.
6. www.boston.com/news/special/faith_based/faith_based_organizations_totaldow.
7. Ibid.
8. The 10/40 window is located between latitudes 10 and 40 degrees north of the equator and includes the Middle East, North Africa, Central and South East Asia. www.abwe.org/serve/ministry_focus/1040_window.asp; accessed 18 October 2006.
9. Information taken from www.boston.com/news/special/faith_based_organizations_totaldow; accessed 25 June 2007.
10. Richard Land, interview with the author, 19 July 2007, Washington DC.
11. Ibid.
12. Ambassador John Bolton, interview with the author, 19 July 2007, Washington DC.
13. Colin Powell's action cable to USAID mission directors and population, health and nutrition officers: 'Implementation of USAID Policies and Programs on HIV/AIDS and Trafficking', 24 December 2002, cited in Kaplan, 2005: 229–30.
14. Barry Lynn, interview with the author, 18 July 2007, Washington DC.
15. Ibid.
16. John Bolton, interview with the author, 19 July 2007, Washington DC.
17. Focus on the Family, 'Our Mission Vision and Guiding Principles', www.focusonthefamily.com/aboutus/A000000408.cfm; accessed 10 February 2007.
18. Dr Janice Crouse, interview with the author, 18 July 2007, Washington DC.
19. Ibid.

20. Ibid.
21. Bill Saunders, interview with the author, 16 July 2007, Washington DC.
22. John Bolton, interview with the author, 19 July 2007, Washington DC.

Chapter 5

1. Peter Schwartz and Doug Randall (2003), 'An abrupt Climate Change Scenario and Its Implications for United States National Security', Department of Defense, cited in Phillips 2006: 88.
2. 'Nationwide Survey Shows Concerns of Evangelical Christians over Global Warming', www.ellisonresearch.com; accessed 1 October 2007.
3. The Evangelical Climate Initiative (2006), 'Climate Change: An Evangelical call to Action', www.christiansandclimate.org/statement; accessed 18 April 2008.
4. *New American Standard Bible.*
5. 'A Letter to the National Association of Evangelicals on the Issue of Global Warming', www.interfaithstewardship.org; accessed 1 September 2007.
6. The Great Warming Interview, 'Interview with Richard Cizik', www.thegreatwarming.com/revrichardcizik.html; accessed 4 October 2007.
7. Cornwall Declaration, www.interfaithstewardship.org/pages/printcornwall.htm; accessed 7 October 2007.
8. Richard Land, interview with the author, 19 July 2007, Washington DC.
9. Ibid.
10. Ibid.
11. The Great Warming Interview, 'Interview with Richard Cizik'.

Chapter 6

1. All quotations from the Bible are taken from *The Bible: Authorized King James Version* (Oxford: Oxford University Press, 1998).
2. BBC News, 'US Military Aid for Middle East', 30 July 2007, http://news.bbc.co.uk/1/hi/world/middle_east/6922664.stm; accessed 14 October 2007.
3. John Bolton, interview with the author, 19 July 2007, Washington DC.
4. Richard Land, interview with the author, 19 July 2007, Washington DC.
5. Religion & Ethics Newsweekly, 'Anti Islam', 20 February 2002, www.pbs.org/wnet/religionandethics/week616/cover.html; accessed 14 October 2007.
6. Pat Robertson, remarks about Islam on *700 Club*, Christian Broadcasting Network, 21 October 2006.
7. Jerry Falwell interviewed by Bob Simon in 'Zion's Christian Soldiers', CBS, 3 October 2002, www.cbsnews.com/stories/2002/10/03/60minutes/main524268.shtml; accessed 21 December 2006.
8. Dennis Ross, interview with the author, 20 July 2007, Washington DC.
9. CUFI Membership Update for 7 May 2007.

10. CUFI Membership Update for 11 June 2007.
11. Comments recorded by the author at Night to Honor Israel, Washington CUFI summit, 17 July 2007.
12. John Bolton, interview with the author, 19 July 2007.
13. CUFI Membership Update for 29 January 2007.
14. S. Con. Res. 88, 'Expressing Solidarity with Israel in the Fight against Terrorism', 107th Congress, 5 December 2001.
15. H. Res. 392, 107th Congress, 2 May 2002.
16. H. Res. 713, 108th Congress, 15 July 2004.
17. S.J. Res. 12, 110th Congress, 25 April 2007.
18. Richard Land, interview with the author, 19 July 2007, Washington DC.
19. Vision America email to the White House about the Middle East peace process, https://secure2.convio.net/va/site/Advocacy?cmd=display&page=UserAction&id=314; accessed 25 January 2008.
20. BBC News, 'Israel confirms settlement plans', 23 December 2007, http://news.bbc.co.uk/1/hi/world/middle_east/7158072.stm; accessed 25 January 2008.

Chapter 7

1. Remarks by President Bush at Islamic Center of Washington, 17 September 2001, Washington DC.
2. Jerry Falwell speaking on *700 Club*, Christian Broadcasting Network, 13 September 2001.
3. Barry Lynn, interview with the author, 18 July 2007, Washington DC.
4. Remarks by George Bush and King Abdullah of Jordan, the Oval Office, Washington DC, 28 September 2001.
5. Remarks at the Good Shepherd Community Church, Boring, Oregon, October 2003.
6. CNN Larry King Live, 'What Would Jesus Do About War with Iraq?', broadcast at 9 p.m. EST on 11 March 2003.
7. 'Road Map is a Life Saver for Us: PM Abbas Tells Ha'aretz', 26 June 2003, as cited in Kaplan, 2005: 9.
8. 'President Bush Discusses Freedom in Iraq and Middle East', National Endowment for Democracy, Washington DC, 6 November 2003.
9. Richard Land, interview with the author, 19 July 2007, Washington DC.
10. www.gnn.tv/headlines/2725/Stations_of_the_Cross_The_Emergence_of_Faith_Based_news; accessed 4 March 2006.
11. 'US Christian Missions in the Middle East', *Los Angles Times*, 18 March 2004.
12. 'In 20 Years, There Will Be No More Christians in Iraq', *Guardian*, 6 October 2006.
13. A copy of the video was posted on YouTube, www.youtube.com/watch?v=uT2BE5RS01E&eurl=; accessed 21 December 2006 (the video has been repeatedly removed and resubmitted). Information is also available from 'Questionable Mission: A Christian Embassy Campaign at the Pentagon Tests Constitutional

Boundaries', *Washington Post*, 6 January 2007. See also Chris Hedges, 'America's Holy Warriors', http://alternet.org/story/46211/; accessed 16 February 2007.

14. Barry Lynn, interview with the author, 18 July 2007, Washington DC.
15. 'Evangelicals, Muslims Meet', *Washington Times*, 11 July 2007.
16. Jerry Falwell speaking on *60 Minutes*, CBS, 6 October 2002.
17. Author's notes taken at Christians United for Israel Washington DC/Israel Summit, Wardman Marriott Hotel, Washington DC, 17 July 2007.
18. Pew Forum on Religion & Public Life Analysis, 'Prospects for Inter-Religious Understanding', prepared for delivery at the International Conference on Faith and Service, 22 March 2006, Washington DC.
19. Richard Land, interview with the author, 19 July 2007, Washington DC.
20. US Department of State fact sheet on counterterrorism, 11 October 2005, www.state.gov/s/ct/rls/fs/37191.htm; accessed 12 August 2007.
21. See the 'Pew Global Attitudes Project 2007', Pew Research Center, Washington DC.

Conclusion

1. Janice Crouse, interview with the author, 18 July 2007, Washington DC.

References

Aaby, P., and Hvalkof, S. (1982), *Is God an American?* Copenhagen: International Working Group for Indigenous Affairs.

Abrams, E., ed. (2001), *The Influence of Faith: Religious Groups and U.S. Foreign Policy*, Lanham MD/Oxford: Rowan & Littlefield/Ethics and Public Policy Center.

Albright, M. (2007), *The Mighty and the Almighty: Reflections on America, God, and World Affairs*, New York: Harper Perennial.

Alden, M (2005), 'Educating America's Right', *Crossing Continents*, BBC Radio 4, http://news.bbc.co.uk/go/pr/fr/-/1/hi/programmes/crossing_continents/4311709.stm; accessed 1 September 2007.

Allin, D., and Simon, S. (2003), 'The Moral Psychology of US Support for Israel', *Survival*, vol. 45, no. 3, Autumn: 123–44.

Alter, A. (2003), 'Groups Weigh Risks, Morality of Evangelizing in Postwar Iraq, *Religion News Service*, The Pew Forum on Religion & Public Life, http://pewforum.org/news/display.php?NewsID=2282; accessed 18 October 2006.

Americans United (2007), 'Bring Me the Head of Rich Cizik! Religious Right Demands Ouster of NAE Official', http://blog.au.org/2007/03/08/bring-me-the-head-of-rich-cizik-religious-right-demand; accessed 1 October 2007.

Anderson, D. (2002), 'Conservative Protestant Leaders Back Bush on Iraq', *Religion News Service*, http://pewforum.org/news/display.phpNewsID=1600; accessed 6 August 2007.

Arkin, W. (2003), 'The Pentagon Unleashes a Holy Warrior', *Los Angeles Times*, 16 October.

Armey, R. (2006), 'Christians and Big Government', *FreedomWorks*, 12 October, www.freedomworks.org/processor/printer.php?issue_id=2731; accessed 9 July 2007.

Baker, J. (1992), 'Securing the Democratic Peace', *US Department of State Dispatch*, issue 2, 13 April.

Barry, T. (2007), 'America's Crusaders', Right Web Analysis, Silver City NM: International Relations Center, 23 February.

Baxter, S. (2003), 'Aids Cash Inspired by Christian Right', *Sunday Times*, 9 February.

BBC News (2006), 'Lebanon: Key Facts', http://news.bbc.co.uk/1/shared/spl/hi/guides/456900/45697/html/default.stm; accessed 23 November 2006.

Beaumont, P. (2007), 'Providing a Place of Sanctuary and Solace for the Faithful on the Frontline', *Guardian*, 21 February.

Beliles, M., and McDowell, S. (1989), *America's Providential History*, San Francisco: Providence Foundation.

Berlet, C. (2005), 'The Christian Right, Dominionism, and Theocracy', www.publiceye.org/christian_right/dominionism.htm; accessed 14 August 2007.

Biddison, J. (2006), 'Evangelicals Misled on Climate Change', *Townhall.com*, 28 February, www.townhall.com; accessed 2 October 2007.

Blumenthal, M. (2006), 'Israel, the U.S., and the Christian Right: The Menage à Trois from Hell', *Huffington Post*, 10 August, www.huffingtonpost.com/max-blumenthal/israel-the-us-and-the-c_b_26995.html; accessed 17 April 2008.

Blumenthal, M. (2007a), 'With the Party of Dobson', *Nation*, www.thenation.com/doc/20061009/party_of_dobson; accessed 21 October 2006.

Blumenthal, M. (2007b), 'Bush Met with Dobson and Conservative Christian Leaders to Rally Support for Iran Policy', 14 May, http://rawstory.com; accessed 15 May 2007.

Boston, R. (2006), 'The Religious Right and American Freedom', *Americans United for Separation of Church and State*, June, www.au.org/site/News2?page=NewsArticle&id=8255&news_iv_ctrl=0&abbr=cs_; accessed 16 April 2008.

Boston, R. (2007), 'The Religious Right after Falwell', *Americans United for Separation of Church and State*, July/August, www.au.org/site/News2?abbr=cs_&page=NewsArticle&id=9216; accessed 14 August 2007.

Broadway, B. (2004), 'The Evangelical–Israeli Connection', *Washington Post*, 27 March.

Broder, J. (2007a), 'At Its Session on Warming, U.S. Is Seen to Stand Apart', *New York Times*, 28 September.

Broder, J. (2007b), 'At Climate Meeting, Bush Does Not Specify Goals', *New York Times*, 29 September.

Brog, D. (2006a), *Standing with Israel*, Lake Mary FL: Front Line.

Brog, D. (2006b), 'Jews and Evangelicals Together', http://article.nationalreview.com/?q=ZDFiODgxY2ZkZjNhY2JmMmFjN2RkN; accessed 19 April 2007.

Brog, D. (2006c), 'David Brog on Why Christians Support the Jewish State', *Haaretz.com*, 7 May.

Brooks, D. (2007), 'Heroes and History', *New York Times*, 17 July.

Brouwer, S., Gifford, P., and Rose, S. (1996), *Exporting the American Gospel: Global Christian Fundamentalism*, London and New York: Routledge.

References

Brown, D. (2005), 'Group Awarded AIDS Grant Despite Negative Appraisal', *Washington Post*, 16 February.

Brozan, N. (1987), 'Politics and Prayer: Women on a Crusade', *New York Times*, 15 June.

Buncombe, A. (2004), 'The Bible College that Leads to the White House', *Independent*, 21 April.

Bunting, M. (2005), 'Bono Talks of US Crusade', *Guardian*, 16 June.

Bunting, M., and Burkeman, O. (2002), 'Pro Bono', *Guardian*, 18 March.

Bush, G.W. (2005b), 'Remarks by the President to the National Endowment for Democracy', 6 October, www.ned.org/events/oct0605–Bush.html; accessed 2 February 2006.

Buss, D., and Herman, D. (2003), *Globalizing Family Values: The Christian Right in International Politics*, Saint Paul: University of Minnesota Press.

Butler, J. (2006), *Born Again: The Christian Right Globalized*, London: Pluto Press.

Canellos, P., and Baron, B. (2006), 'A US Boost to Graham's Quest for Converts', *Boston Globe*, 8 October.

Capitol Advantage (2007), *Congress at your Fingertips:* 110*th Congress: Ist Session*, Washington DC: Capitol Advantage.

Carnes, T. (2003), 'The Bush Doctrine', *Christianity Today*, May.

Carney, J. (2006), 'The Rise and Fall of Ralph Reed', *Time Magazine*, 23 July.

Carothers, T. (1999), *Aiding Democracy Abroad*, Washington DC: Carnegie Endowment for International Peace.

Carothers, T. (2007), *U.S. Democracy Promotion During and After Bush*, Washington DC: Carnegie Endowment for International Peace.

Castelli, E. (2005), 'Praying for the Persecuted Church: US Christian Activism in the Global Arena', *Journal of Human Rights* 4: 321–51.

CBS (2003), 'Zion's Christian Soldiers', *CBS News*, 8 June, www.cbsnews.com/2002/10/03/60minutes/524268.shtml; accessed 19 February 2007.

CFI (Christian Freedom International) (2006), *Annual Report* 2006, www.christian-freedom.org/pdf/annual_report.pdf; accessed 20 June 2007.

Christian Century (2007), 'NAE Rebuffs Critics, Affirming Cizik and a Wider Agenda', *Christian Century*, 3 April.

Cizik, R. (2007), 'The Great Warming: Interview with Rev. Richard Cizik', www.thegreatwarming.com/revrrichardcizik.html; accessed 4 October 2007.

Clarke, R. (2004), *Against All Enemies*, London: Free Press.

Clarkson, F. (2007), 'Bush's Religious Right Swat Team Takes Aim at Methodists', 6 February, www.talk2action.org/2007/2/6/152631/1600; accessed 16 February 2007.

Clifford, C. (1992), *Counsel to the President*, New York: Anchor Books.

Clinton, W. (1993), 'American Foreign Policy and the Democratic Ideal', *Orbis*, vol. 37, no. 4, Fall.

Colby, G., and Dennett, C. (1995), *Thy Will Be Done*, London: HarperCollins.

Colson, C. (2002), 'Drawing the Battle Lines: We Need to be Informed and Discerning about the Islamic Worldview', *Christianity Today* 46, 17 January.

Cooperman, A. (2007), 'McCain Makes Play for Evangelicals' Support', *Washington*

Post, 7 June, A08.

Cornwall Alliance (2006), *A Call to Truth, Prudence, and Protection of the Poor: An Evangelical Response to Global Warming*, Burke VA: Cornwall Alliance for the Stewardship of Creation.

Cornwell, R. (2006), 'Evangelists' Coalition Demands White House Acts on Environment', *Independent*, 9 February.

Croft, S. (2007), '"Thy Will be Done": The New Foreign Policy of America's Christian Right', *International Politics* 44: 692–710.

Crouse, J. (2002), 'United States Reverses Clinton Endorsement of the International Criminal Court', *Concerned Women for America*, 1 January, www.cwfa.org/articledisplay.asp?id=1959&department=CWA&categoryid=nation; accessed 22 January 2008.

Dahl, R. (1971), *Polyarchy, Participation and Opposition*, New Haven CT: Yale University Press.

DeMar, G., and Leithart, P. (1988), *The Reduction of Christianity*, Fort Worth TX: Dominion Press.

de Soto, A. (2007), 'End of Mission Report', confidential report leaked to the *Guardian*, 13 May.

de Tocqueville, A. (1998), *Democracy in America*, London: Wordsworth.

Diamond, S. (1989), *Spiritual Warfare: The Politics of the Christian Right*, Cambridge MA: South End Press.

Diamond, S. (1995a), 'The Threat of the Christian Right', *Z Magazine*, http://wwzena.secureform.com/Znet/ZMag/articles/july95diamond.htm; accessed 18 October 2006.

Diamond, S. (1995b), *Roads to Dominion: Right-Wing Movements and Political Power in the United States*, New York: Guilford Press.

Dobson, J. (2005), 'Good News Regarding Families around the World', www.focusonthefamily.com/docstudy/newsletters/A000000762.cfm; accessed 25 March 2007.

Dobson, J. (2006a), 'Mr. Armey, You've Become a Bitter Man', *FoxNews.com*, 31 October, www.foxnews.com/0,3566,226522,00.html; accessed 9 July 2007.

Dobson, J. (2006b), 'Focus on the Family Broadcast: Dr. Dobson Says "The Big Tent Will Turn Into a Three-Ring Circus"', *Citizenlink.com*, www.citizenlink.org/clspecialalert/A000002993; accessed 11 November 2006.

Domke, D. (2004), *God Willing? Political Fundamentalism in the White House, the War on Terror and the Echoing Press*, London: Pluto.

Doyle, M. (1983a), 'Kant, Liberal Legacies and Foreign Affairs', *Philosophy and Public Affairs*, vol. 12, no. 3: 205–35.

Doyle, M. (1983b), 'Kant, Liberal Legacies and Foreign Affairs, Part 2', *Philosophy and Public Affairs*, vol. 12, no. 4: 323–53.

Durham, M. (2004), 'Evangelical Protestantism and Foreign Policy in the United States after September 11', *Patterns of Prejudice*, vol. 38, no. 2: 709–24.

Economist (2006), 'Halleluja! The Rise of Pentecostalism Could Change the Face of Kenya', *Economist*, 20 July.

Eggen, D. (2002), 'Alleged Remarks on Islam Prompt an Ashcroft Reply', *Washington Post*, 14 February.

Evans, G., and Newnham, J. (1998), *The Penguin Dictionary of International Relations*, London: Penguin.

Firestone, D. (2002), 'Evangelical Christians and Jews Unite for Israel', *New York Times*, 9 June.

Foreign Policy (2007), 'The Failed State Index 2007', *Foreign Policy*, July/August.

Fox, J., and Sandler, S. (2006), *Bringing Religion into International Affairs*, London: Palgrave Macmillan.

FRC/FOF (Family Research Council/Focus on the Family) (2007), 'Vote Scorecard: 109th Congress 2nd Session', *FRC and Focus on the Family Action*, Washington DC: FRC/FOF.

Frum, D. (2003), *The Right Man: An Inside Account of the Surprise Presidency of George W. Bush*, London: Weidenfeld & Nicolson.

Fukuyama, F. (1989), 'The End of History?', *National Interest* 16, Summer: 3–18.

Fukuyama, F. (1992), *The End of History and the Last Man*, London and New York: Penguin.

Fukuyama, F. (2006), *After the Neocons: America at the Crossroads*, London: Profile Books.

Gilgoff, D. (2007), 'A New Crusade for GOP Evangelicals', *Los Angeles Times*, 25 March.

Glanz, J., and Rubin, A. (2007), 'Blackwater Shootings "Murder", Iraq Says', *New York Times*, 8 October.

Glazov, J. (2006), 'Standing with Israel', *FrontpageMagazine.com*, www.frontpagemag.com/Articles/ID=22701; accessed 19 April 2007.

Goldberg, M. (2007), *Kingdom Coming: The Rise of Christian Nationalism*, New York: W.W. Norton.

Goodstein, L. (2007), 'Evangelical's Focus on Climate Draws Fire of Christian Right', *New York Times*, 3 March.

Gorski, E. (2007), 'Baptists Approve Global Warming Measure', *ABC News*, http://abcnews.go.com/print?id=3275501; accessed 2 October 2007.

Grant, G. (1985), *Bringing in the Sheaves*, Chicago: Christian Liberty Press.

Grant, G. (1987), *The Changing of the Guard*, Fort Worth TX: Dominion Press.

Green, J. (2001), 'God's Foreign Policy', *Washington Monthly*, November.

Green, J., Smidt, C., Guth, J., and Kellstedt, L. (2005), 'The American Religious Landscape and the 2004 Presidential Vote: Increased Polarization', Washington DC: Pew Forum on Religion and Public Life.

Guttman, N. (2007), 'Top Bush Advisor Says Rice's Push for Mideast Peace Is "Just Process"', *Jewish Daily Forward*, 11 May.

Hagee, J. (2006), 'Bible FAQ', www.sacornerstone.com/faq_biblical.asp; accessed 12 July 2006.

Hagee, J. (2007), *Jerusalem Countdown*, Lake Mary FL: Front Line.

Hasdorff, T. (2006), 'Testimony before the Subcommittee on Africa, Global Human Rights and International Operations, House International Relations Committee',

28 September, www.usaid.gov/press/speeches/2006/ty060928.html; accessed 13 July 2007.

Haynes, J. (2007), *An Introduction to International Relations and Religion*, Harlow: Pearson Longman.

Hedges, C. (2007), 'America's Holy Warriors', *Truthdig*, http://alternet.org/story/46211; accessed 16 February 2007.

Hehir, J. (2001), 'Religious Freedom and U.S. Foreign Policy: Categories and Choices', in E. Abrams (ed.), *The Influence of Faith: Religious Groups and U.S. Foreign Policy*, Lanham MD/Oxford: Rowan & Littlefield/Ethics and Public Policy Center.

Henderson Blunt, S. (2006), 'Shakeup at Patrick Henry College', *Christianity Today*, May, www.christianitytoday.com/ct/article_print.html?id=38739; accessed 1 September 2007.

Hertzke, A.(2006), *Freeing God's Children*, Lanham MD: Rowman & Littlefield.

Hodge, W. (2007), 'U.N. Chief Urges Fast Action on Global Climate Change', *New York Times*, 25 September.

Holley, J. (2007), 'Harnessed the Political Power of Evangelicals', *Washington Post*, 16 May: A01.

Horowitz, D. (2006), 'Evangelicals Seeing the Error of "Replacement Theology"', *Jerusalem Post* Online Edition, www.jpost.comSatellite?cid=1139395642585; accessed 27 March 2007.

Horowitz, M. (1995), 'New Intolerance Between the Crescent and the Cross', *Wall Street Journal*, 5 July.

House, W., and Ice, T. (1988), *Dominion Theology: Blessing or Curse?* Oregon: Multnomah Publications.

Huckabee, M. (2008), 'America's Priorities in the War on Terror', *Foreign Affairs*, January/February.

Hunter, J. (2007), 'Faith and Science Can Complement Each Other to Accomplish a Common Cause', *Christian Science Monitor*, 8 February.

Huntington, S. (1991), *The Third Wave: Democratization in the Late Twentieth Century*, Norman and London: University of Oklahoma Press.

Huntington, S. (1993), 'The Clash of Civilizations?', *Foreign Affairs*, vol. 72, no. 3: 22–49.

Huntington, S. (1997), *The Clash of Civilizations and the Remaking of World Order*, New York: Simon & Schuster.

Huntington, S. (2005), *Who Are We?* London: Free Press.

Hurlburt, (2001), 'Global Injustice: A Case Against the International Criminal Court', *Concerned Women for America*, 2 May, www.cwfa.org/articledisplay.asp?id=1975&department=CWA&categoryid=nation; accessed 22 January 2008.

Hvalkof, S. (1984), 'On the Summer Institute of Linguistics and its Critics', *Current Anthology*, vol. 25, no. 1, February: 124–6.

Hvalkof, S., and Stipe, C. (1984), 'On the Summer Institute of Linguistics and Its Critics', *Current Anthropology*, vol. 25, no. 1, February: 124–6.

IASPS (Institute for Advanced Strategic and Political Studies) (1996), 'A Clean Break: A New Strategy for Securing the Realm', www.israelecoNo.my.org/strat1.htm; accessed 21 October 2006.

ICC (International Christian Concern) (2007), 'The Hall of Shame 2007', http://ww.persecution.org/suffering/pdfs/HallofShame2007.pdf; accessed 1 July 2007.

ICEJ (International Christian Embassy Jerusalem) (2006a), 'A Defence of Christian Zionism', www.icej.org/article.php?id=3464; accessed 21 October 2006.

ICEJ (International Christian Embassy Jerusalem) (206b), 'Foundations of Christian Zionism', www.icej.org/article.php?id=2807; accessed 21 October 2006.

IMFA (Israel Ministry of Foreign Affairs) (2006) 'Israel Among the Nations: North America', http://mfa.gov.il/MFA/Facts+About+Israel/Among+te+Nations/ISRAEL+AM; accessed 11 April 2007.

Inhofe, J. (2003), 'The Science of Climate Change', Senate floor statement, 28 July, http://inhofe.senate.gov/pressrelease/climate.htm; accessed 1 October 2007.

Inhofe, J. (2004), 'Partisan Environmental Groups', Senate floor statement, 4 October, http://inhofe.senate.gov/pressrelease/epwgroups.htm; accessed 1 October 2007.

Inhofe, J. (2005), 'Climate Change Update', Senate floor statement, 4 January, http://inhofe.senate.gov/pressrelease/climateupdate.htm; accessed 1 October 2007.

Inhofe, J. (2006), 'Inhofe to Blast Global Warming Media Coverage in Speech Today', Senate floor statement, 25 September, http://inhofe.senate.gov/pressrelease/globalwarming.htm; accessed 1 October 2007.

Institute for First Amendment Studies (1998), 'Council for National Policy: unofficial information page', www.publiceye/ifas/cnp/index.html; accessed 2 September 2007.

IPCC (Intergovernmental Panel on Climate Change) (2007), *Climate Change 2007: The Physical Science Basis*, Geneva: Intergovernmental Panel on Climate Change Secretariat.

John Paul II (2003), 'Address of his Holiness Pope John Paul II to the Diplomatic Corps', 13 January, www.vatican.va/holy_father/john_paul_ii/speeches/2003/january/documents/hf; accessed 28 July 2007.

Kant, I. (1970), 'Perpetual Peace', in Hans Reiss (ed.), *Kant's Political Writings*, Cambridge: Cambridge University Press.

Kaplan, E. (2005), *With God on Their Side*, New York and London: New Press.

Kirkpatrick, D. (2007), 'Christian Right Labors to Find '08 Candidate', *New York Times*, 24 February.

Klein, R. (2006), 'A Piece of Hollywood is Converted into a Call to Christianity', *Boston Globe*, 11 October.

Kline, S. (2004), 'The Culture War Gone Global: "Family Values" and the Shape of US Foreign Policy', *International Relations*, vol. 18, no. 453: 453–66.

Kranish, M. (2006), 'Religious Right Wields Clout: Secular Groups Losing Funding Amid Pressure', *Boston Globe*, 9 October.

Krauthammer, C. (1991), 'The Unipolar Moment', *Foreign Affairs*, vol. 70, no. 1: 23–33.

Kristof, N. (2000), 'The 2000 Campaign; The 1988 Campaign; for Bush, Thrill was in Father's Chase', *New York Times*, 29 August.

Kuo, D. (2006), *Tempting Faith: An Inside Story of Political Seduction*, New York: Free Press.

LaHaye, T., and Jenkins, J. (1995), *Left Behind*, Carol Stream IL: Tyndale House.

Land, R. (2007), *The Divided States of America*, Nashville: Thomas Nelson.

Layklin, M. (2003), 'Water Shortage Works to Chaplain's Advantage', *Miami Herald*, 7 April.

Leaming, J., and Boston, R. (2004), 'Behind Closed Doors', Americans United for Separation of Church and State, www.au.org/site/News2?abbr=cs_&page=NewsArticle&id=6949&news_iv_ctrl; accessed 14 August 2007.

Lindsey, H. (2005), 'Signs from the Heavens', www.hallindsey.org/index2.php?option=com_content&task=view&id=90&pop=1&p; accessed 4 October 2007.

Lindsey, H. (2006), *The Greatest Works of Hal Lindsey: The Late Great Planet Earth/Satan is Alive and Well on Planet Earth*, New York: Inspiration Books.

Lindsey, H. (2007a), 'Al Gore: 180 degrees Off Kilter – WMD', www.hallindsey.org/index2.php?option=com_content&task=view&id=143&pop=1&; accessed 4 October 2007.

Lindsey, H. (2007b), 'More Hot Air from the U.N.', *WorldNetDaily*, www.worldnetdaily.com/news/article.asp?ARTICLE-ID=54505; accessed 4 October 2007.

Lipset, S.M. (1973), *American Exceptionalism: A Double-Edged Sword*, New York: W.W. Norton.

Luo, M., and Goodstein, L. (2007), 'Emphasis Shifts for New Breed of Evangelicals', *New York Times*, 21 May.

Lynch, C. (2002), 'Islamic Bloc, Christian Right Turn up to Lobby UN', *Washington Post*, 17 June.

Lynn, B. (2006), *Piety and Politics: The Right-wing Assault on Religious Freedom*, New York: Harmony Books.

Macalister, T. (2007), 'Shell Lures Bush's Environmental Advisor', *Guardian*, 5 February.

MacAskill, E. (2007), 'Tehran the Target of Huge Arms Deal, Says Rice', *Guardian*, 1 August.

McClymond, M. (2005), 'We're Not in Kansas Anymore: The Roots and Routes of World Pentecostalism', *Religious Studies Review*, vol. 31, no. 3, July–October: 163–9.

MacLeod, L., and Hurlburt, C. (2000), 'Exposing CEDAW', www.CWA.org/article display.asp?1971&department=CWA&categoryid=nation; accessed 26 August 2006.

McMahon, R. (2006), 'Christian Evangelicals and U.S. Foreign Policy', *Council for Foreign Relations*, www.cfr.org/publication/11341/; accessed 19 January 2008.

Maddox, G. (2003), 'The "Crusade" against Evil: Bush's Fundamentalism', *Australian Journal of Politics and History*, vol. 49, no. 3: 398–411.

Mansfield, S. (2004), *The Faith of George W. Bush*, New York: Penguin/Strang Communications.

Marsden, L. (2005), *Lessons from Russia: Clinton and US Democracy Promotion*, Aldershot: Ashgate.

Martin, W. (1999), 'The Christian Right and American Foreign Policy', *Foreign Policy*, Spring.

Mayer, J. (2004), 'Christian Fundamentalists and Public Opinion Toward the Middle East: Israel's New Best Friends? *Social Science Quarterly*, vol. 85, no. 3: 695–712.

Mearsheimer, J., and Walt, S. (1993), 'Keeping Saddam in a Box', *New York Times*, 2 February.

Mearsheimer, W., and Walt, S. (2003), 'An Unnecessary War', *Foreign Policy* 134, January–February: 50–59.

Mearsheimer, J., and Walt, S. (2006a), 'The Israel Lobby and U.S. Foreign Policy', http://ksgNo.tes1.harvard.edu/Research/wpaper.nsf/rwp/RWP06-011; accessed 3 June 2006.

Mearsheimer, J., and Walt, S. (2006b), 'The Israel Lobby', *London Review of Books*, vol. 28 no. 6, 23 March.

Mearsheimer, J., and Walt, S. (2007), *The Israel Lobby and U.S. Foreign Policy*, London: Allen Lane.

MEPI (Middle East Partnership Initiative) (2005), 'The Middle East Partnership Initiative Story', *Middle East Partnership Initiative*, http://mepi.state.gov/outreach/index.htm; accessed 26 September 2007.

Milligan, S. (2006), 'Together but Worlds Apart', *Boston Globe*, 10 October.

Mission Network News (2005), 'Christians are Ministering the Love of Jesus to Muslims Wracked by War and Persecution', 17 March, www.persectionproject.org/pdfs/Published%20Article%20(MNN%20–%20Chrstian3%20Ministering.pdf; accessed 20 June 2007.

Monkerud, D. (2005), 'The Religious Right Determining U.S. Foreign Policy', http://rightweb.irc-online.org/rw/698; accessed 14 August 2006.

NAE (National Association of Evangelicals) (2004), 'For the Health of the Nation: An Evangelical Call to Civic Responsibility', Washington DC: National Association of Evangelicals.

Natsios, A. (2005), 'Conversation: Andrew Natsios', www.pbs.org/newshour/bb/fedagencies/july-dec05/natsios_12–27.html; accessed 26 July 2007.

Netanyahu, B. (1994), *A Place among the Nations*, New York: Bantam Books.

North, G. (1989), *Introduction to Christian Economics*, Phillipsburg NJ: P&R Publishing.

Northcott, M. (2004), *An Angel Directs the Storm: Apocalyptic Religion and American Empire*, London: I.B. Tauris.

Norris, P. (1996), *Electoral Change Since 1945*, Oxford: Blackwell.

NSC (National National Security Council) (2006), *The National Security Strategy of the United States of America*, Washington DC: National Security Council.

Oldfield, D. (2004), 'The Christian Right's Influence and How to Counter It', *Foreign Policy in Focus*, March.

Olsen, T. (2004), 'Patrick Henry College's Plan is Working, Says *The New York Times*', *Christianity Today*, March, www.christainitytoday.com/ct/2004/march-web-only/3–8–12.0.html; accessed 1 September 2007.

Onishi, N. (2002), 'Africans Fill Churches that Celebrate Wealth', *New York Times*, 13 March.

Palast, G. (2003), *The Best Democracy Money Can Buy*, London: Robinson.

Perkins, J. (2006), *Confessions of an Economic Hit Man*, London: Ebury Press.

Perlstein, R. (2004), 'The Jesus Landing Pad', *Village Voice*, 18 May, www.village-voice.com/news/0420,perlstein,53582,1.html; accessed 14 October 2007.

Perry, M. (2007), 'Elliott Abram's Uncivil War', *Conflicts Forum* 13, March.

Perry, M., and Woodward, P. (2007), 'Document details "U.S." Plan to Sink Hamas', *Asia Times*, 16 May.

Pew Forum (2006a), *Spirit and Power: A 10-Country Study of Pentecostals*, Washington DC: Pew Forum on Religion and Public Life.

Pew Forum (2006b), 'Pentecostalism in Africa', *The Pew Forum on Religion & Public Life*, www.pewforum.org/surveys/Pentecostal/africa; accessed 9 September 2007.

Pew Forum (2006c), 'Pentecostalism in Latin America', *The Pew Forum on Religion & Public Life*, www.pewforum.org/surveys/Pentecostal/latinamerica; accessed 9 September 2007.

Pew Forum (2006d), 'Pentecostalism in South Korea', *The Pew Forum on Religion & Public Life*, www.pewforum.org/surveys/Pentecostal/countries/CountryID=194; accessed 9 September 2007.

Pew Forum (2006e), *Many Americans Uneasy with Mix of Religion and Politics*, Washington DC: Pew Forum on Religion and Public Life.

Pew Research Center (2007), 47-*Nation Pew Global Attitudes Survey*, Pew Global Project Attitudes, Washington DC: Pew Research Center.

PFAW (People for the American Way) (2006), 'Focus on the Family', *People for the America Way*, www.pfaw.org/pfaw/general/default.aspx?oid=4257; accessed 14 August 2007.

PFAW (People for the American Way) (2007a), 'Concerned Women for America', *People for the America Way* www.pfaw.org/pfaw/general/default.aspx?oid=22376; accessed 14 August 2007.

PFAW (People for the American Way) (2007b), 'Eagle Forum', *People for the America Way* www.pfaw.org/pfaw/general/default.aspx?oid=3152; accessed 14 August 2007.

Phillips, K. (2006), *American Theocracy: The Perils and Politics of Radical Religion, Oil, and Borrowed Money in the 21st Century*, London: Viking.

Philo, G. (1990), *Seeing and Believing: The Influence of Television*, London: Routledge.

Phiri, I., and Maxwell, J. (2007), 'Gospel Riches', *Christianity Today*, www.ctlibrary.com/46571; accessed 10 September 2007.

Pizzo, S. (2004), 'The Christian Taliban', *AlterNet*, www.alternet.org/story/18259; accessed 2 August 2007.

PNAC (Project for the New American Century) (1997), 'Statement of Principles', www.newamericancentury.org/statementof principles.htm; accessed 25 March 2003.

PNAC (Project for the New American Century) (1998), 'Letter to President Clinton on Iraq', www.newamericancentury.org/iraqclintonletter.htm; accessed 23 January 2008.

PNAC (Project for the New American Century) (2002), 'Open Letter to President Bush', www.newamericancentury.org/Bushletter-040302.htm; accessed 7 June 2007.

Powell, C. (1992), 'US Forces: Challenges Ahead', *Foreign Affairs*, vol. 72, no. 5: 32–45.

Pulliam, S. (2006), 'Arguing for God', *Christianity Today*, April, www.christianitytoday.com/ct/2006/aprilweb-only/116–52.0.html; accessed 1 September 2007.

Rennie, D. (2003), 'God Put Bush in Charge, Says the General Hunting bin Laden', *Daily Telegraph*, 17 October.

Rollin, B. (2001), 'A Curriculum of Faith', *Religion and Ethics NewsWeekly*, 27 April, www.pbs.org/wnet/religionandethics/week435/cover.html; accessed 1 September 2007.

Rosin, H. (2005), 'God and County', *New Yorker*, 27 June.

Rosin, H. (2007), *God's Harvard: A Christian College on a Mission to Save America*, San Diego and New York: Harcourt Books.

Rushdoony, R. (1973), *Institutes of Biblical Law*, Phillipsburg NJ: P&R Publishing.

Russell Mead, W. (2006), 'God's Country', *Foreign Affairs*, September/October.

Russett, B. (1993), *Grasping the Democratic Peace: Principles for a Post-Cold War World*, Princeton, NJ: Princeton University Press.

Russett, B. (2005), 'Bushwacking the Democratic Peace', *International Studies Perspectives*, vol. 6, no. 4: 395–408.

Ruthven, M. (2004), *A Fury for God: The Islamist Attack on America*, London: Granta Books.

Sachs, P. (2006), 'Democrats, Evangelicals Team up on Global Warming', *Religion News Service*, 30 June.

Salpeter, E. (2002), 'Rev. Vines called Mohammed a Demon-possessed Pedophile', *Ha'aretz*, 17 July.

Saunders, B. (2007), 'Why do you Persecute Me? The Worldwide Struggle for Religious Freedom', www.frc.org/get.cfm?i=WT07CO1v; accessed 27 June 2007.

Scahill, J. (2007), *Blackwater: The Rise of the World's Most Powerful Mercenary Army*, New York: Nation Books.

Sharansky, N. (2004), *The Case for Democracy*, New York: Public Affairs.

Shea, N. (1997), *In the Lion's Den: A Shocking Account of Persecution and Martyrdom of Christians Today and How We Should Respond*, Nashville: Boardman & Holman.

Shea, N. (2005a), 'Kingdom's Religious Wrongs: The Religious Tyranny in Saudi Arabia is Not Just Saudi's Business', *National Review Online*, 25 April, http://article.nationalreview.com/?q=ODcyMGMxOTJiYjM3ZGQ5NWFiZ TM4OWUzWU1N2ZiNWU=; accessed 9 July 2007.

Shea, N. (2005b), 'Saudi Stories: Peeling Back the Slick Western Imaging', *National Review Online*, http://article.nationalreview.com/?q=N2VkYzMoNjVjZGQ1MGVkNzhjMzllYWU1NGM4OTI2Njk=; accessed 9 July 2007.

Shea, N. (2006a), 'Monitoring Respect for Human Rights Around the World: A Review of the "County Reports on Human Rights Practices for 2005"', evidence before the subcommittee on Africa, Global Human Rights and International Operations of the House Committee on International Relations, 16 March, www.house.gov/international-relations; accessed 10 June 2007.

Shea, N. (2006b), 'This is a Saudi Textbook (After the Intolerance Was Removed)', *Washington Post*, 21 May.

Shea, N. (2006c), 'The Plight of Religious Minorities: Can Religious Pluralism Survive?', evidence before the subcommittee on Africa, Global Human Rights and

International Operations of the House Committee on International Relations, 30 June, www.house.gov/international-relations; accessed 10 June 2007.

Shea, N. (2007), 'Religious Freedom in Egypt: Recent Developments', briefing before the Task Force on Religious Freedom of the United States House of Representatives, Washington DC: United States Commission on International Religious Freedom.

Shupe, A., and Heinerman, J. (1985), 'Mormonism and the New Christian Right: An Emerging Coalition? *Review of Religious Research*, vol. 27, no. 2, December: 146–57.

Simes, D. (2003), 'America's Imperial Dilemma', *Foreign Affairs*, November/December.

Singer, P. (2004), *The President* of *Good and Evil*, London: Granta Books.

Sizemore, B. (2006), 'Blackwater USA Says it Can Supply Forces for Conflicts', *Virginia-Pilot*, 30 March.

Smith, M. (2003), 'Homeschooling Grows in the Black Community', HSLDA website, 13 June, www.hslda.org/docs/news/hslda/200306/200306130.asp; accessed 14 October 2003.

Stockman, F. (2006), 'For Those Excluded, Loan Program is No Success', *Boston Globe*, 10 October.

Stockman, F., Kranish, M., Canellos, P., and Baron, K. (2006), 'Bush Brings Faith to Foreign Aid', *Boston Globe*, 8 October.

Stone, P. (2006), 'Reed in the Rough', *National Journal*, 7 July.

Street, J. (2001), *Mass Media*, *Politics and Democracy*, London: Palgrave Macmillan.

Superville, A. (2003), 'Bush Broadens Global Gag Rule on Abortion', *Associated Press*, 29 August.

Talhelm, J. (2006), 'Evangelical Leader: GOP Abandoned Voters', *Washington Post*, 9 November,.

TBN (Trinity Broadcasting Network) (2007), 'Trinity Broadcasting Network bringing faith and family networks to Asia-Pacific region', *Trinity Broadcasting Network*, www.tbn.org/index.php/7.html?nid=200; accessed 9 September 2007.

Theocracy Watch (2005), 'Christian Zionism', www.theocracywatch.org/christian_zionism.htm; accessed 19 February 2007.

Thomas, S. (2005), *The Global Resurgence of Religion and the Transformation of International Relations*, New York: Palgrave Macmillan.

Tooley, M. (2006), 'Religious Climate Change?', *Weekly Standard*, 5 May.

Trammel, M. (2007), 'Making Air Waves', *Christianity Today*, February, vol. 51 no. 2: 26–33.

Unruh, B. (2007), 'Dobson Says "No Way" to McCain Candidacy', *WorldNetDaily*, www.worldnetdaily.com/news/article.asp?ARTICLE_ID=53743; accessed 16 February 2007.

USAID (United States Agency for International Development) (2005), 'Faith-Based and Community Initiatives', www.usaid.gov/about_uusaid/presidential_initiative/faithbased.html; accessed 3 July 2007.

USAID (United States Agency for International Development) (2006), 'United States International Food Assistance Report 2006', Washington DC: USAID.

USAID (United States Agency for International Development) (2007), 'Expanding outreach to the Muslim world', www.usaid.gov/press/speeches/2007/sp070627; accessed 3 July 2007.

USDOS (United States Department of State) (2006), *International Religious Freedom Report* 2006, Bureau of Democracy, Human Rights and Labor, Washington DC: US Department of State.

USDOS (United States Department of State) (2007), *International Religious Freedom Report* 2007, Bureau of Democracy, Human Rights and Labor, Washington DC: US Department of State.

Vineyard, A. (2003), 'Shutting Down the Feminists', www.beverlylahayeinstitute.org/articledisplay.asp?id=3553&department=BLI&categoryid=nation; accessed 25 March 2007.

Wagner, D. (2003a), 'Christians and Zion: British Stirrings', www.information-clearinghouse.info/article4959.htm; accessed 21 October 2006.

Wagner, D. (2003b), 'Christian Zionists, Israel and the "Second Coming"', www.informationclearinghouse.info/article4930.htm; accessed 21 October 2006.

Wagner, D. (2003c), 'A Heavenly Match: Bush and the Christian Zionists', www.infrmationclearinghouse.info/article4960.htm; accessed 21 October 2006.

Wallis, J. (2005), *God's Politics: Why the American Right Gets it Wrong and the Left Doesn't Get It*, Oxford: Lion Hudson.

Weber, T. (2004), 'On the Road to Armageddon: How Evangelicals Became Israel's Best Friend', *Beliefnet*, www.beliefnet.com/story_15165.html; accessed 10 August 2007.

Wicker, C. (2000), 'Dumfounded by Divorce', article on the Barna Research Group survey 1999, www.adherents.com/largecom/baptist_divorce.html; accessed 23 January 2008.

Wilcox, C., and Larson, C. (2006), *Onward Christian Soldiers?* Boulder CO: Westview Press.

Wilson, B. (2007), '"Pro Israel" Christian Leader Blames Jews for the Holocaust', www.talk2action.org/2007/3/5/105015/2167; accessed 26 March 2007.

Woodward, B. (2003), *Bush at War*, London: Simon & Schuster.

Woodward, B. (2004), *Plan of Attack*, London: Simon & Schuster.

Zahavy, T. (2006a), '"It's Not Our Agenda": An Interview with Abraham Foxman', *New Jersey Jewish Standard*, 31 August.

Zahavy, T. (2006b), '"Christians are Hearing the Message": An Interview with David Brog', *New Jersey Jewish Standard*, 31 August.

Zunes, S. (2002), 'The Swing to the Right in U.S. Policy toward Israel and Palestine', *Middle East Policy*, vol. 9, no. 3, September: 45–64.

Zunes, S. (2004), 'US Christian Right's Grip on Middle East Policy', *Asian Times*, 14 July.

Index

Index

Index

Index

Index